世界历史名篇译读

自由与权利

梅祖蓉 编著

人民出版社

目　　录

前　　言

历史名篇的阅读，若求理想状态，须在三个方面努力。一是读通，或说读顺，知其字、词、句的基本含义；二是读懂，求其历史背景或其诞生的缘由；三是读透，理解其思想、学术价值乃至其历史与现实意义。

这由通至透的境界，说来不费功夫，其实难于实践，就笔者而言，实可谓“望尽天涯路”、不知其究竟止于何处的过程。静安先生学问三境界的总括，道尽问学之艰难与甘苦，亦说尽学人之追求。由是，笔者不揣冒昧，远望“灯火阑珊处”，不惜上下求索，勉力求知，绝不敢说已达“衣带渐宽终不悔”乃至于“蓦然回首”的境界；然而山高水长，今已迈出一小步的欣喜，令笔者大胆奉献给读者一部不成熟的文选阅读心得。

就笔者所见，目前国内提供给史学新生的《世界历史文选》大多以编为主，辅之以字词释义、作者与选文背景简介、翻译练习，偶尔可见篇幅不大的导读。这是可以理解的，毕竟这样可以为学习者提供更多选篇，并且突出其目的：提高阅读外文文献的能力。然而，笔者却欲在此传统之外，尝试另一类风格的文选译读。一方面，保留“世界历史文选”注重外语学习的传统；另一方面，将更多历史元素注入其中，并以某一主题为统领，遴选名篇文献，以期达到系统性学术训练的目的。譬如本卷“自由与权利”，即以西方政治思想史上两个最基本的概念“自由”与“权利”为主题，说明它们如何成为人们争取、维护公平与正义的工具，其概念本身又如何演变发展。细心的读者会发现，各篇之间，从《我有一个梦》到1215年《大宪章》，有着内在的关联。

基于此思路，《世界历史名篇译读》的体例与结构就必然与传统的《世界历史文选》颇为相异。所谓《名篇译读》，顾名思义，有原文、译文、解读。为便于读者延伸阅读，解读末尾还提供了推荐书目，并就推荐理由有所陈述，有别于简单的书名列举。“原文”部分（TEXT），在文本之外，给出两类注释：页边注,以英文释义难字与词[①];页下注,给出有关作者、地名、人名、历史事件、特定术语的知识性注释。译文,除了林肯《葛底斯堡演讲》引用朱曾汶译本外,均为笔者参考诸多版本后自译。之所以要给出译文,是为读者提供一种参照或学习英语的路径。常习英语的人,往往发现,有成就的译家多建议初学者找来经典译作,仔细对比原文,体味翻译之道与翻译之难。笔者在读威廉·夏伊勒(William Shiler)所著《第三帝国的兴亡——纳粹德国史》(*The Rise and Fall of the Third Reich:A History of Nazi Germany*)时,特意找来董乐山主译的中译本,与原著对照着读,真是受益匪浅。譬如"Hitler was the fate of the German People"一句,董先生译作"希特勒是德国人民的劫数",把通常译为"命运"的"fate"改译为"劫数",准确地传递出德国人民命中注定、在劫难逃的原文意图;再如"beside himself with excitement and joy"这一短语,如译为"因为兴奋和快乐而发狂"也未为不可,但难免显得欧化,不像是地道的汉语表达方式,董乐山则以"乐极忘形"译出,将一个标准的英语结构不露痕迹地化为汉语结构,叫人拍案叫绝。通过这样的对比,笔者知道,想要提高英文水平,参考他人的译作是一种有效的方式。课堂教学中,我也经常发现,学生们对于外文文本的理解往往出现很大的偏差,如果让他们养成比照的习惯,也许可以少走弯路,哪怕是通过批评的方式。正是出于这个原因,我在"文选解析"中也将部分引文以中英文对比的方式列出,一来令读者体会原文之美,二来提供一个批评的靶子,令笔者与读者共同在批评中成长。

各篇选文的次序安排,我也突破了按时间先后来排的常例。缘何如此?主要是出于难易程度的考虑。所选 5 篇文献,最难的是 1215 年《大宪章》,如果按年代早晚将它置于最前,对于部分读者来说,也许会出现理解上的障碍。它是产生于英国中古时期的文献,其中又涉及西欧封建社会封君与封臣间的权利与义务,理解起来,需要有相当的知识储备。因此笔者考虑再三,决定按照循序渐进、先易后难的思路,逐一地从《我有一个梦》开始,最后解读《大宪章》。这样一来,正好形成了本书的一个特色:倒叙的手法。

---

① 英文释义在《牛津高阶英汉双解词典》《韦氏高阶英语词典》《韦氏大学英语词典》"牛津在线英语词典"(http://en.oxford dictionaries.com)中选取较为简明的一种,有时稍加编辑。

倒叙有倒叙的好处。先看《我有一个梦》,原文文本提到了林肯的《解放宣言》与美国《独立宣言》,笔者的解读也以之为起点,这就为后面的《葛底斯堡演说》与《独立宣言》埋下伏笔。第2篇《葛底斯堡演说》的解析,重点是林肯如何提升《独立宣言》的地位与价值,所以第3篇顺理成章地跟上了《独立宣言》;而《独立宣言》在世界上的影响首先及于法国,恰如美国历史学家卡尔·贝克尔(Carl Becker)所言,美国《独立宣言》启发了法国人想要有一份权利宣言的愿望①,这个愿望在1789年的法国大革命中得以实现。因此,第4篇紧接着读法国《人权与公民权宣言》(简称《人权宣言》)。最后,无论是美国《独立宣言》,还是法国《人权宣言》,其理论源头都离不开英国《大宪章》,而前面那些文选解析已经为理解《大宪章》做了诸多准备与铺垫,所以接下来无论从解析理路与难易程度来说,都可以来读《大宪章》了。这样的排序恰好也满足了按国别来分的原则。

同样出于难易程度的考虑,各篇文选的解析篇幅稍有差异,最长的是《大宪章》,4万余字;其次是《人权与公民权宣言》,3万8千字;《我有一个梦》只有不到2万字的解析篇幅。依据著作结构讲究均衡的美学标准,这样安排,稍嫌不美,但这是不得已的结果。《译读》原属课堂教学的产物,是笔者对"世界历史文选"双语课大胆改革后的成果,各篇文选的解析篇幅取决于听众的理解能力与反馈意见。文选难,则解析长;文选易,则解析短。若为求均衡而勉强增削篇幅,并非不可以,然而笔者认为无必要。

最后要诚挚地感谢加拿大劳里埃大学(Wilfrid Laurier University)布莱恩·蔡森(Blaine Chaisson,中文名柴国松)教授。作为以英语、法语为母语,同时又通晓中文、俄文的历史学家,Blaine总是不厌其烦地回答我各种各样的问题,帮助我搜求资料;这份文稿完成后,他又通读全稿,修正了其中不尽妥当的英文表达,令人感激不尽。当然,文中缺漏与错误之处,均系我一人造成,责任自负。恳请读者批评、指正!

梅祖蓉

2017年1月16日晨于开封

---

① Carl Becker, *Declaration of Independence: A Study in the History of Political Ideas*, New York: Harcout, Brance and Company, Inc., 1922, p, 232.

I HAVE A DREAM
《我有一个梦》

I HAVE A DREAM

Martin Luther King, Jr.①

I am happy to join with you today in what will go down in history as the greatest demonstration for freedom in the history of our nation.

Five score years ago, a great American, in whose symbolic shadow we stand today, signed the Emancipation Proclamation②. This momentous decree came as a great beacon light of hope to millions of Negro③slaves who had

---

① Martin Luther King, Jr.(马丁·路德·金,1929.1.15~1968.4.4),出生于美国南部佐治亚州亚特兰大市(Atlanta, Georgia),中产阶级家庭背景,自幼接受良好教育,大学阶段主修神学与社会学。1954年继承其父衣钵,在阿拉巴马州蒙哥马利(Montgomery, Alabama)的一个浸礼会教堂(Baptist Church)担任牧师(a pastor)。1955年于波士顿大学获神学博士学位。1955年底,蒙哥马利公车抵制运动(Montgomery Bus Boycott)发起,金被推选为抵制运动的领导人,自此投身美国民权运动,并于1957年组建"南方基督教领导大会"(Southern Christian Leadership Conference, SCLC)。其哲学思想以"爱"为核心,积极主张非暴力抵抗。1963年8月28日,马丁·路德·金参与领导"华盛顿游行"(March on Washington for Jobs and Freedom)。游行末,他发表演说"I Have a Dream",从此又以其卓越的演说才能著称于世。1964年获诺贝尔和平奖。1968年4月4日,在田纳西州孟菲斯(Memphis, Tennessee),马丁·路德·金遇刺身亡,年仅39岁。短暂一生,他发表了大量演说与文章,著有*Stride Toward Freedom: The Montgomery Story*(1958),*Why We Can't Wait*(1964),*Where do we go from here: Chaos or Community?*(1967)等作品。他去世后,美国许多城市将其生辰日——1月15日——定为节日。1986年,这一天成为美国的国家节日。此处所引演说词出自Clayborne Carson ed., *The Autography of Martin Luther King, Jr.*, New York: Intellectual Property Management, Inc., 2013, pp.223~227.

② 1863年1月1日,美国第16任总统亚伯拉罕·林肯签署并颁布《解放宣言》,宣布南方反叛军控制地区的黑奴获得自由。

③ 尽管在日常生活中,"negro"一词含贬义,但首字母大写的"Negro"不同。20世纪初,从牙买加来到美国的黑人民族主义领袖马库斯·加维(Marcus Garvey, 1887~1940)倡议将黑人的贬称"negro"首字母大写以示对黑人的尊重,获国际社会与美国官方支持。

been seared in the flames of withering injustice. It came as a joyous daybreak to end the long night of their captivity.

But one hundred years later, the Negro still is not free. One hundred years later, the life of the Negro is still sadly crippled by the manacles of segregation and the chains of discrimination. One hundred years later, the Negro lives on a lonely island of poverty in the midst of a vast ocean of material prosperity. One hundred years later, the Negro is still languished in the corners of American society and finds himself an exile in his own land.

And so we've come here today to dramatize a shameful condition. In a sense we've come to our nation's capital to cash a check. When the architects of our republic wrote the magnificent words of the Constitution and the Declaration of Independence①, they were signing a promissory note to which every American was to fall heir. This note was a promise that all men, yes, black men as well as white men, would be guaranteed the "unalienable Rights" of "Life, Liberty and the pursuit of Happiness"②.

It is obvious today that America has defaulted on this promissory note insofar as her citizens of color are concerned. Instead of honoring this sacred obligation, America has given the Negro people a bad check, a check which has come back marked "insufficient funds". But we refuse to believe that the

sear: to burn, scorch and damage with strong and sudden heat

wither: (of a plant) to become dry and weak

manacle: either one of a set of two metal rings designed to lock around a person's wrists or ankles; handcuff

segregation: the practice or policy of keeping people of different races, religions, etc., separate from each other

languish: to be or live in a state of depression or decreasing vitality

dramatize: to show (something that might not be noticed) in a clear and effective way

fall: used when something passes to someone in a way that doesn't involve choice

① "Constitution"指《美利坚合众国宪法》(*The Constitution of the United States of America*),1787年由制宪会议制订,1789年获各州批准并生效。"Declaration of Independence"指美国《独立宣言》,发表于1776年7月4日。

② "unalienable Rights" of "Life, Liberty and the pursuit of Happiness"取自美国宪法。首字母大写表示强调。

bank of justice is bankrupt. We refuse to believe that there are insufficient funds in the great vaults of opportunity of this nation. So we've come to cash this check, a check that will give us upon demand the riches of freedom and the security of justice.

vault: room, especially in a bank, used for keeping valuable safe

We have also come to this hallowed spot① to remind America of the fierce urgency of Now. This is no time to engage in the luxury of cooling off or to take the tranquilizing drug of gradualism②. Now is the time to make real the promises of democracy. Now is the time to rise from the dark and desolate valley of segregation to the sunlit path of racial justice. Now is the time to lift our nation from the quicksands of racial injustice to the solid rock of brotherhood. Now is the time to make justice a reality for all of God's children③.

tranquilize: to use a drug to cause a person or animal to become relaxed and calm

quicksand: a situation that is dangerous of difficult escape from

It would be fatal for the nation to overlook the urgency of the moment. This sweltering summer④ of the Negro's legitimate discontent will not pass until there is an invigorating autumn of freedom and equality. Nineteen sixty-three is not an end, but a beginning. Those who hope that the Negro needed to blow off steam and will now be content will have a rude awakening if the nation returns to business as usual. There will be

blow off steam: release surplus energy or emotion from being restrained

① "hallowed spot"（圣地）指林肯纪念堂（Lincoln Memorial）。它是"华盛顿游行"的最后一站，也是马丁·路德·金发表演说之地。黑人齐聚于此，以示对他们心中的圣人亚伯拉罕·林肯的崇敬。

② "gradualism"（渐进主义）反对游行、示威、静坐等较为激进的民权运动方式。

③ 意指上帝面前，人人平等。

④ "sweltering summer"（酷热的夏季）一语双关。1963 年夏，美国南方异常炎热；1963 年夏，又是美国诸多城市，尤其是在南方，发生严重种族冲突的时候，黑人与白人的关系异常紧张。

neither rest nor tranquility in America until the Negro is granted his citizenship rights. The whirlwinds of revolt will continue to shake the foundations of our nation until the bright day of justice emerges.

tranquility: state of being quiet and peaceful

But there is something that I must say to my people, who stand on the warm threshold which leads into the palace of justice: in the process of gaining our rightful place, we must not be guilty of wrongful deeds. Let us not seek to satisfy our thirst for freedom by drinking from the cup of bitterness and hatred. We must forever conduct our struggle on the high plane of dignity and discipline. We must not allow our creative protest to degenerate into physical violence. Again and again, we must rise to the majestic heights of meeting physical force with soul force.

warm: fresh

plane: level of thought, existence or development

The marvelous new militancy which has engulfed the Negro community must not lead us to a distrust of all white people, for many of our white brothers, as evidenced by their presence here today①, have come to realize that their destiny is tied up with our destiny. They have come to realize that their freedom is inextricably bound to our freedom. We cannot walk alone. And as we walk, we must make the pledge that we shall always march ahead. We cannot turn back.

pledge: solemn promise; vow

There are those who are asking the devotees of civil rights, "When will you be satisfied?" We can never be satisfied as long as the Negro is the victim of the unspeakable horrors of police brutality. We can never be satisfied as long as our bodies, heavy with the fatigue of travel, cannot gain

① 当日参与游行的白人约 6 万之众。

lodging in the motels of the highways and the hotels of the cities. We cannot be satisfied as long as the Negro's basic mobility is from a smaller ghetto① to a larger one. We can never be satisfied as long as our children are stripped of their selfhood and robbed of their dignity by signs stating "for whites only."② We cannot be satisfied as long as a Negro in Mississippi cannot vote and a Negro in New York believes he has nothing for which to vote③. No, no, we are not satisfied, and we will not be satisfied until "justice rolls down like waters, and righteousness like a mighty stream."

I am not unmindful that some of you have come here out of great trials and tribulations. Some of you have come fresh from narrow jail cells. Some of you have come from areas where your quest for freedom left you battered by the storms of persecution and staggered by the winds of police brutality. You have been the veterans of creative suffering. Continue to work with the faith that unearned suffering is redemptive.

tribulation: a state of great trouble or suffering

stagger: cause (someone) to move unsteadily from side to side; walk with weak unsteady steps, as if you are about to fall

Go back to Mississippi, go back to Alabama, go back to South Carolina, go back to Georgia, go back to Louisiana④, go back to the slums and ghettos of our northern cities, knowing

① "ghetto"是北方州各城市专为黑人或其他有色人种而建的聚居区，有译为"隔都"者。

② "For Whites Only"（仅供白人），种族隔离的标识；见于候车室、餐厅、剧院、公园、图书馆、俱乐部、医院、学校等公共场所。

③ 以密西西比与纽约州的黑人为例，意味深长。密西西比州位于美国南方，南方州的黑人由于形形色色的法律规定而在事实乃至法律上被剥夺了选举权，而密西西比是黑人受歧视与迫害最严重的州之一。纽约州位于北方，北方州的黑人在法律上享有选举权，也在事实上能够参与投票，但是，黑人在国家权力体系中的作用微不足道，即便有选举权也改变不了他们的命运。以这两州为例，一方面表明美国南北方在种族政策上的差异，另一方面也揭示：无论南方还是北方，黑人都需为改变自己的命运而努力。

④ 密西西比、阿拉巴马、南卡罗来纳、佐治亚、路易斯安那这5个州是通常所说的南方腹地州（Deep South，亦称"深南方"），种族歧视与迫害最为严重。有时，"Deep South"还包括佛罗里达和德克萨斯州，语境不同，所指范围亦有差异。

that somehow this situation can and will be changed.

Let us not wallow in the valley of despair, I say to you today, my friends: so even though we face the difficulties of today and tomorrow, I still have a dream. It is a dream deeply rooted in the American dream.①

wallow: to roll oneself about in a lazy manner; to spend time without making any effort to change situation, feelings, etc.

I have a dream that one day this nation will rise up and live out the true meaning of its creed—we hold these truths to be self-evident, that all men are created equal②.

I have a dream that one day on the red hills of Georgia③ the sons of former slaves and the sons of former slave owners will be able to sit down together at the table of brotherhood.

I have a dream that one day even the state of Mississippi, a state sweltering with the heat of injustice, sweltering with the heat of oppression, will be transformed into an oasis of freedom and justice.

oasis: a pleasant or peaceful area or period in the midst of a difficult or hectic place or situation.

I have a dream that my four little children will one day live in a nation where they will not be judged by the color of their skin but by the content of their character.

I have a dream today!

---

① 从此段起，演说进入“我有一个梦”的主题；但这个“梦”并非马丁·路德·金事先准备好要说的内容，而属即兴发挥。当时，台下有听众向他喊道：“告诉他们，我们有一个梦”（Tell them, we have a dream）。回应观众的请求，金放下讲稿，开始大声讲述黑人的梦想。此段中“still”一词就透露出了当时的情形。

② 何谓“American dream”？机会平等、自由竞争、努力工作，寻找自己的幸福。这就是美国梦！然而，对于黑人来说，他们在获得与白人平等的身份之前，不可能实现这样的梦。因此，马丁·路德·金首先用美国《独立宣言》所宣示的“不言而喻的真理：人人生而平等”（we hold these truths to be self-evident, that all men are created equal）作为讲述其“梦”的起点。随后几段是历史性的追忆。

③ Red Hills 横跨佐治亚与佛罗里达州。18 世纪初，美国白人驱逐、杀害居住于在这里的印第安人，并开始定居于此，种植棉花，施行奴隶制度。此处提示黑人为奴的历史。

I have a dream that one day, down in Alabama, with its vicious racists, with its governor having his lips dripping with the words of interposition[①] and nullification[②]; one day right there in Alabama little black boys and black girls will be able to join hands with little white boys and white girls as sisters and brothers.

I have a dream today!

I have a dream that one day every valley shall be exalted, and every hill and mountain shall be made low, the rough places will be made plain, and the crooked places will be made straight and the glory of the Lord shall be revealed and all flesh shall see it together[③].

exalt: raise to a higher position

This is our hope. This is the faith that I go back to the South with. With this faith, we will be able to hew out of the mountain of despair a stone of hope.

hew: to shape sth by cutting with a sharp tool (such as an ax)

With this faith, we will be able to transform the jangling discords of our nation into a beautiful symphony of brotherhood. With this faith, we will be able to work together,

jangle: to make a ringing metallic sound, typically a discordant one

① 1896年5月，美国联邦最高法院在“普莱西对弗格森”(Plessy v. Ferguson)一案中作出“隔离但平等”(Separate but Equal)的裁决。1954年5月，该裁决由联邦最高法院在“布朗对托皮卡”(Brown v. Board of Education of Topeka)案中宣布废除。自此，种族隔离制度的合法性被推翻。但是，布朗裁决遭到了南方各州白人种族主义者的强烈抵制，他们呼吁南方各州政府插在联邦最高法院与白人之间，抵制布朗裁决的执行，使之归于无效。1956年4月起，阿拉巴马、密西西比、佐治亚、田纳西、南卡罗来纳、弗吉尼亚、阿肯色、佛罗里达、路易斯安那等南方州先后通过法案，同意以“插入”(Interposition)策略抵制布朗裁决，宣布布朗裁决无效。

② “nullification”指州政府如认定联邦法令违宪，便可拒绝执行。作为一种政治、法律思想，它在美国南方由来已久。19世纪上半叶，美国政治家约翰·卡尔洪恩(John Calhoun)主张最为激烈与坚决。

③ 此段从“Every valley shall be exalted”直到结尾，均出自《圣经·旧约》“以赛亚书”(Isaiah)第40章第4至5节(通常以40:4~5表示)，“以赛亚书”对之有特别说明：“这是耶和华亲口说的”。马丁·路德·金拥有神学博士学位，身为牧师，引用《圣经》是他的习惯。这一段也是他布道时常常引用的段落。另：前文“unearned suffering is redemptive”亦出自《圣经》。

to pray together, to struggle together, to go to jail together, to stand up for freedom together, knowing that we will be free one day.

This will be the day, this will be the day when all of God's children will be able to sing with new meaning: "My country 'tis of thee, sweet land of liberty, of thee I sing. Land where my fathers died, land of the Pilgrim's pride, from every mountainside, let freedom ring!"① And if America is to be a great nation, this must become true.

'tis: that is

thee: used as a singular form of "you" when it is the object of a verb or preposition

Pilgrim: one of the people who traveled by boat from England and created the first permanent settlement in New England at Plymouth in 1620

And so let freedom ring from the prodigious hilltops of New Hampshire.

prodigious: amazing or wonderful

Let freedom ring from the mighty mountains of New York.

Let freedom ring from the heightening Alleghenies of Pennsylvania.

Let freedom ring from the snow-capped Rockies of Colorado.

Let freedom ring from the curvaceous slopes of California.

curvaceous: having an attractively curved shape

But not only that②

Let freedom ring from Stone Mountain of Georgia.

---

① "My Country, 'tis of thee"是一首在美国传唱百余年的爱国歌曲，又名"America"，歌词由塞穆尔·史密斯(Samuel Francis Smith)于1831年创作。美国官方于1931年将"The Star-Spangled Banner"定为国歌之前，"My Country, 'tis of thee"一直是美国国歌之一。演说中所引是它的第一段歌词。

② 前文"let freedom ring"指自由的歌声从美国东部、西部与中部，即美国全境响起；从这里起，以下三句"Let freedom ring"让自由之声响起的地方转入对美国黑人来说意味尤其深长的地区：Stone Mountains of Georgia，刻有南部邦联总统杰斐逊·戴维斯(Jefferson Davis)、南部邦联名将罗伯特·李(Robert E.Lee)与托马斯·杰克逊(Thomas Jackson)三人的巨型浮雕，均为骑在马上的姿态；Lookout Mountain of Tennessee，1863年美国内战战场之一；Mississippi，既是美国南方棉花种植带(又称Black Belt)的中心，也是美国黑人受歧视与迫害最严重的地区之一。

Let freedom ring from Lookout Mountain of Tennessee.

Let freedom ring from every hill and molehill of Mississippi.

From every mountainside, let freedom ring!

And when this happens, when we allow freedom to ring, when we let it ring from every village and every hamlet, from every state and every city, we will be able to speed up that day when all of God's children, black men and white men, Jews and Gentiles, Protestants and Catholics, will be able to join hands and sing in the words of the old Negro spiritual: "Free at last! Free at last! Thank God Almighty, we are free at last."

hamlet: a small settlement, generally one smaller than a village

Gentile: a person who is not Jewish

spiritual: a religious folk song that was sung originally by African-Americans in the southern United States

译文

我有一个梦

马丁·路德·金

今天,我高兴地与大家参与到这将载入史册的行动。它是我国历史上最伟大的为自由而举行的游行。

100年前,一位伟大的美国人签署了《解放宣言》。今天,我们站在他雕像前。这个重大的法令是如灯塔的光芒,为千百万黑奴带来了希望——他们在严酷的不义之火中备受煎熬。宣言的到来,宛如欢乐的黎明,结束了黑人不得自由的漫漫长夜。

但是,100年后的今天,黑人依然不是自由的。100年后的今天,黑人的生活依然悲哀地为种族隔离的桎梏所困、为种族歧视的锁链所拘。100年后的今天,在一片物质丰裕的大洋环绕中,黑人生活在一个穷困的孤岛上。100年后的今天,黑人仍然蜷缩于美国社会的角落,不得伸展,仿佛在家园中流亡。

因此,我们今天来到这里,要向大家展示这令人羞愧的现状。从某种意义上说,今天我们是为了兑现一张支票而汇聚首都。当共和国的缔造者们将伟大的字句写入美国《宪法》与《独立宣言》时,他们签下了一张支票,一张每个美国人都有权承接的支票。它承诺:赋予所有人——白人以及黑人——生存、自由和追求幸福的权利,保证他们享有这些不可剥夺的权利。

现在来看,对于美国的有色公民来说,美国显然并未兑现这张支票。它不仅未曾遵从这神圣的义务,反而给黑人开了一张空头支票,一张盖上"资金不足"的印章便给退回的支票。但是,我们不相信,正义的银行已然破产。我们不相信,在这个满是机会的国家里,会有"资金不足"。因此,我们来兑现这张支票,一张让我们有权要求自由之丰裕、正义之保障的支票。

我们来到这片圣地，也是为了提醒美国，情势现已非常紧迫。现在已不能再侈谈冷静，或者用渐进主义的说辞平息情绪。现在是实现民主的诺言的时候；现在是从种族隔离的荒暗阴谷走出、进入种族平等的光明大道的时候；现在是让我们的国家脱离种族不平等的险境，而让它立基于博爱之坚石的时候；现在是让所有上帝的子孙得享真实的正义的时候。

忽视了此刻的紧迫，将令这个国家面临毁灭。这个令黑人感到义愤的酷暑将不会过去，除非令人振奋的自由与平等的秋天就要来临。1963 年，不是征途的结束，而是开始。如果美国一如既往，那些认为黑人过去需要抒发愤懑、现在应该感到满足的人将会猛然醒悟。如果黑人不被赋予作为公民的权利，美国将无有宁日。暴乱的旋风将继续摇撼这个国家的根基，直到正义的光明之日出现。

但有些话我必须要说，说给那些站在通往正义殿堂的新的起点上的人们：在争取我们应得的位置时，一定不要因错误的行动而犯下罪行。请勿因渴求自由而从苦恨与敌意中舀取一杯来饮。我们必须永远以高度的尊严、严明的律己之态进行斗争。我们不能允许我们开创性的抗议降格为肉体上的暴力行为。当我们用灵魂的力量一次次地面对肉体上的暴力时，我们的境界必然上升至庄严的高度。

令人赞叹的战斗精神已然充盈了黑人社会，但绝不能让它导向对所有白人的不信任。因为许多白人兄弟已经意识到，他们的命运与我们的命运紧密相连。他们今天到场就证明了这一点。他们已经意识到，我们的自由与他们的自由密不可分。我们不能单独行进。就在我们前行的时候，我们必须立下庄严的誓言：我们当一直向前。我们不能后退。

有人向热心民权运动者发问："你们什么时候才能满意？"我们永远都不会满意，只要黑人未能免于警察的残暴，被他们难以言说的暴行所害。我们永远都不会满意，只要我们旅途劳顿、疲惫不堪，却不能在公路旁的汽车旅馆以及城里的旅馆寻得住处。我们永远都不会满意，只要黑人的活动范围仅限于从一个专为他们而建的小安置区挪到一个大点儿的安置区。我们永远都不会满意，只要我们的孩子因为"仅供白人"的标牌而失去自我、而被剥夺尊严。我们永远都不会满意，只要密西西比有一位黑人不能投票、纽约有一位黑人认为其投票毫无益处。是的！是的！我们现在不满意，将来也不会满意，除非正义如水之顺流、公正如江河滔滔。

我注意到了，今天来到这里的人中，有的饱经磨难，有的刚刚走出狭小的牢房，有的来自种族迫害与警察暴行的风暴区——他们在要求自由时，受到了严厉的摧折。你们是非同寻常的磨难的长期经历者。带着信念继续行进吧，要相信：承受这些不应承受的磨难是会得救的。

回到密西西比，回到阿拉巴马，回到南卡罗来纳，回到佐治亚，回到路易斯安那，回到北方城市的贫民窟与安置区去吧！要知道，总有一天，这种状况能够也必将被改变。

请勿在绝望的峡谷漫无目的地徘徊。我的朋友们，我今天要对你们说，即使我们现在与将来会面对诸多困难，我依然有一个梦想——一个深植于美国梦中的梦想。

我梦想有一天，这个国家会崛起，彻底实现其信念的真实含义——“人人生而平等，这是我们认为不言而喻的真理”。

我梦想有一天，在佐治亚的红山上，从前那些奴隶与奴隶主的子孙能坐在一起，叙话如兄弟。

我梦想有一天，甚至连密西西比这个因充斥着非正义与压迫的热浪而令人痛苦难当的州，也将转变为一片自由与正义的绿洲。

我梦想有一天，我的四个小孩将生活在一个不以其肤色，而以其品格来评判他们的国度里。

今天，我有一个梦！

我梦想有一天，就在阿拉巴马，这个有着邪恶的种族主义者的州（该州州长满口“插入抵制”、“裁决无效”）发生转变。梦想有一天，就在那里，黑人的孩子能与白人的孩子手牵着手，如同兄弟姐妹。

今天，我有一个梦想！

我梦想有一天，峡谷上升山岳降，崎岖之地化平川，曲折之路转通途，让上帝的光辉显露，所有的生灵都能望见。

这就是我们的希望。正是因为它，我将回到南方。有了这个信念，我们就能从绝望的山岭中劈出一块希望之石。

有了这个信念，我们就能把这个国家嘈杂刺耳的争吵变为一曲优美的博爱交响曲。有了这个信念，我们将能同工作，同祈祷，同斗争，同入狱，共同坚持自由；并且知道，终有一天，我们会自由。

当这一天来临，上帝的所有子孙都会以新的意义唱响这首歌："你啊，我的祖国，美好的自由之地，我为你歌唱。这里是我的父辈们死去的地方，是新英格兰开拓者的骄傲，让每一个山麓啊，响彻了自由之声。"如果美国要成为一个伟大的国家，就必须实现这个梦。

因此，请让自由之声从新罕布什尔州巍峨的山顶响起！

让自由之声从纽约州的大山响起！

让自由之声从宾夕法尼亚高耸的阿利根尼山脉响起！

让自由之声从科罗拉多冰雪覆盖的落基山响起！

让自由之声从加利福尼亚蜿蜒的群峰响起！

不止如此

还要让自由之声从佐治亚州的石头山响起！

让自由之声从田纳西州的望山响起！

让自由之声从密西西比的每一座小山与丘陵响起，从每一片山坡响起！让自由之声响起！

当所有这些都发生，当我们让自由之声从所有的乡村、州县、城市、各州响起时，这一天就能够加速到来。那时，上帝的所有子孙——黑人与白人、犹太人与非犹太人、新教徒与天主教徒——都将携手共唱一首歌曲，用的是美国南部古老的黑人圣歌的曲辞："终于自由了！终于自由了！感谢全能的主，我们终于自由了！"

解　析

为什么我有一个梦?

1963 年往前推一百年,也就是 1863 年,第 16 任美国总统亚伯拉罕·林肯(Abraham Lincoln)颁布《解放宣言》(*Emancipation Proclamation*)。随后几年内,第 13、14、15 宪法修正案(The 13th,14th,15th Amendment to the Constitution)相继在国会通过并获得批准——奴隶制被废除、所有美国黑人都获得了公民身份,并且规定美国公民的投票权不能因其种族、肤色或曾经被奴役而被剥夺①。

但是,正如美国黑人学者杜波依斯(W.E.Du Bois)所言,"被解放了的黑人只是在阳光下稍站片刻,就又回到了奴隶制"(The slave went free;stood a brief moment in the sun;then move back again toward slavery)②。从 1870 年开始,南方各州相继制定了各种各样对黑人加以歧视与迫害的法律,总称为吉姆·克劳法(Jim Crow Laws),譬如人头税(Poll Tax)③、祖父条款(Grandfather

---

① 第 15 条宪法修正案第一款原文如下:The right of citizens of the United States to vote shall not be denied or abridged by the United States or by any State on account of race,color,or previous condition of servitude.

② W.E.B.Du Bois,*Black Reconstruction in America*:*1860-1880*,New York:The Free Press,1992,p.30.

③ 自 19 世纪晚期,人头税就成为佛罗里达、阿拉巴马、田纳西、阿肯色、路易斯安那、南卡罗来纳、北卡罗来纳、弗吉尼亚、德克萨斯(1902 年)等州选民登记的必要条件(a prerequisite to voter registration),要求登记选民者至少缴纳 1.50 ~1.75 美元的税金方可有资格参与选举。佐治亚还规定了按累进方式计算的人头税(1877 年)。人头税虽不分种族,面向所有 21~60 岁的男子,然而无力缴纳人头税的黑人在其人口比例中大大超出贫穷的白人在白人人口中的比例。因而,人头税的设置主要是为了限制黑人投票。这一限制同时还伴随着其他关于投票资格的限制,比如"祖父条款"(要求登记选民的男子证明其父或祖父在奴隶制被废除之前曾在未纳税的情况下投过票)、文化测试等。

Clause)、文化测验(Literacy Test)等。这些吉姆·克劳法剥夺黑人本该享有的权利,其目的是为了维护白人至上原则(White Supremacy),一种在北美大陆已盛行了两个半世纪的社会与文化传统。1896 年,美国联邦最高法院在"普莱西对弗格森"(Plessy v.Ferguson)一案中确认"隔离但平等"原则(Separate but Equal),种族隔离与歧视制度从此具有了合法性。从那时起,在种族隔离与歧视制度下生活的黑人不但在法律上失去了与白人平等的公民身份,即便是每一个美国公民所应享有的不可剥夺的权利,也被剥夺了;美国《宪法》所谓"保证我们自己和子孙后代的幸福"(Secure the blessings of liberty to ourselves and our posterity),对于黑人而言,只是一个不敢奢望的梦。但是,随着自由与民主理念在全世界的推进,随着人们对第二次世界大战种族主义恶行的反思,黑人获得了争取自由与幸福权利的机会,民权运动(Civil Rights Movement)因此而展开。就在这样一个渴望甩开二等公民身份、获得与白人平等的公民权的运动中,黑人自然而然地有了一个深深植根于美国梦中的梦(a dream deeply rooted in the American dream):一个希望人人生而平等的梦(a dream of that all men are created equal);一个希望能与白人并肩而坐、叙话如兄弟的梦(a dream of sitting down together at the table of brotherhood);一个渴望自己的孩子不因肤色而被歧视、只依其品格而加以评判的梦(a dream of that our children will not be judged by the color of their skin but by the content of their character);一个黑人与白人的孩子可以手拉手,亲近如兄弟姊妹般的梦(a dream of that black boys and girls and white boys and girls will be able to join hands with each other as sisters and brothers)。总而言之,一个希望生活在美好的、充满自由与正义的绿洲上的梦(a dream of living on the oasis of freedom and liberty,a sweet land of liberty)。

华盛顿游行(March on Washington for Jobs and Freedom)——《我有一个梦》的诞生

作为美国黑人自由运动史一份重要的文献,《我有一个梦》诞生于一场伟大的为自由而行的运动。这就是 1963 年的华盛顿游行(March on Washington for Jobs and Freedom)。这场游行因何而发起?

前面提到了民权运动。民权运动从20世纪初开始,历经艰难,终于在1954年5月17日取得了最具转折意义的重大胜利。美国联邦最高法院在"布朗对托皮卡"(Oliver Brown et al v.Board of Education of Topeka)一案中作出裁决①,即通常所说的布朗裁决(Brown Decision)——一个关于种族隔离学校是否正义的裁决。法官们一致认定,"在教育上实施种族隔离本质上就是不平等的(Separate education facilities are inherently unequal);这样的隔离背离了美国宪法所承诺给予公民受法律平等保护的原则"(such segregation is a denial of the equal protection of the laws ganranteed by the Fourteenth Amendment);并宣布"公共教育领域的隔离但平等原则从此不应存在"(We conclude that in the field of public education the doctrine of separate but equal has no place)②。这就在法律上否认了种族隔离与种族歧视的正当性。种族隔离墙从此被推倒。

然而,民权运动从一开始就遇到了白人种族主义者(White racists)的强烈抵制(White Resistance),尤其是在美国南方。

从19世纪末到20世纪50年代,因参与或支持黑人自由运动者,无论黑人还是白人,屡屡受到私刑迫害(the persecution of lynching),杀人者往往逍遥法外。布朗裁决一宣布,便遭到白人种族主义者的谴责与蔑视。他们将布朗裁决宣布的这一天——5月17日——称之为"黑色星期一"(Black Monday),并迅即组织反攻。密西西比州出现了以维护"白人至上"为宗旨的"白人市民理事会"(White Citizens' Council),专以对抗种族融合为务,该组织很快就覆盖到其他州;"三K党"(Ku Klux Klan)的活动也倍加猖獗,其成员身着白袍,风帽蒙面,先是以焚烧十字架作为警示,恫吓不成,再加以人身暴力、焚烧房屋,乃至于谋杀。1956年3月,来自11个南方州的101名国会议员在美国联邦参议院(Senate)联名发布《南方宣言》(*The Southern Manifesto*),公开呼吁南

---

① 该案由联邦最高法院集合了来自堪萨斯、南卡罗来纳、弗吉尼亚、特拉华、哥伦比亚特区的5个上诉案件合并而成。

② Richard Kluger, *Simple Justice: The History of Brawn V. Board of Education and Black America's Struggle for Equality*, New York: Alfred Knopf, 2004, pp.790~798.

方各州"采取一切所谓的合法手段抵制布朗裁决,即强制性的种族融合"(to resist forced integration by any lawful means)①。在这些人的煽动下,当年4月起,南方各州纷纷通过法案,宣布"布朗裁决"在该州无效。1957年9月在阿肯色州小石城(the city of Little Rock, Arkansas),为阻止9名黑人中学生(Little Rock Nine)入读白人学校,州长沃佛·福布斯(Orval Faubus)调动地方武装阿肯色州国民卫队(Arkansas National Guard),挑起了小石城危机(Little Rock Crisis),白人与黑人间发生了激烈对抗,最后竟迫使总统艾森豪威尔(Dwight David Eisenhower)动用联邦军队全副武装保护黑人学生入学②。1963年6月12日,就在肯尼迪(John F.Kennedy)总统发表电视讲话,表示支持民权运动,呼吁国会议员通过《民权法》议案的第二天,麦德加·埃弗斯(Medgar Evers)——美国最有影响的民权组织"全国有色人种协进会"(National Association for the Advancement of Colored People, NAACP)在密西西比州的地方领导人,在他家门口被"白人市民理事会"授意枪杀③。埃弗斯的死燃起了黑人的愤怒之火,许多城市发生了严重的种族冲突,1963年的夏天因此成为马丁·路德·金所说"一个酷热的夏季(a sweltering summer)"。

就在这种背景下,早已在酝酿并于1963年春知会肯尼迪总统将要组织一次大规模游行的民权运动元老,也是马丁·路德·金在民权运动上的导师及战友,菲利普·伦道夫(A.Philip Randolph)抓住时机,争取到了其他民权领袖

---

① *Congressional Record*, 84th Congress Second Session. Vol.102, Part 4(March 12, 1956). Washington, D.C.: Governmental Printing Office, 1956. pp.4459~4460.

② 值得一提的是,阿肯色州小石城在美国南方并非种族对立尤为严重的地区,州长沃佛·福布斯的态度原本也较为温和,布朗裁决出来之后,小石城的公立学校还为促进种族融合做了不少准备工作。然而就在第一批黑人学生准备入读白人学校时,福布斯一改以往温和态度而采取措施抵制种族融合,用他自己的话说,"来维持或恢复这个地方的和平与良好秩序"(to maintain or restore the peace and good order of this community)。促使他改变立场的原因在于他不得不迎合在白人中普遍而根深蒂固的种族主义。当时,他正面临州长选举,其对手是一个极力反对种族融合的强硬分子,颇受选民欢迎,福布斯若想连任,必须表明抵制种族融合,否则无法获得白人选票。小石城危机结束后,福布斯高票当选,第二次连任阿肯色州州长。

③ Medgar Evers(1925~1963),密西西比州杰出的民权运动领导人。他曾参与第二次世界大战,为国奉献,却在军营中遭受种族隔离。战争结束后,他回到家乡,投身民权运动,所司职责深为白人种族主义者仇视,譬如调查暗杀黑人的真相并将之公布于众、寻觅与保护证人、为黑人争取入读白人学校的权利、动员并训练黑人参与投票等。

对游行计划的支持。6 月 22 日,包括伦道夫与金在内的 6 位民权运动领导人(Six Big)[①]会晤肯尼迪,并在 7 月 2 日正式宣布:将于 8 月 27、28 日两天举行命名为"March on Washington for Jobs and Freedom"的大规模和平游行。游行如期进行,约 25 万人——白人、黑人以及其他有色人种——参加。8 月 28 日,游行队伍汇聚林肯纪念堂(Lincoln Memorial)前,马丁·路德·金最后一个发表演讲,这就是"I Have a Dream"。令人赞叹的是,这篇节奏铿锵、富于感染力的演说,有一半的内容系即兴发挥。演说一出,即刻家喻户晓。

《我有一个梦》的思想基础

20 世纪美国黑人民权运动史上,影响最大的两个人物要算马丁·路德·金与马尔卡姆·X(Malcolm X)[②]。两人均以充满智慧、善于演说而知名。从个人魅力上说,也许马尔卡姆更胜一筹。他英俊、潇洒;经历坎坷,却有学者的风度;思想深邃不在金博士之下。不过,这两个人的思想反映美国民权运动两支不同的路向。马尔卡姆以思想激进见著,体现民权运动中具有强烈黑人民族主义的一支;马丁·路德·金的思想温和执中,代表民权运动的主流[③]。《我有一个梦》正是民权运动主流思想的充分表达。

首先,它以美国《宪法》与《独立宣言》承诺给美国公民的合法权利作为基本纲领。这就是不可剥夺的生命、自由与追求幸福的权利(unalienable rights of Life, Liberty and pursuit of Happiness)。在马丁·路德·金等民权领袖看

① 其他 4 位领导人分别为:James Farmer,"种族平等大会"(Congress of Racial Equality)主席;John Lewis,"学生非暴力合作委员会"(Student Nonviolent Coordinating Committee)主席;Roy Wilkins,"全国有色人种协进会"主席;Whitney Young,"全国城市联盟"(National Urban League)主席。

② Malcolm X(1925~1965),原名 Malcolm Little,20 世纪下半叶美国现代黑人民族主义的代表,黑人自由运动中与公民权运动阵营颇为对立的黑人领袖。1948 年,加入黑人宗教组织"伊斯兰国度"(Nation of Islam),改宗伊斯兰教,遵从该组织要求,将姓氏改为"X"。笔者有意未将"X"译出。其原因在于:伊斯兰国度成员以"X"为姓,是为表示黑人曾屈身为奴,文化上丧失其源、不知其姓的历史。1965 年 2 月 21 日,马尔科姆在纽约曼哈顿被谋杀。

③ 需要指出,20 世纪 60 年代,即便是马丁·路德·金的思想,在美国主流社会看来,依然是激进的。这里所言"马丁·路德·金的思想温和执中",只是在整个民权运动阵营内相对而言。

来,正是宪法与独立宣言的承诺为美国这个国家建立了一个正义的银行(a bank of Justice);每一个美国公民都有资格从这个银行中提取自由的丰裕与正义的保障(Every American citizen shall have right to demand the riches of freedom and the security of justice);而遵从共和国缔造者(the architects of our republic)的承诺则是美国政府的责任或者说神圣的义务(to honor this sacred obligation);但是,美国未曾履行这神圣的义务,致使建国之父的诺言成为一张空头支票(a bad check which has come back marked "insufficient funds")。不过,黑人们不愿意相信正义的银行已然破产(They refuse to believe that the bank of justice is bankrupt)。尽管他们对种族压迫深感愤怒,却对这个国家依然抱有信心,因此他们汇聚首都,前来兑现这张支票(We've come to our nation's capital to cash a check)。他们相信,严酷的夏季过去后,平等与自由的秋天将会来临(The sweltering summer will be followed by an invigorating autumn of freedom and equality);黑人将获得作为美国公民的权利(The Negro is granted his citizenship rights);民主的诺言终将成为现实(The promises of democracy will be made real);所有上帝的子孙也终将感受到正义的光明(For all of God's children, the bright day of justice emerges)。简言之,这个国家将充分而真实地体现其天赋人权的政治信念(This nation will rise up and live out the true meaning of its creed——we hold these truths to be self-evident)。

其次,以种族融合(Racial Integration)作为民权运动的目标。奉行人人生而平等的原则,不因肤色、种族、宗教信仰、所出生的国家以及从前的身份等而相互歧视,脱离种族隔离的阴郁深谷(to rise from the dark and desolate valley of segregation),在各个方面与白人或其他有色人种和谐共处、亲密无间。这样的社会,在民权运动的主流看来,才能让美国迈上阳光照耀下的正义之路(the sunlit path of racial justice)。因此,马丁·路德·金在演讲中表达出他的融合梦:梦想有一天,从前那些奴隶与奴隶主的子孙能如兄弟般并肩而坐(I have a dream that one day the sons of former slaves and the sons of former slave owners will be able to sit down together at the table of brotherhood);梦想有一天,黑人与白人的孩子能如兄弟姐妹般手挽着手(I have a dream that one day little black boys and black girls will be able to join hands with little white boys and white girls as sisters and brothers);梦想有一天,所有的白人都意识到:白人的自由与黑人的自由密不可分(They come to realize that their freedom is inextricably bound to our freedom)、黑人的命运与白人的命运息息相关(Their destiny is tied up with our destiny)。他相信,只要怀抱着兄弟般的博爱情谊,就能得到白人兄弟的支持与联合,使这个国家不再立于种族不平等的险滩之上(It will be able to lift our nation from the quicksands of racial injustice),最终实现种族间平等的融合。

最后,但绝非最不重要,以非暴力抵抗作为争取权利或自由的战斗哲学。演讲词中有一段话语说给为自由而战的黑人:在争取应得的位置时,一定不要因错误的行动而犯下罪行。请勿因渴求自由而从苦恨与敌意中舀取一杯来饮。我们必须永远以高度的尊严、严明的律己之态进行斗争;绝不允许我们开创性的和平抗议降格为肉体上的暴力行为(But there is something that I must say to my people, to those who stand on the threshold which leads into the palace of justice, in the process of gaining our rightful place, we must not be guilty of wrongful deeds. Let us not seek to satisfy our thirst for freedom by drinking from the cup of bitterness and hatred. We must forever conduct our struggle on the high plane of dignity and discipline. We must not allow our creative protest to degenerate into physical violence)。这是马丁·路德·金对于圣雄甘地非暴力抵抗(nonviolent resistance)精神的追随,也是马丁·路德·金以爱代替恨的宗教思想的表达。

然而,非暴力抵抗的哲学、以爱代替恨的宗教大爱,知犹不易,行更艰难。1963 年的美国,黑人的愤怒情绪积蓄至深,随时即可大规模喷发。夏季尚未来临,种族压迫与反抗的热浪已席卷美国。4、5 月间,阿拉巴马州伯明翰市的民权游行(Birmingham Campaign)遭到严厉镇压。每平方英寸水压达 100 磅的高压水龙头将游行者掀翻在地,其中主要是中小学生;警察甚至放出了恶犬;包括马丁·路德·金在内,近 3000 人被捕。游行尚未平息,企图暗杀金与其家人的爆炸案接连发生,愤怒的抗议者开始与警察发生暴力冲突。这一年的春与夏,约 930 余起抗议示威在美国一百多个城市此起彼伏,难以止歇①。频繁的种族冲突中包括许多行为激进的黑人,和平抗议大有演为暴乱之势。

---

① Clayborne Carson, etc., *The Struggle for Freedom*, p.471.

一向不赞成非暴力抵抗策略的马尔科姆向黑人呼吁，“只要有人向黑人放狗，黑人就应该杀了它，不管那是四条腿的狗还是两条腿的狗”（If anybody sets a dog on a black man, the black man should kill that dog—whether he is a four-legged dog or a two-legged dog）①。这引起了金的焦虑。他目睹这个国家的根基正在被摇撼、社会的安宁将要失去（There will be neither rest nor tranquility in America; the whirlwinds of revolt will continue to shake the foundations of our nation）。但他不愿意看到这样危险的局面。他希望，民权运动的抗议目标是邪恶本身而非行恶之人；对于行恶之人，须怀着以爱代替恨的信念，勇敢地承受痛苦而不还击。在他看来，承受不应受的痛苦（to suffer the unearned suffering），不还手也不报复，才是内心强大有尊严的表现；才能体现正义必将如水之顺流、公正必将如江河滔滔的信念（with the faith that justice rolls down like waters and righteousness like a mighty stream）。因此他呼吁，所有为自由而战的黑人表现出高度的尊严与严明的律己之态，勿将公民不合作（Civil Disobedience）的创造性形式——非暴力抵抗或和平抗议——降格为肉体上的暴力行为；通过以爱代替恨的崇高行为，表现抗议者灵魂的力量（to reach the majestic heights of meeting physical force with soul force）。

但是问题在于，“我怎么去爱一个对我怀着敌意的种族”？（How could I love a race of people who hated me?）。这个连马丁·路德·金自己也被困扰数年的问题同样摆在其他黑人面前。马丁·路德·金最终依靠宗教的力量解决了这个问题。他说，他把爱那些恨他的人视为一个基督徒的义务——“It was my duty as a Christian to love him”②。不过，对于在种族迫害的风暴中深受伤害的其他人，并非个个都能接受以爱代替恨的哲学。

马丁·路德·金的梦是所有美国人的梦吗？

当然不是。尽管金的梦很美好，但在思想激进的黑人看来（更不用说思

---

① Manning Marable, *Malcolm X: A Life of Reinvention*, New York: Penguin Books, 2012, p.238.

② Clayborne Carson, ed., *The Autography of Martin Luther King, Jr.* p.7.

想保守的白人),他的梦非但不切实际,甚至显得虚伪。

种族融合?黑人们问自己,“我真的想融进一个对我充满仇恨、随时要将我房屋烧毁的白人社会吗?”(Do I really want to be integrated into a burning house?)①。1619年,第一批来自非洲的黑人被锁链拴着登上了北美大陆,从此作为奴隶在这片土地上生存。他们被剥削、被压迫了近两个半世纪。其间,美国革命喊出了“人人生而平等”、“一切人都享有不可剥夺的天赋权利”的口号,并将其作为美国的立国原则。然而,奴隶制却在这人人生而平等与自由的国度被保留下来。直到内战结束,黑奴才出乎意料地得到解放。但是,解放不等于平等。它甚至使得白人社会更加仇视黑人。种族隔离制度因此在南方成为维系社会秩序的传统;“三K党”也因此在南方横行肆虐,时时威胁黑人的生命、毁灭黑人的财产。黑人在这个传统包裹下与恐惧的气氛中为佣、为工、为二等公民,从未呼吸到自由的空气,只觉得自己低人一等。白人也确实是这样高傲地看待他们的。而这与白人社会一直宣扬的平等、自由与公平原则是多么冲突!除了虚伪,许多黑人不知道怎样描述这种美国文明。在他们看来,“白人的天堂就是黑人的地狱”(The white man's Heaven is the black man's Hell)②;那种从未履行口头上所宣扬的价值观的社会与文明,根本不值得黑人接受与融合进去。现在谈种族融合,岂不是要求“四百年来受尽苦难的美国黑人就应这样仅以接受美国现在的文明而了结?”(The four-hundred-year travail of the American Negro should result merely in this attainment of the present level of the American Civilization?)③。

至于非暴力抵抗的战斗哲学,在那些对美国社会的自由、平等与正义已深感绝望的人眼里,根本就是痴人做梦。在他们看来,正义的银行已然破产,“美国已是一片无望的国土、一个无可救赎的民族”(America was an hopeless, irredeemable nation)④;指望以非暴力战斗哲学赢得白人的同情与让步,争得

---

① James Baldwin, *The Fire Next Time*, New York: Dell Publishing, 1985, p.127.

② James Baldwin, *The Fire Next Time*, p.64.

③ James Baldwin, *The Fire Next Time*, p.129.

④ Peniel E.Joseph, *Waiting'til The Midnight Hour: A Narrative History of Black Power in America*, New York: Holt Paperbacks, 2007, p.66.

黑人的自由,无异于“指望不经耕耘就有收获;未经雷电就会下雨;未有狂潮怒啸便成其为海洋”(They want crops without plowing up the ground;they want rain without thunder and lightning;they want the ocean without the awful roar with its many waters)①。因此,他们对马丁·路德·金的梦嗤之以鼻,嘲笑说:“你的梦不是我的梦(Your dream is not my dream)”。马尔卡姆·X对金提出严厉的批评,说他“装腔作势,以为自由就是坐在白人身旁喝咖啡(King is a poseur who defined freedom as drinking coffee next to whites)”②。就在金发表演说“我有一个梦”的当天,马尔卡姆·X对游行组织者之一巴亚德·拉斯廷(Bayard Rustin)言道:“金的这个梦在他梦醒之前就会变成一场噩梦(This dream of King's is going to be a nightmare before it is over)”③。

那么,对于这些思想激进的黑人来说,他们的梦是什么?是先去除强制性的种族隔离(It is to lift the forced racial segregation),再与白人社会自愿隔离(to practice self-segregation);是建立“国中国”(a nation within a nation),由黑人掌握权力,实现种族自治。在他们看来,“是权力,而不是道德,横亘其间,不让美国黑人得到上帝允诺的自由”(Power,not morality,stood between black Americans and the promise of freedom)④。

显然,这样的黑人梦对美国社会的繁荣与稳定势必构成威胁。马丁·路德·金清楚地预见到了这一点。因此,他在演讲中提醒美国人民和政府,现在已到了情势非常紧迫的时候(We have come to this hallowed spot to remind America of the fierce urgency of now),到了民主的诺言必须真实地实现的时候(Now is the time to make real the promises of democracy)。倘若对此危险情势视若罔闻,美国将面临灾难性后果(It would be fatal for the nation to overlook

① Kwame Ture and Charles V.Hamilton, *Black Power: The Politics of Liberation in America*, New York: Vintage Books, 1992, p.xviii.说明:这段话原本出自19世纪美国著名黑人弗里德里克·道格拉斯(Frederick Douglass)之口。1857年8月3日,道格拉斯发表演说,鼓励美国黑人通过暴力手段争取自由(参见 Robert Levine ed., *Frederick Douglass: A Heroic Slave*, New Haven: Yale University Press, 2015, pp.133~134)。一个多世纪之后,反对非暴力运动策略的黑人拿它来宣扬暴力抵抗的合理性。

② Peniel E.Joseph, *Waiting'til The Midnight Hour*, pp.79-80.

③ Manning Marable, *Malcolm X: A Life of Reinvention*, New York: Penguin Books, 2012, p.257.

④ Peniel E.Joseph, *Waiting'til The Midnight Hour*, pp.55-56.

the urgency of the moment);倘若不赋予黑人以公民权,美国社会将永无宁日(There will be neither rest nor tranquility in America until the Negro is granted his citizenship)。

值得欣慰的是,美国政府与人民接受了金的提醒。华盛顿游行当日,肯尼迪总统邀请黑人领袖到白宫,向他们表示:"我也有一个梦,梦见有一天,新的《民权法案》能够在参、众两院通过"①。来年春季,第24条宪法修正案(The 24th amendment to the Constitution of the United States)首先获得批准,它禁止以缴纳人头税作为公民参与选举的条件②。随后,《公民权法》(*Civil Rights Act*)在国会通过。1965年,肯尼迪总统的继任者,林登·约翰逊(Lyndon Johnson)又签署了《选举权法》(*Voting Rights Act*),黑人作为美国公民的权利得到了较为确实的法律保障,种族歧视的时代终于开始走向末路。至少,所有美国人都已经认识到,种族歧视在政治上是不正确的。

同时也不能忽视的是,玫瑰色的梦没有消除白人与黑人间的敌意。"我有一个梦"演讲发表仅仅18天后,阿拉巴马州伯明翰市,4名黑人学生被当场炸死,15人受伤。同年11月,肯尼迪总统遇刺。尽管美国人对其原因争议纷纷,但在黑人看来,这位帮助他们获享正当权利的总统被谋杀,意味着自由梦不可避免的透着血色猩红;如果说美国可以得到救赎,那也必定是一场血色救赎(bloody redemption)。随后的数年,美国各城市不断上演着因种族冲突与黑人自由运动的分裂而导致的暴乱场面,其中包括马尔科姆·X的被谋杀(1965年2月21日);而最严重的暴乱之一发生在马丁·路德·金遇刺身亡(1968年4月4日)后。他的死引发了美国一百多个城市的大规模种族冲突,46人死亡,3000多人受伤。

---

① 林达:《我也有一个梦想》,北京:生活·读书·新知三联书店,2013年,第366页。

② 第24条宪法修正案如下:The right of citizens of the United States to vote in any primary or other election for President or Vice President, for electors for President or Vice President, or for Senator or Representative in Congress, shall not be denied or abridged by the United States or any State by reason of failure to pay any poll tax or other tax.值得指出的是,第24条宪法修正案获得批准、生效后,依然有5个州——弗吉尼亚、阿拉巴马、德克萨斯、阿肯色、密西西比(Virginia, Alabama, Texas, Arkansas, and Mississippi)保留了有关选举权限定资格的人头税。

延伸阅读

林达：《我也有一个梦想》，北京：生活·读书·新知三联书店，2013年。林达是一对美籍华人夫妇共用的笔名。男的叫丁耀富，女的叫李晓琳。1991年，二人前往美国。随后数年间，以书信体形式写下“近距离看美国”系列。因其清新流畅的文笔，富有洞见的议论，被誉为“中国的托克维尔”（1831年5月至1832年2月，法国人托克维尔与其挚友古斯塔夫·德·博蒙游历美国。回国后，托克维尔先后出版《论美国的民主》上、下两卷，记录其在美9个月的观察所得）。该系列之一《我也有一个梦想》浅易而生动地叙述了美国社会的种族关系演进史（主要是白人与黑人），对于理解美国民权运动的背景与过程，提供了别开生面的视野。

Clayborne Carson, ed., *Autobiography of Martin Luther King, Jr.*, New York: Warner Books, Inc., 1999（克莱伯恩·卡森编：《马丁·路德·金 自传》，马乐梅、张安恩、杨婕译，南昌：江西人民出版社，2009年）。依据马丁·路德·金本人的文字辑选而成的自传，虽非十分全面，但充分体现了金的宗教与政治思想。编者克莱伯恩·卡尔森系美国斯坦福大学历史学荣誉教授，大学期间曾亲身参与美国民权运动，譬如1963年“华盛顿游行”，并由此奠定他终身的志业：研究非裔美国人自由运动史。1985年，卡尔森受马丁·路德·金的遗孀科丽塔·司格特·金（Coretta Scott King）的委托，主持“马丁·路德·金文集工程”，逐渐成为著名的马丁·路德·金研究专家，目前已编纂、出版《马丁·路德·金文集》1~7卷。2000年，由他所编撰的《马丁·路德·金自传》音像版获音乐界“格莱美”奖（Grammy Award）。

David Garrow, *Bearing the Cross: Martin Luther King, Jr. and the Southern Christian Leadership of Conference*, New York: Rerennial Classics, 1999. 马丁·路德·金的自述中其实有不合或隐蔽事实之处，学界早期对金的评价也往往将

之圣人化。《背负十字架》通过客观地呈现金的私人与公共生活,真实叙述了金的一生及其思想,表明金并非 20 世纪的汤姆大叔。通过此书,读者亦可了解 20 世纪五六十年代美国民权运动发展历程。

Manning Marable, *Malcolm X: A Life of Reinvention*, New York: Penguin Books, 2012. 欲图全面理解马丁·路德·金以及美国民权运动,必须同时了解马尔科姆的一生及其思想。他二人都为美国黑人的自由与权利奉献了生命,虽然其思想基础与战斗策略大有差异,但都在生命的晚期开始理解对方,由此可以看出美国黑人运动的发展方向与不同阵营的殊途同归处。曼宁·马拉布尔是美国历史学家中对马尔科姆研究最深者之一。这本书不仅跟踪、论述了马尔科姆一生思想的变化或者说重塑,也告诉人们如何正确理解马尔科姆:他并非黑人暴力运动的积极推动者,他只是反对一味的非暴力抵抗。

Peniel E.Joseph, *Waiting'til The Midnight Hour: A Narrative History of Black Power in America*, New York: Holt Paperbacks, 2007. "黑人权力运动"(Black Power Movement)是美国黑人自由运动中最为激进的一支,马丁·路德·金对它反对尤力。它因何而起,又如何发展,最后怎样结局?约瑟夫为读者提供了细致的分析。

James Baldwin, *The Fire Next Time*, New York: Dell Publishing, 1985. 20 世纪 60 年代是美国历史上种族关系最复杂、白人与黑人间的冲突最为剧烈的时期。经历数世纪压迫的美国黑人想什么、恨什么、怕什么、渴求什么?他们又如何看待自己在美国社会中的地位?如何以各种方式面对自己的命运?读此书当可对读者理解其时的美国社会与种族关系有所帮助。这本书发表于 1963 年,被称为 20 世纪 60 年代最有影响的关于黑人与白人种族关系的评论。作者鲍德温是 20 世纪美国有名的黑人文学家与社会评论家,与理查德·莱特(Richard Wright)和拉里夫·埃里森(Ralph Ellison)齐名。后两人的代表作《土生子》(*Nation Son*)与《看不见的人》(*Invisible Man*)对于美国白人了解黑人以及黑人了解自己起到了照镜子般的作用。

Eyes on the Prize, 14 集电视纪录片,再现了 1954 年布朗裁决以来直到 1985 年期间的美国民权运动历程,曾在美国公共电视台(Public Broadcast Service, PBS)黄金时段播放。其叙事视角不以人们所熟知的民权领袖譬如马

丁·路德·金为中心，而主要呈现普通人在这场运动中的贡献。它将小人物的英雄故事采入镜头。其目的乃为说明：民权运动属于普通人，如果没有他们的勇气与参与，种族歧视问题永远得不到解决，马丁·路德·金等只是民权运动的产儿，而非创造者。第6集《通往自由之桥》(*Bridge to Freedom*)获1988年"奥斯卡奖"(Academy Awards)提名。伴随纪录片发行的还有两大本提供了丰富背景材料的书：Juan Williams, *Eyes on the Prize: American Civil Right Years 1954~1965*, New York: Penguin Books, 1987; Henry Hampton and Steve Fayer, ed., *Voices of Freedom: An Oral History of the Civil Rights Movement from the 1950s through the 1980s*, New York: Bantam Books, 1990.

约翰·霍普·富兰克林：《美国黑人史》，张冰姿等译，北京：商务印书馆，1988年。富兰克林(John Hope Franklin)是20世纪美国著名的黑人历史学家(1915~2009)，是黑人中较早在哈佛大学获得博士学位者(1941年)，以其对非裔美国人史研究的开创性贡献而享有盛名。1995年，富兰克林获得美国公民最高荣誉，由克林顿总统授予其"总统自由勋章"。他最有名的著作是 *From Slavery to Freedom: A Story of Negro Americans*，初版于1947年，至今已出至第12版。这里所介绍的《美国黑人史》即译自其第5版(中译本取其副标题为书名)，系国内读者所见到的为数不多的综合性美国黑人史著作之一。

THE GETTYSBURG ADDRESS
《葛底斯堡演说》

THE GETTYSBURG ADDRESS[①]

Abraham Lincoln[②]

proposition: statement that expresses a judgment or an opinion

Four score and seven years ago[③]our fathers[④]brought forth on this continent[⑤], a new nation[⑥], conceived in Liberty, and dedicated to the proposition that all men are created equal.

Now we are engaged in a great civil war[⑦], testing whether

---

① 此为亚伯拉罕·林肯于1863年11月19日在葛底斯堡国家烈士公墓落成典礼上的演说。演说词引自 Philip Stern ed., *The Life and Writings of Abraham Lincoln*, New York: The Modern Library, 2000, 系林肯在演讲后的亲笔定稿，也就是最通行的 Bliss Text(葛底斯堡演说词约有5个版本)。葛底斯堡位于宾夕法尼亚州西南，美国内战时，是为该州交通咽喉，地扼东西南北，战略意义重大，如今已成为著名的历史文化旅游城市。它象征着“联邦不可裂解的国家信念与原则”(national idea and principle of the indissolubility of the Union)，见 James McPherson, *Hallowed Groud: A Walk at Gettysburg*, New York: Crown, 2003, p.2.

② 亚伯拉罕·林肯(1809.2.12~1865.4.15)，美国第16任总统(1861年3月至1865年4月)，内战时领导联邦军队获胜，保持了美利坚合众国的统一。

③ 即1776年7月4日北美13个英属殖民地联合发表《独立宣言》，宣布脱离母国，美利坚合众国成立之时。

④ “our fathers”指美国建国之父。

⑤ “this continent”指北美大陆。

⑥ 有学者指出，“nation”一词是林肯为强调合众国不只是一个政治联合体(political union)，而是一个在美国《联邦宪法》制定之前便已产生的国家，而精心选用的。它在演说中共出现5次，说明林肯意图将美国立国的原则——一切人生而平等与自由——置于最为重要的位置。参见 David Herbert Donarld, *Lincoln*, New York: Simon & Schuster Paperbacks, 1995, p.462.

⑦ 即1861年4月爆发的南北战争，持续至1865年4月，以南部邦联无条件投降结束。南北战争最多用的名称为“内战”。不过，内战时，参与南部邦联的各州(共11个)称其为“南部独立战争(War for Southern Independence)”或“北方侵略战争(War of Northern Aggression)”等；南部邦联政府则以“美利坚邦联州与美利坚联合州之间的战争(War Between the Confederate States of America and United States of America)”或“国与国之间的战争(War Between the States)”指代。因此时南部各州实已宣布独立，并成立了联合政府。内战后，“War Between the States”普遍为南方州所用，但“States“的含义已发生变化，不指国而指州(中译亦应调整为“州之间的战争”)。在北方，内战期间及其后，“反叛战争(War of the Rebellion)”亦常为人所用；黑人则称之为“自由战争(Freedom War)”。用名不同，体现各方对战争意义理解之不同。

that nation, or any nation so conceived and so dedicated, can long endure. We are met on a great battle-field of that war. We have come to dedicate a portion of that field, as a final resting place for those who here gave their lives that that nation might live. It is altogether fitting and proper that we should do this.

altogether: completely

But, in a larger sense, we can not dedicate—we can not consecrate—we can not hallow—this ground. The brave men, living and dead, who struggled here, have consecrated it, far above our poor power to add or detract. The world will little note, nor long remember what we say here, but it can never forget what they did here.①It is for us the living, rather, to be dedicated here to the unfinished work which they who fought here have thus far so nobly advanced. It is rather for us to be here dedicated to the great task remaining before us—that from these honored dead we take increased devotion to that cause for which they gave the last full measure of devotion—that we here highly resolve that these dead shall not have died in vain—that this nation, under God, shall have a new birth of freedom—and that government of the people, by the people, for the people, shall not perish from the earth.

consecrate: to devote somebody or something to a special purpose

hallow: to make somebody or something holy; honor as holy

measure of: degree of something

---

① 这里的对比修辞——living and dead, add and detract, no long remember/never forget, 是林肯常用也是他擅长的演说技巧。不妨另举两例:例 1. 1861 年 2 月 22 日林肯在费城独立大厅即兴演说,其中一段:"Now, my friends, can this country be saved upon that basis? If it can, I will consider myself one of the happiest men in the world if I can help to save it. If it cann't be saved upon that principle, it will be truly awful. But, if this country cannot be saved without giving up that principle—I was about to say I would rather be assassinated on this spot than to surrender it."例 2. 1865 年 3 月 4 日第二次总统就职演说中一段:"Both parties deprecated war; but one of them would make war rather than let the nation survive; and the other would accept war rather than let it perish. And the war came."

译文

葛底斯堡演说[1]

亚伯拉罕·林肯

八十七年前，我们的先辈们在这个大陆上创立了一个新国家，它孕育于自由之中，奉行一切人生来平等的原则。

我们正从事一场伟大的内战，以考验这个国家，考验任何一个孕育于自由和奉行上述原则的国家是否能够长久存在下去。我们在这场战争中的一个伟大战场上集会。烈士们为使这个国家能够生存下去而献出了自己的生命，我们来到这里，是要把这个战场的一部分奉献给他们作为最后安息之所。我们这样做是完全应该而且非常恰当的。

但是，从更广泛的意义上说，这块土地我们不能够奉献，不能够圣化，不能够神化。那些曾在这里战斗过的勇士们，活着的和去世的，已经把这块土地圣化了，这远不是我们微薄的力量所能增减的。我们今天在这里所说的话，全世界不大会注意，也不会长久地记住，但勇士们在这里所做过的事，全世界却永远不会忘记。毋宁说，倒是我们这些还活着的人，应该在这里把自己奉献于勇士们已经如此崇高地向前推进但尚未完成的事业。倒是我们应该在这里把自己奉献于仍然留在我们面前的伟大任务——我们要从这些光荣的死者身上汲取更多的献身精神，来完成他们已经完全彻底为之献身的事业；我们要在这里下定最大的决心，不让这些死者白白牺牲；我们要使国家在上帝福佑下自由的新生，要使这个民有、民治、民享的政府永世长存。

---

① 译文取自亚伯拉罕·林肯：《林肯选集》，朱曾汶译，北京：商务印书馆，2010年，第277~278页。

解　　析

葛底斯堡战役(Battle of Gettysburg)——葛底斯堡演说诞生之源

林肯这篇演说发表于葛底斯堡国家烈士公墓落成典礼(Consecration of the National Cemetery at Gettysburg)。这个典礼是为了纪念美国内战(American Civil War)爆发以来规模最大、也是最具转折意义的一场战役——葛底斯堡战役;也是为了纪念那些在战场上奉献生命的众多勇士,向他们表示敬意,“把这个战场的一部分奉献给他们作为最后安息之所”(We have come to dedicate a portion of that field,as a final resting place for those who here gave their lives that that nation might live)。

葛底斯堡战役发生在 1863 年 7 月 1 日至 3 日宾夕法尼亚州的葛底斯堡镇。在此之前,联邦军队(Federal Army,or Union Army)虽然不乏胜绩,但在东线战场上,由罗伯特·李将军(General Robert Lee)指挥的南部邦联部队(Confederate Army)屡屡挫败联邦军队(或称北军)①,以至于内战持续两年后,北方依然看不到胜利的希望,一度士气衰落、民心颓废。尤其是 1863 年四五月间的钱瑟勒斯维尔一役(Battle of Chancellorsville,Virginia)②,素有“灰狐狸”

---

① 美国内战战场布局分东、西两线(Eastern Theater & Western Theater)。东线包括弗吉尼亚、西弗吉尼亚、马里兰、宾夕法尼亚、哥伦比亚特区、北卡罗来纳沿海城防与港口。西线指阿拉巴马、佐治亚、佛罗里达、密西西比、北卡罗来纳大部、肯塔基、南卡罗来纳、田纳西,以及密西西比河以西路易斯安那地区。

② 钱瑟勒斯维尔战役发生于 4 月 30 日 至 5 月 6 日,主要战场邻近斯波齐尔韦尼亚县(Spotsylvania County,Virginia)钱瑟勒斯维尔村(village of Chancellorsville)。指挥南北方军队作战的分别是罗伯特·李、约瑟夫·胡克尔少将(Major General Joseph Hooker),麾下士兵一为 6 万,一为 13 万 3 千。交战结果,南部邦联获胜。这一役因此被称为李将军的完美战役。不过,李将军也在这一战中损失了他最重要的臂膀之一托马斯·杰克逊中将(Lieutenant General Thomas J. “Stonewall” Jackson),后者在内战开始不多久就因勇猛无畏而得名“石墙”(Stonewall)。

(Grey Fox,a nickname of Robert Lee)之称的罗伯特·李在其家乡弗吉尼亚州依靠仅及联邦军队一半的兵力获胜,创下了战无不胜的神话。趁此战果,李向南部邦联总统杰斐逊·戴维斯(Jefferson Davis,President of Confederate States of America)提出一项大胆的计划:率军北攻,进入宾夕法尼亚州,将战火燃向尚未经历过内战侵扰的北方,继而对联邦首都华盛顿构成威胁。李有着一石三鸟的盘算。一来,减轻部队驻扎在南方而给家乡带来的补给压力;二来,迫使华盛顿与南部邦联代表坐在谈判桌前,承认邦联的独立(The Independence of the Confederacy);三来,通过战场上的胜利,说服重要的欧洲国家主要是英法两国,放弃中立态度,转而支持南部邦联,承认其主权国家的地位。因此而言,无论就南方还是北方,这都是一场令人揪心的战役。

两军布阵中,葛底斯堡成为决定灰狐狸能否北上的必经之路①。对于罗伯特·李来说,不幸的是,葛底斯堡战役以及随后结束的维克斯堡战役(Battle of Vicksburg,Mississippi,1863 年 4 月~7 月 4 日)②,将其北上之路彻底堵死。这头"灰狐狸"以为颇有把握获胜,并希望将之作为谈判砝码使南部邦联得以独立的一场战役,反而成为令北方佬(Yankees)从此士气大振、将要在南方长驱直入的一首哀歌。尽管内战随后又持续了两年,但葛底斯堡一役将罗伯特·李不可战胜的神话打破,反叛各州脱离联邦而独立的企图自此化为泡影,他们希望借助战场上的优势获得英、法两国政府支持的愿望也落了空。失败的消息传来,南部邦联军械署长约西亚·戈加斯(Josiah Gorgas, chief of Confederate ordnance)在其日记中悲叹,"邦联摇摇欲坠,行将溃矣!"(The Confederacy totters to its destruction)。葛底斯堡与维克斯堡战役胜利的消息传到英国,美国驻英大使之子,也是其秘书的亨利·亚当斯(Henry Adams)则欢呼:"反叛者灾难已定,任何成功的指望都无可挽回其败局;他们现在得承认,让外国政府来干预的想法全都已然走到尽头"(The disasters

---

① 葛底斯堡并非罗伯特·李预先定下的战斗地点,而是在两军布阵过程中形成的决战胜负的战场。

② 关于维克斯堡战役的战略意义,联邦军队总指挥尤利西斯·格兰特(Ulysses S.Grant)如是评论:"维克斯堡陷落之时,南部邦联的命运就已定下了"(The fate of Confederacy was sealed when Vicksburg fell)。见 James McPherson, *Battle Cry of Freedom: The Civil War Era*, London: Penguin Books,1990,p.637.

of the rebels are unredeemed by even any hope of success; it is now conceded that all idea of intervention is at an end)①。最终,美利坚合众国的完整与统一得以保全。

内战期间,约有 237 场战役发生。葛底斯堡是伤亡最惨重的一役。仅仅 3 天时间,伤亡人数达 51,000 人。北方,投入战斗的波多马克兵团(Army of the Potomac)丧失了超过四分之一的生力军(23,000 Union casualties, more than one-quarter of the army's effectives)。南方损失更重,28,000 人阵亡、受伤或失踪,李将军派出的部队,主要是北弗吉尼亚兵团(Army of Northern Virginia),折损了三分之一还多。毁灭生命的炮声在 120 公里外的匹兹堡(Pittsburg, Pennsylvania)都能听到。对此,战斗双方谁也无法释怀。四十年后,一位南方老兵 J.M.波克(J.M.Polk)依然时时为阵亡战友的魂灵环绕;艾利斯·斯皮尔(Ellis Spear)——北方缅因第 20 步兵团的军官——多年后回首往事,那堆积如山的尸首与被烧焦、肿胀的士兵与马匹遗骸,历历在目②;南军著名将领、在葛底斯堡一役中担任重要角色的詹姆斯·郎斯特里特(James Longstreet),提起 7 月 3 日那一天,将之视为"生命中最悲伤的日子之一"(That day at Gettysburg was one of the saddest day of my life)③。他明知自己的人将被牺牲,却不得不命令他们继续向前。志愿参与战地救护,战后因其小说《小妇人》(*Little Women*)而闻名的路易莎·奥尔科特(Louisa Alcott)也在她的《战地医院速记》(*Hospital Sketches*)中,记下了她对葛底斯堡战役的感受:她知道了什么是真正的战争。

战略上的重大转折意义、战场上前所未有的伤亡记录,令美国人尤其是宾夕法尼亚人无法忘怀这场战役。战事结束后,他们在葛底斯堡建起了一座国家烈士公墓,安葬并纪念牺牲者。公墓落成之日,1863 年 11 月 19 日,作为国家行政首脑的林肯受邀在典礼上说"几句恰当的话"(a few appropri-

① James McPherson, *Battle Cry of Freedom*, p.665.

② Glenn W. Lafantasie, *Gettysburg Heroes: Perfect Soldiers, Hallowed Ground*, Bloomington: Indiana University Press, 2008, p.8.

③ James McPherson, *Battle Cry of Freedom*, p.661.

ate remarks)①。借此机会,林肯发表了一个演说。他并非典礼上第一个发表演说的人——在他前面,还有蜚声遐迩的演说家、时任哈佛大学校长的爱德华·艾佛瑞特(Edward Everett);他所用的时间也比艾佛瑞特长达两小时的演讲短得多——不到两分半钟。但这短短两分半钟的演说成为了林肯一生中最著名的演讲,也使现在的人们几乎忘记:当时还有一位大名鼎鼎、滔滔不绝的演说者排在林肯前面。林肯的演说词中有这样一句话:“我们今天在这里所说的话,全世界不大会注意,也不会长久地记住”(The world will little note, nor long remember what we say here)。显然,林肯犯了一个错误,因为这个世界马上就注意到了他所说的话,并且永远地记住了它。这篇演说的重要性,正如许多评论者所言,绝不亚于葛底斯堡战役本身。

自由的新生(New Birth of Freedom)——葛底斯堡演说之主旨

葛底斯堡演说最富有深意且被传播最广的一句话是“自由的新生”。它是全文主旨所在,也是林肯为内战确立的一个新的目标:“要使这个国家得到自由的新生”(This nation shall have a new birth of freedom)。林肯为何将“自由的新生”视为如此重要的国家使命?

端在于这个国家“孕育于自由之中”(conceived in liberty),而在它诞生之日起,身上便有了一块污点——奴隶制,共和政体的长袍因此被“染污,在泥中拖曳”(Our republican robe is soiled and trailed in the dust)。这显然是一种半自由半奴隶的状态(half free and half slave)。而这半自由半奴隶的状态,林肯早在1858年就已认定,对于联邦,其危险就如同“裂开的房子是站不住的”(A house divided against itself cannot stand, this government cannot endure perma-

① 林肯于11月4日接到邀请信,信上写道:It is the desire that, after the oration, you, as Chief Executive of the nation, formally set apart these grounds to their sacred use by a few appropriate remarks。需要在此一提的是,作为美国总统的林肯在这次典礼上角色次要,并非主持典礼的委员会有意轻慢他,而是遵循了当时的传统——联邦政府并无责任与义务参与州政府事务,林肯本人亦不以为怪。

nently half slave and half free)①。

林肯判断准确。这所"房子"终因奴隶制正确与否的争论而裂开大缝,引发内战②。欲求延续并扩展奴隶制的 11 个南方州先后以各种理由发表"独立宣言",并组成了美利坚联盟(Confederate States of America,即 Confederacy)或称南部邦联,以武力相要挟,要与联邦政府谈判,退出联邦;联邦政府则不能容忍国家的分裂与解体,坚决捍卫合众国的统一。这才有了延续 4 年之久的内战。正如林肯在第二次总统就职演说中(The Second Inaugural Address)中所剖析的那样,"双方虽然都想避免战争,但其中的一方宁愿开战也不愿让国家生存下去,而另一方则宁愿应战也不愿让国家灭亡。于是战争就爆发了"(Both parties deprecated war,but one of them would make war rather than let the nation survive;and the other would accept war rather than let it perish.And the war came)③。

因此,内战伊始,联邦政府的目标只是为保全联邦,而非其他。这一点,林肯在 1862 年,即战争开始不久,阐述明确。他说,"我在这场斗争中的最高目标是拯救联邦,而非为保全奴隶制,也非为摧毁奴隶制。如果我能拯救联邦而不解放任何一个奴隶,我愿意这样做;如果为了拯救联邦要我解放所有奴隶,我愿意这样做;如果为了拯救联邦,需要我解放一部分奴隶而让另一部分人继续为奴隶,我也愿意这样做"(My paramount object in this struggle is to save the Union,and is not either to save or to destroy slavery.If I could save the Union without freeing any slave,I would do it;and if I could save it by freeing all the slaves,I would do it;and if I could save it by freeing some and leaving others alone,I would also do that)④。不言而喻,解放黑奴不是林肯应战的目的。但是问题在于:林肯始终是反奴隶制的。他多次公开地指出,奴隶制在道德上、社会上和政治上

① Allan Nevins ed.,*The Life and Writings of Abraham Lincoln*,New York:The Mordern Library,1940,p.300,347.

② 美国内战起因复杂,但有一点须明确:它不是为了解放黑奴或者说废除奴隶制,而是基于奴隶制正确与否的争论而引发的国家分裂与否的对立。

③ Allan Nevins ed.,*The Life and Writings of Abraham Lincoln*, p.624.

④ Allan Nevins ed.,*The Life and Writings of Abraham Lincoln*,p.538.

都是错误的。他有一句名言,"如果奴隶制不是错误的,那没有一样东西是错误的了"(If slavery is not wrong,nothing is wrong)。在他看来,这种制度使共和有失公正、使自由显得伪善、使好人也为私利而牺牲正义。既如此,他为何不将废除奴隶制作为战争目标?这是因为他看到,奴隶制的存在是这个国家的实际需要(the necessity of this nation)。美国立国以来,黑人占美国人口比例五分之一到八分之一不等,集中在美国南部。对于南方蓄奴州,"这些奴隶形成了一种特别的、重大的利益"(These slaves constituted a peculiar and powerful interest)。其利益之重大与特别,令建国之父也不得不容忍奴隶制的存在,只能通过法令如1787年的《西北土地法令》(*Northwestern Ordinance*)禁止奴隶制扩张到没有实行奴隶制的准州,只能授权国会废除奴隶贸易。其意不言自明:通过限制奴隶制让它逐渐地萎缩、消亡。但是他们的愿望没有达成。奴隶制在美国不但没有消亡,反倒发展了,最后竟威胁到联邦的存续与完整。而这种危险林肯是早就注意到了的。既如此,他为什么还不肯提出废除奴隶制?原因无他。太难!林肯早就坦言,对于建国之父也没能解决的问题,他"也不知道该怎么办,哪怕让他拥有人世间所有的权力"(If all earthly power were given me,I should not know what to do as the existing institution)。因此,在内战之初,他的想法是:不去动它,最好是让它"回到建国之父给它规定的地方,好好地待在那里"(Let us return it to the position our fathers gave it,and there let it rest in peace)。[①] 可是战争局势的发展让他不得不改变初衷。

首先,随着反叛州的顽抗与内战的旷日持久,黑奴的解放,"已成为军事上的必要之举;对联邦的保全绝不可少的措施"[②],为了强化联邦军队的力量,尤其是削弱南方叛乱州的作战能力与经济基础,联邦政府需要"诱使黑人全都从反叛者那里投奔到我们这里来"[③]。与此同时,他还要让反叛各州明白,"不要指望可以花上十年时间试图推翻联邦政府;万一输了,还可以毫无损失地回到联邦"[④]。其次,为赢得英、法两国外交上的支持,尤其是英国,奴隶制

① Allan Nevins ed.,*The Life and Writings of Abraham Lincoln*,p.600,624,279,300.

② James M.McPherson,*Battle Cry of Freedom*,p.504.

③ 亚伯拉罕·林肯:《林肯选集》,第293页。

④ James M.McPherson,*Battle Cry of Freedom*,p.503.

的废除在道义上也成为一个必不可少的条件。以热爱自由自称的英国人,总以禁止跨大西洋奴隶贸易和废除西印度群岛的奴隶制自豪;如果联邦政府不举起废奴的旗帜,宣称为自由而战,如何与正在争取获得英国政府承认其独立的南部邦联竞争,向英国人显示北方联邦在道义上的优势,从而赢得其支持?就在 1862 年 10 月,英国内政大臣威廉·格莱斯通(Chancellor of the Exchequer William Gladstone)还出于现实利益的考虑,发表了一番近乎承认南部邦联独立的言论。他说:"对于奴隶制,我们有我们的看法,并且因此可能支持或反对南方;不过,毫无疑问,杰斐逊·戴维斯和南方的其他领导人已经建立起了军队,看起来他们还正在建立海军;他们所建立起来的,不是什么别的,而是一个国家"(We may have our opinions about slavery, we may be for or against the South; but there is no doubt that Jefferson Davis and other leaders of the South have made an army; they are making, it appears, a navy; and they have made what is more than either, they have made a nation)①。这对于林肯,不能不说是一个无法掉以轻心的警示。再者,南方的黑人们不待林肯宣布解放令,已经开始了自我解放。他们或者逃到北方,加入联邦军队;或者在北方军队进入南方时,自愿跟着队伍后面,为其服务。由这诸多方面的战争形势所决定,1863 年 1 月 1 日,林肯签署了《解放宣言》(*Emancipation Proclamation*)。

不过,历史的演进常常越出原定轨道。作为一种军事需要的《解放宣言》在它发布之后,就因其内含的自由意象而转变、上升为一种政治信仰的表达。对于黑奴,《解放宣言》就像一把火炬,照亮了他们黑暗的世界。他们把它理解为林肯给予其自由的承诺。林肯对此当然不能否认,尤其是它能使半自由半奴役的国家以完全自由的形象挺立于北美大陆时。因而,奴隶制的废止从解放宣言发布的那一刻起就已经从军事策略上的不得不行转变为政治哲学上的必需之理、必行之事。就在葛底斯堡演说近三个月前,林肯致信伊利诺伊州的家乡人民,表示"允诺以自由的诺言既已作出,就必须信守"(The promise, ie,. the promise of freedom, being made, must be kept)②。内战的第二个目

① William J.Cooper, Jr., *Jefferson Davis, American*, New York: Vintage Books, 2001, p.435.

② Allan Nevins ed., *The Life and Writings of Abraham Lincoln*, p.581.

标——令这个国家获得“自由的新生”——升起于硝烟尚在弥漫的战场。

不难看出,林肯现在所决意获得的不仅是军事上的胜利——平定企图裂解联邦的反叛,他还要在制度上拔除反叛发生的根源——奴隶制,以拯救这自由的国家得以诞生的原则;而在尚未可能从法律上废除奴隶制的 1863 年,他决意先在思想上散播下革命的种子——这个国家必须获得自由的新生。

要种下一颗怎样的种子才能生出结实的花苗?在一个已然以自由自诩的社会,什么样的观念注入才能使美国人意识到其自由需要新生?林肯在葛底斯堡演说中只说了一句——“要使这个民有、民治、民享的政府永世长存”(Government of the people, by the people, for the people, shall not perish from the earth)①。但这短小的一句就足以令人警醒自问。

首先,何为“民有、民治、民享的政府”?它必然是自治而非专制的政府。自治而非专制的政府必然以反对、废除专制为天职。内战前的美国是自治的吗?显然不是。从白人自己管理自己来看,它是自治的;但白人在管自己之外,还管别人——黑奴,这就超出了自治,是为专制。这种专制能否容许它继续存在?林肯认为不能。因为“没有一个人能好到这种程度,能够不获得一个人的同意就统治那个人”(No man is good enough to govern another man without that other's consent);不容许专制发生也“是美国共和主义的原则与靠山”(This is a leading principle, the sheet anchor of American republicanism)②。若要共和真实、自治而非专制的政府建立,非要使黑人获得自由不可。

其次,“民有、民治、民享的政府”为谁之政府?它必然是自由人的政府,由自由人所拥有和治理的政府。这些自由人是谁?当然不只是白人,还有黑人。倘若黑人不被包括在内,那四百多万居住于美国各州、获得了自由的黑人

---

① “民有、民治、民享的政府”并非林肯首创。在他之前,美国政治家与思想家丹尼尔·韦伯斯特(DanielWebster),以及西奥多·帕克尔(Theodore Parker)均有类似提法。1830 年,韦伯斯特在一次演讲中称“the American government made for the people, made by the people, and answerable to the people”;帕克尔也曾在一次布道中将民主定义为“a government of all the people, by all the people, for all the people”(参见 David Herbert Donald, *Lincoln*, New York: Simon & Schuster Paperbacks, 1995, p.461)。不过,民有、民治、民享的政府概念只是浮在他二人的言论中,并未在其理论中生根;是林肯通过葛底斯堡演说将其深化为一种政府理念。

② Allan Nevins ed., *The Life and Writings of Abraham Lincoln*, p.290.

将如何自治、又将如何久安于联邦之内？再者，若无黑人在内，白人的自由又将如何保障？

再次，“民有、民治、民享的政府”是由各州而联合的政府，还是由全体美国公民所拥有的政府？林肯无疑是在确认，联邦政府是全体美国公民的政府；它所遵从的是作为整体的美国人的意志，而非各州的意志。换言之，政治意义上的民族概念——美国人，由于林肯的“民有、民治、民享政府”的提出而在独立战争之后再次得到强调，并因其内涵的扩大而获得新生。无怪乎美国历史学家加里·威尔斯(Garry Wills)如此评述葛底斯堡演说之革命性意义：“内战之前，The United States(合众国)是一个复数名词(The United States are a free government)；葛底斯堡演说之后，合众国就变成了一个单数名词(The United States is a free government)”①。

总之，葛底斯堡演说已表现出林肯摧毁奴隶制的决心，尽管他只字未提奴隶制(这是一个成熟的政治家政治智慧的表现。《解放宣言》的颁布并未使美国人在心理上做好废除奴隶制的准备。宣言颁布后，联邦军队中不少士兵主动或受家人鼓动逃离部队，他们不愿为废除奴隶制而战；来自南伊利诺伊州的两个团因逃兵过多不得不迫使格兰特将军将之解散②。林肯讲求实效、深谙政治得失之道。他不会在时机尚未成熟时推出其政治主张)。然而一场观念乃至制度的革命显然在酝酿中。内战前对他还太难的政治问题——这个半自由半奴隶的国家能否永存下去，现在他已决意去解决；内战伊始他不打算触动的奴隶制，他也决意要去动一动了。

奉行一切人生来平等的原则(Dedicated to the proposition that all men are created equal)——葛底斯堡演说之纲领

何以实现“自由的新生”？林肯在演讲一开头就拿出其总纲领——“奉行一切人生来平等的原则”。

---

① Garry Wills, *Lincoln at Gettysburg*, p.110.

② James McPherson, *Battle Cry of Freedom*, pp.594~595.

"一切人生来平等"是美国建国之父在《独立宣言》(*The Declaration of Independence*)中确认为不言而喻的真理,并因之将一切人享有造物主赋予的某些不可剥夺的权利——生命、自由与追求幸福的权利,也确认为不言而喻的真理(*We hold these truths to be self-evident: That all men are created equal; that they are endowed by their Creator with certain unalienable rights; that among these are life, liberty and the pursuit of happiness*)。

然而,这个不言而喻的真理,即一切人生来平等的天赋权利说,在美利坚合众国政体初建时,由于实际存在着奴隶制的需要,并未成为一项法律义务。

唯因其未成为一项法律义务,奴隶制的支持者不肯承认和接受它。他们或者以嘲笑的口吻将之贬为"表面好看的泛论"(glittering generalities);或者诡辩说:建国之父所说的一切人是指欧洲人,不包括黑人;"黑人不是人,《独立宣言》里没有他们一席之地"(Negroes are not men; having no part in the Declaration of Independence);有的干脆声称,《独立宣言》所确认的一切人生来平等是个"不言而喻的谎言"(a self-evident lie)。[①] "谎言"说的代表人物约翰·卡尔霍恩(John Calhoun)声称,一切人生来平等的学说"没有一句符合真实。宣言第一句——一切人生来,就是绝对不真实的。人并不是生来的,婴儿才是生来的。婴儿逐渐长大才成了人"[②]。在他看来,人不仅生来不平等,这种不平等还必须被视为人类进步的主要条件之一。他断言,人类文明的一切进展都源自于人与人之间存在不平等;自由也并非人生来就拥有的天赋权利,而是"一种并非一切人都配得上的特权和奖赏,个人或人种应该用事实证明他们有资格享受这种特权和奖赏"[③]。总之,一切人生来平等的天赋权利说要么被全盘否定,要么被解释为与奴隶制并行不悖的理论。

尽管林肯与其同时代的几乎所有白人一样有种族优越感:他不肯将《独立宣言》的原意解释为"一切人在一切方面都生来平等"(I don't understand the Declaration to mean that all men were created equal in all respects),他也"不赞成以任何方式使黑人在社会上和政治上与白人完全平等(I am not in favor

---

① Allan Nevins ed., *The Life and Writings of Abraham Lincoln*, pp.388~414.

② 梅里亚姆:《美国政治学说史》,朱曾汶译,北京:商务印书馆,1988 年,第 120 页。

③ 梅里亚姆:《美国政治学说史》,第 120~123 页。

of bringing about in any way the social and political equality between the white and the black races)”,并认为二者“体质上的差别将永远不允许他们在完全平等的基础上一起生活(There is a physical difference between the two, which, in my judgment, will probably forever forbid their living together upon the footing of perfect equality)”。但他是奉《独立宣言》为“自由宪章”的思想者,认定一切人生来平等是自由政体所赖以建立的基本与伟大的原则;他也是怀抱基督教慈善准则(The Christian rule of charity)的基督徒,反对将黑人需要的东西剥夺(Give to him that is needy rather than take from him that is needy);他“不能理解,为什么白人占了优等地位,黑人就应该被剥夺一切”(I do not perceive that because the white is to have the superior position the Negro should be denied everything)。[①] 他又是将提高人的地位作为政府之目的的政治家,希望给予一切人自由的开端与公平的机会。因而他无法容忍上述奴隶制辩护士的言说或理论。在他看来,这些人在贪得无厌地从黑人身上榨取利润时,将其祖先写下的自由宪章也取消和撕毁了;其目的是要破坏一切人生来平等的自由政体准则,代之以另一个不同的准则,即“否认人生来平等,硬说一种人有天赋的、道义上和宗教上的权利去奴役另一种人”[②];尽管他们把奴役他人说成是一种神圣的自治权利,实则是在吹灭人类理智、道德与自由之光。他反复强调,即便说白人优越于黑人,也“绝对没有理由去说黑人没有资格享有《独立宣言》列举的各种天赋权利”(There is no reason in the world why the Negro is not entitled to all the natural rights enumerated in the Declaration of Independence);无论白人、黑人,“在吃以自己双手挣来的面包而不用任何人批准的权利方面,……是一样的(But in the right to eat the bread, without the leave of anybody else, which his own hand earns, he is my equal, and the equal of every living man)”。[③]

因此,还在1858年时,林肯就在与斯蒂芬·道格拉斯(Stephen Douglas)的辩论中吁请美国公民,“把所有那些关于某个人、某个人种是劣等因而必须处于劣等地位的诡辩统统丢掉,……在这块土地上团结得像一个民族,直到我

---

① Allan Nevins ed., *The Life and Writings of Abraham Lincoln*, p.357, 381, 362, 385, 382.

② 亚伯拉罕·林肯:《林肯选集》,第115页。

③ Allan Nevins ed., *The Life and Writings of Abraham Lincoln*, p.362.

们再一次站起来宣布一切人生来平等”(Let us discard all this quibbling about this man and the other man, this race and the other race being inferior, and therefore they must be placed in an inferior position.Let us discard all these things, and unite as one people throughout this land, until we shall once more stand up declaring that all men are created equal)①。到了1863年,当美国联邦因种族主义奴隶制之争而陷入一场已持续两年的内战时,他更深信,87年前由先辈们建立的自由政体,只有奉行它所赖以建立的伟大基本原则——一切人生来平等(It dedicates to the proposition that all men are created equal),并将之确立为一项法律义务,才能也将必能获得自由的新生(A new nation brought forth on this continent by our fathers four score and seven years ago, conceived in Liberty, shall have a new birth of freedom)。

问题在于,如何将《独立宣言》所宣示的天赋权利说确立为法律义务?《独立宣言》虽属国家重要文件,但它不是正式法律文本;美利坚合众国宪法才是这个国家正在施行的法律,而它承认了奴隶制的存在(尽管宪法文本未出现“奴隶”二字,总以他词替代),并且将黑人事实上作为财产处理。在没有通过宪法修正案废除奴隶制之前,黑奴作为他人的财产而不享有人的权利,这在法律上是成立的。奉行一切人生来平等的原则,让黑人享有他不可剥夺的天赋权利,除非先让他恢复了人的身份;又除非论证出《独立宣言》具有优先于美国宪法的效力。林肯正是这么做的。

黑人是人还是财产?林肯首先依据社会生活的事实指出,即便是奴隶主也大多没有把黑人完全等同于财产。否则,为什么他们同意把在非洲从事奴隶买卖的人绞死,而没有提出把在非洲买卖野马、野牛的人绞死?为什么他们蔑视奴隶贩子,不愿与之打交道;而不会拿那样的态度对待贩卖玉米、烟草与棉花的人?这都是因为他们意识到黑人也是人。假如说黑人不是人,那些值钱的自由黑人——他们全都是奴隶的后代,或者自己就曾是奴隶——为什么没有主人?或者被人买卖,而任由他们自由地生活、跑动?这是因为白人内心

---

① Allan Nevins ed., *The Life and Writings of Abraham Lincoln*, p.354.

的正义感告诉他们,黑人也有自己的天赋权利。[①]

他还依据美国宪法暗指奴隶与奴隶制的措辞指出,国家的法律文本也将黑人认定为人——宪法中凡是暗指奴隶的地方,都称他为"人"(Wherever the slave is alluded to in the Constitution he is called a person);并且说明,制宪者们这么做的目的,"就是不让宪法里有一种可以把人当财产的想法"(This mode of alluding to slaves and slavery, instead of speaking of them, was employed on purpose to exclude from the Constitution the idea that there could be property in man)[②]。

确认了黑人具有人的地位,也就确认了他们在《独立宣言》中占有一席之地,而不是如斯蒂芬·道格拉斯之流所言,黑人在《独立宣言》中没有份。依据《独立宣言》确认的不言而喻的真理——一切人生来平等,黑人与白人一样享有其不可剥夺的天赋权利。

然而在美国宪法中,黑奴在事实上是作为财产被处理的。如何理解这种既把黑人当人又把黑人当财产的矛盾做法,又如何解决宪法与《独立宣言》的冲突?

林肯一生对宪法上的奴隶制有过多次阐述。他指出,那是建国之父们出于实际需要,不得不屈从于不平等的社会传统,而向现实作出的妥协。然而这种妥协不仅不意味着他们放弃了《独立宣言》的理想——一切人生来平等的政治信仰,反而说明,在宪法中保留奴隶制于他们只是一种暂时性的制度安排,一种无法达至理想时的权宜之策,一种希望在将来可能得到修正的解决方法。修正的方向便是不把黑人当做财产看,恢复他们作为人的地位,并享受一切人生来平等的天赋权利。

至于宪法与《独立宣言》的冲突如何解决,林肯创造性地通过论证《独立宣言》与宪法的关系,确立了《独立宣言》优先于美国宪法的地位,从而在思想与法理上跨越了宪法不可挑战的障碍。在林肯看来,诞生于1776年的《独立宣言》是建国之父为自由社会规定的准则,这个准则为所有人尊重、关心,并

① 亚伯拉罕·林肯:《林肯选集》,第72~73页。

② Allan Nevins ed., *The Life and Writings of Abraham Lincoln*, p.450.

为它出力，即使它从未得到完全实现，人们也总在一步步向它靠近。换言之，《独立宣言》所声明的是美国人永恒的理想，而1787年制定的美国宪法只是为实现此理想的临时一步。当这一步走得不大理想，或者可能迈入歧途时，就应根据《独立宣言》的总精神——一切人生来平等的原则——加以改变。林肯特别强调，建国之父把一切人生来平等这个主张放在《独立宣言》中不是为了与英国分离，宣布独立；而是为防止"自由人民重新回到专制主义那条可恶的老路上去(Its authors meant it to be a stumbling block to all those who might seek to turn a free people back the hateful path of despotism)，是为将来的专制者特意设立的绊脚石、硬钉子(a hard nut to crack)"①。

就是这样，通过重新诠释《独立宣言》与宪法的关系，林肯将这个国家必须奉行的政治原则、法律纲领确立下来——一切人生来平等，无论他是黑人还是白人。依据这一纲领，所有人都应享有不可剥夺的基本权利。凡与这一纲领相违背的，都应加以修正。人们似乎又听到了《独立宣言》起草者托马斯·杰弗逊(Thomas Jefferson)的话："除了与生俱来的、不可剥夺的人的权利，没有什么是不可以改变的"(Nothing is unchangeable but the inherent and unalienable rights of man)②。

毋庸讳言，林肯的反奴隶制学说并非出于深刻的哲理分析，在这一点上，他不及同时代人威廉·钱宁(William Channing)与弗朗西斯·韦兰(Francis Wayland)③；他那一切人在某些方面生来平等的有限平等论也远不及激进废奴主义彻底，他身边的不少政治家比如国务卿威廉·西华德(William Seward)、参议员撒迪厄斯·斯蒂文斯(Thaddeus Stevens)等都比他主张激烈；但他那平易不艰深的语言风格、基于人性而展开的朴实论述、为自由人的自由而解放黑奴的自由升华论，以及务实、坚定、灵活的论述策略，使他的理论深入人心。通过触及美国政治最根本的问题，尤其是《独立宣言》中关于"一切人生来平等"的原则，林肯深刻地改变了美国人的政治思想。又因为他身为总统，拥有无可匹敌的政治权威，他成了美国历史上第一个将平等理论转变为现

① Allan Nevins ed., *The Life and Writings of Abraham Lincoln*, p.334.

② Thomas Jefferson, *Political Writings*, Cambridge: Cambridge University Press, 1999, p.386.

③ 梅里亚姆：《美国政治学说史》，第113～115页。

实的政治家。奉行一切人生来平等的政治纲领发表不久,美国人的社会生活与政治制度就被重塑。内战尚未结束,国会提出并通过了第十三条宪法修正案(The Thirteenth Amendment to the Constitution of the United States,1865 年 1 月 31 日),奴隶制永被废除。奴隶制的废除又为美国黑人获得公民身份,即第十四条宪法修正案,平等地享有公民权奠下了基石。

生、死、重生(Birth,death,rebirth)——葛底斯堡演说之宗教隐喻

对于林肯的葛底斯堡演说,没有人吝惜其赞美词。有学者赞叹,"它是这样的优美,以至于最鲁钝的耳朵也能听到音乐在流淌(It is so beautiful that even the dullest ear can hear its music);它是如此的卓越,以至于其对手有时也不得不承认这篇小小的演说词深刻地改变了美国人思考最根本的政治问题的方式(It is so significant that even his rivals can sometimes admit that his little speech made a profound change in the way Americans framed their most fundamental political questions)"①。一篇小小的演说词,因何具有如此强大的感染力?盖因其修辞朴素而动人,如同诗歌;用词简练、精准、充满节奏感和韵律美,仿佛一首乐曲;尤其值得一提的是,演说词内含着强烈的宗教感召力。

据美国学者 A.埃尔莫尔(A.Elmore)言,林肯是第一个在公开演说或声明中引用"上帝"的总统②。是否第一,颇难认定。然而林肯经常在演说中引用《圣经》,确然无疑。因何如此?一是他自幼熟读《圣经》③,记忆力惊人,又常接触宗教界人士,将其用词、隐喻等顺手拈来,为我所用,实属自然。二是,林肯生活在一个《圣经》被广泛诵读的时代。19 世纪中叶的美国人,识字的、不识字的,也都和林肯一样,熟悉《圣经》。无论文人、武夫,或者奴隶,譬如文坛魁首拉尔夫 · 爱默生(Ralph Emerson),南方邦联名将托马斯 · 杰克逊

① A.E.Elmore,*Lincoln's Gettysburg Address*,p.6.

② A.E.Elmore,*Lincoln's Gettysburg Address*,p.x.

③ 下文所引《圣经》文本系詹姆斯钦定版(King James Bible),也就是林肯所生活的时代人们所用的版本。

(Thomas Jackson)，黑奴反叛领袖纳特·特拿(Nat Turner)等，都很自然地用《圣经》的语调说话①。在此背景下，演说者利用圣经用词与隐喻强化其演说力量，顺理成章。葛底斯堡演说又恰好被安排在一个最宜表现宗教情感的场合——安葬烈士的典礼上。因此之故，林肯有意让演说贯穿了圣经的主题，满载着圣经的语言。

《圣经》"新约"(*New Testament*)开首四福音书(Four Gospels)——《马太福音》(*Gospel of Matthew*)、《马可福音》(*Gospel of Mark*)、《路加福音》(*Gospel of Luke*)、《约翰福音》(*Gospel of John*)——俱都以基督的诞生、受难、重生为主题，葛底斯堡演说通篇也以出生、生命的奉献、新生为线索建构国家意象。

第一句："我们的先辈们在这个大陆上创立了一个新国家，它孕育于自由之中"(our fathers brought forth on this continent, a new nation, conceived in Liberty)，这是国家的出生。

第二段第一句："现在我们正从事一场伟大的内战，以考验这个国家，……是否能够长久存在下去"(Now we are engaged in a great civil war, testing whether that nation, can long endure)；第二句："烈士们为使这个国家能够生存下去而献出了自己的生命"(for those who here give their lives that that nation might live)，这是国家在受难，烈士们为联邦与自由的保存献出了生命。

最后一句："我们要使国家在上帝福佑下得到自由的新生，要使这个民有、民治、民享的政府永世长存"(that this nation, under God, shall have a new birth of freedom, and that government of the people, by the people, for the people, shall not perish from the earth)，这是国家的重生与自由政体之原则的永存，正如基督复活后，圣子永生不灭。

不只是生、死、重生的意象与《圣经》主题暗合，即便是表现生、死、重生的词也取自《圣经》，而且在有意无意间地使词义延伸，用意深刻。

美利坚合众国的"孕育"与"诞生"，林肯选的是"conceived"与"brought forth"。"brought forth"不仅在《圣经》中用于描述诞生，譬如圣母玛利亚头生

① Nathan O. Hatch and Mark A. Noll, eds., *Bible in America: Essays in Cultural History*, New York: Oxford University Press, 1982, p.79.

子即耶稣的出世①;还在《旧约》(*Old Testament*)"撒母耳记"(上)(*Samuel 1*)12:8(chapter 12,verse 8)中出现,记述的是以色列人从埃及奴隶制下逃离得救的事②。凡是熟悉圣经的耳朵,听到这个词,都不会不想到美国的奴隶制——这场内战的根源,以及这个国家能否因战争而得救、如何得救。圣经中,"conceived"则数次与"brought forth"相伴随,说明圣母玛利亚如何因圣灵而受孕。林肯用这两个词,焉知未有将合众国的诞生比喻为基督出世之意?"孕育于自由之中"、"所怀的孕是从圣灵来的"(that which is conceived in her is of the Holy Ghost),二者何其相似,不能不令人产生此种联想。

这一联想又因林肯用"dedicate"(奉献)指代生命在战场上的消灭而被强化。"dedicate"在圣经中多次出现。它有两层含义:一是向神献祭,二是洗礼。献祭是净化之后的死亡;洗礼即可是精神上的再生,也可是归入死亡之后的新生,所以《罗马书》(*Romans*)6:4 说,"我们藉着洗礼归入死,和他(耶稣)一同埋葬,原是叫我们一举一动有新生的样式,像基督藉着父的荣耀从死里复活一样"(Therefore we are buried with him by baptism into death:that like as Christ was raised up from the dead by the glory of the Father,even so we also should walk in newness of life)。为什么要先归入死?因为有罪。经上说,"死是从罪里来的"。从死里复活就意味着罪身灭绝,得到新生。

内战对于美利坚合众国来说,无疑是一场规模空前的献祭与洗礼,是血与火的献祭与洗礼——葛底斯堡战役,双方战亡五万之众。它的起因是有罪的奴隶制。也许是上帝的意旨使这场战争发生。假如上帝的意旨是要藉此战火的洗礼去除有罪的奴隶制,那么如何"不让这些死者白白牺牲"?除非罪身灭绝,消灭了奴隶制。因此,林肯在演说中宣示,他"下定了最大的决心",要让这个"国家在上帝福佑下得到自由的新生"。尽管他只字未提奴隶制,但意识

---

① 例如《马太福音》(Gospel of Matthew)1:20-21:But while he thought on these things,behold,the angel of the LORD appeared unto him in a dream,saying,Joseph,thou son of David,fear not to take unto thee Mary thy wife:for that which is conceived in her is of the Holy Ghost.And she shall bring forth a son,and thou shalt call his name JESUS:for he shall save his people from their sins.

② 《撒母耳记(上)》(Samuel 1)12:8:When Jacob was come into Egypt,and your fathers cried unto the LORD,then the LORD sent Moses and Aaron,which brought forth your fathers out of Egypt,and made them dwell in this place.

到奴隶制是美国国家之罪的人不会不想到什么是自由的新生。

再如“检验这个国家是否能够长久存在下去”中的“endure”,同样令人将圣经故事与合众国的命运相联系。这个词在《圣经》中多用于“称谢耶和华,因他的慈爱长存”(give thanks unto the LORD,for he is good;for his mercy endureth forever),但在《旧约》“以斯帖记”(*Esther*)8:6 中意指不忍见同族被害、同宗被灭①(For how can I endure to see the evil that shall come unto my people? or how can I endure to see the destruction of my kindred?),而在《马太福音》10:22、24:13 以及《马可福音》13:13 中则指“忍耐到底的必然得救”(he that shall endure unto the end,the same shall be saved)。美国内战不正是一场同族相残的战争吗?在战争与奴隶制中忍耐的人是否应得救?假如上帝慈爱长存,这个孕育于自由之中的国家就应得救;然而怎样得救?美国人不得不想一想。

林肯还在演说末尾“要使这个民有、民治、民享的政府永世长存”一句中,用了“perish”(灭亡)一词,而“perish”在《诗篇》(*Psalms*)102:26 与《约翰福音》6:27 中,是与“endure”同时出现的。林肯似乎在借用圣经,提示人民:不新生,就灭亡。这个已有 87 岁的共和国,能否经得住内战的考验,将“一切人生来平等的原则”奉行到底,确乎要靠能否得到自由的新生。这是个重大的问题,加之演说发生在一个肃穆的场合,所以林肯在演说一开始,就采用了《圣经》表达年份的常用方式——以“two score”表示“forty years”、“four score”表示“eighty years”,以示庄重。他没有说“Eighty seven years ago”(八十七年前),而是说“Four score and seven years ago”。这一短语本身还马上让人想到《诗篇》中的名句,90:10“叹人生转瞬即逝:我们一生的年日是七十岁,如是强壮可到八十岁;但其中可矜夸的不过是劳苦愁烦,转眼成空,我们便如飞而去”(The days of our years are threescore years and ten; and if by reason of strength they be fourscore years, yet is their strength labour and sorrow; for it is soon cut off, and we fly away)。其中关于年日的表达正是“threescore years and ten”、“fourscore years”。

---

① 以斯帖(Esther):波斯王薛西斯(《圣经》中记为“亚哈随鲁”)的王后,犹大人,因为叔父以及整个犹大族将被波斯王宠臣哈曼所害,故而在王施恩时祈求其恩惠,救其同族。

不难看出,葛底斯堡演说从开头到结尾,从主题意象的构建到字词句的选择,通篇都隐含着宗教的寓意。林肯之用意,显然是要通过它唤起民众对内战之根源的反思、对国家命运的关切,并将其拯救国家与自由政体之原则的意志灌入民心。

明晰而抽象、言短而意长——葛底斯堡演说词之风格(The Style of the Speech)

与林肯的其他著名演说一样,葛底斯堡演说词并非匆匆写就,而是他深思熟虑的作品。如何在只能"说几句话"的短时间内,恰当地把自己关于这场战争的看法表达出来,应该是林肯在演说词的准备中一直在考虑的问题。他选择了一种明晰而抽象的表意方式。明晰,是他一贯的特色;抽象,实则出于形势的需要。

葛底斯堡战役的胜利,在林肯看来,虽不意味着战争即将结束,但他相信它已令南部邦联遭受重创①,因此必然想到战后的重建。然而此刻南北双方正胶着在一场血腥的军事对抗中。一方面,他要鼓舞北方的士气与民心,以期赢得军事上的胜利;另一方面,他要为南方州将来回归联邦未雨绸缪,在感情上奠定和平友好的基础。换言之,他要在充满敌意的战争心理中注入一些可令双方握手言和的情感。

因此,林肯在演说中有意避开了具体所指。与艾弗瑞特演说中大量动人心弦的具体事例相比,林肯似乎什么也没有说——没有具体的人名、地名、参战兵团,也没有对某个人或团体的赞美与谴责。然而,他的措辞同样使人感到亲切,并且有些说不清道不明。譬如"那些曾在这里战斗过的勇士"(The brave men, living and dead, who struggled here)一句,在北方人民听来,显然是指联邦军队的士兵,而非叛乱一方。可谁又能说那些"活着的"或"死了的"勇士不包括南部邦联的将士?至少林肯没有这样说。他有意不这样说。因为他需要利用这个含义明晰、指称对象却模糊的词,令南方州将来感到可以融入联

① James McPherson, *Battle Cry of Freedom*, p.666.

邦。他把这场因有罪的奴隶制而引发的南北冲突升华为“一场伟大的内战”（We are engaged in a great civil war），并将其解释为对一个孕育于自由的国家能否长存下去的考验（Testing whether that nation，or any nation so conceived and so dedicated，can long endure），都有这种意图在里头。“不让这些死者白白牺牲”（These dead shall not have died in vain），显然也表达了对南部邦联士兵的惋惜，因为他们毫无疑问也是经受考验的一方。

不消说，南北两方一直为之争论竟至于交火的主题，诸如“奴隶制（slavery）”、“财产（property）”、“合乎宪法（constitutionality）”、“分裂主义（sectionalism）”等都没有出现在林肯的演说中，连“州（states）”也没有提起；有的只是“国家（nation）”、“自由（liberty）”、“奉献（delicate）”、“我们的先辈（our fathers）”等可唤起共鸣的语词。此种基于对国家命运之关切、对自由信念之维护的遣词造句，表达的是抽象的概念，触动的是南北双方对战争的看法。对于北方，是为维护国家的完整与先辈的成就而战；对于南方，是为自由或者说自治政府而战。虽然各自理由不同，但都在相似的概念之下，各自都可以之为据，声明其事业的崇高（尤其值得指出的是：内战结束后近半个世纪，在美国南方，依然有非常多的人为南部各州脱离联邦而辩护，其理由正是维护自由与州权）。因此林肯的演说在充满敌意的战场上无异于一种和解之音。这既是林肯政治目光远大的缘故，也是他内心情感的丰富所致。无怪乎美国历史学家卡尔·贝克尔（Carl Becker）赞叹林肯对于世态人生那“深沉的情感体悟”（profoundly emotional apprehension of experience）[①]。朴质无华而又气度恢弘的林肯在葛底斯堡演说中体贴入微地照顾到了各方的情感与心理。

葛底斯堡演说在美国演说史上被誉为是改变了美国演说传统，因而具有革命性意义的演说。原因之一在于它篇幅短小，仅有 272 个单词。林肯时代的演说，流行长篇大论，譬如爱德华·埃弗瑞特（Edward Everett）那长达两小时的演讲，任何一个不足半小时的演说都会被指为陈腐。然而林肯却以不到 3 分钟的演说改写了美国政治演说的传统。当然，传统能被改变绝不仅因其

① Carl Becker，*Declaration of Independence：A Study in the History of Political Ideas*，New York：Harcourt，Brace and Company，1922，p.216.

小,而因其短小篇幅包含了丰富内涵。若非如此,埃弗瑞特就不会在演讲第二天向林肯表示,“如果我那两小时的演讲能与您在两分钟内谈及的主要思想稍有接近,我就感到高兴了”(I should be glad if I could flatter myself that I came as near to the central ideal of the occasion, in two hours, as you did in two minutes)①。的确,林肯的这次演讲与他第二次就职演说也只用了六百余字一样,虽然惜墨如金,但是“智慧多多”(Lots of wisdom in that document)②。以饱含智慧的语言作为武器,运用于战场内外,是众所周知极富魅力、颇具奇效而又难以做到的。林肯做到了。正因为如此,后世学者代际不断地试图恢复葛底斯堡演说昔日的光彩,呈现它永恒的魅力。然而,正如一位学者指出的那样,“没有一种评论,没有一种分析,能给林肯的演说以生命,给予它们生命的只能是演说者的远大目光,这个人身高出众、瘦骨嶙峋、衣衫不整、举止粗鲁,但却因诚挚端庄而变得光彩夺目”③。对此,我们须有自知之明。

① Allan Nevins ed., *The Life and Writings of Abraham Lincoln*, p.587.

② Garry Wills, *Lincoln at Gettysburg: The Words that Remade America*, p.130.

③ 亚伯拉罕·林肯:《林肯选集》,第 323 页。

延伸阅读

James McPherson, *Battle Cry of Freedom: The Civil War Era*, London: Penguin Books, 1990. 詹姆斯·麦克佛森是美国研究内战史最为出色的历史学家,《内战时代》为其代表作,列入科梅尔·凡·伍德沃德主编《牛津美国史》序列。他以生动流畅的文笔,对墨西哥战争至内战结束这二十年间的美国政治、经济、社会与军事史,做了清晰、系统的叙述与剖析。葛底斯堡战役见第21章"Long Remember: The Summer of'63"。

亚伯拉罕·林肯:《林肯选集》,朱曾汶译,北京:商务印书馆,2010年。一本林肯的书信与演讲集,译文忠实、典雅、流畅,可对照阅读 Allan Nevins ed., *The Life and Writings of Abraham Lincoln*(New York: The Modern Library, 1940),了解林肯一生事业及其书信与演说背景。

Garry Wills, *Lincoln at Gettysburg: The Words that Remade America*, New York: Simon & Schuster, 1993. 此书提供了葛底斯堡演说的发生背景、多份手稿,着重从历史根源揭示葛底斯堡演说词的意涵与风格。

Gabor Boritt, *The Gettysburg Gospel: The Lincoln Speech That Nobody Knows*, 2006. 与以往研究葛底斯堡演说侧重于其政治意义不同,本书乃为宗教视野之解读,提醒当代读者勿要忽略:林肯深受基督教教义影响。

A. E. Elmore, *Lincoln's Gettysburg Address, Echoes of the Bible and Book of Common Prayer*, Southern Illinois University, 2009. 一本依据《圣经》与《公祷书》解释葛底斯堡演说的著作,其中关于前人研究之缺失与优长的议论颇有深度。

David Herbert Donald, *Lincoln*, New York: Simon & Schuster Paperbacks, 1995. 诸多关于林肯的传记中,这一本的特色是忠实、可靠。作者尽其所能采用一手材料,以"解释而非评判"(It seeks to explain rather than judge)的风格再现了林肯的思想、生活以及他眼中的世界。

Carl Sandburg, *Abraham Lincoln*: *The Prairie Years The War Years*, New York: Mariner Books, 2012. 卡尔·桑德堡是20世纪美国著名诗人,他的6卷本《林肯传》(《草原年代》2卷、《战争年代》4卷)也是一种诗性的叙述,然而深得历史学家赞赏。这本《亚伯拉罕·林肯:草原年代与战争年代》是他自己依据6卷本浓缩而成,但篇幅并不短。不愿意花时间读大部头的人,也可以选择戴尔·卡耐基(Dale Carnegie)富于感情色彩的《林肯传》(*Lincoln the Unknown*),读之可粗略知晓林肯政治生涯史,同时约略窥见其情感特征与婚姻生活。

Eric Foner, *The Fiery Trial*: *Abraham Lincoln and American Slavery*, New York: W.W.Norton & Company, 2010. 伟人的特质在于:具有不断成长的能力。林肯正是一个在各种环境乃至危机中成长起来的政治家、美国黑奴"伟大的解放者"(Great Liberator)。不过,林肯尽管生来就是反奴隶制的,却不是生来就决定要废除奴隶制。他是在良知的推动、关于时局的辩论、军事策略的驱使甚至可说逼迫下,逐渐地担起了解放黑人的使命。关于种族关系的见解,他超越于同时代人,但也未曾脱离社会环境。其中过程究竟如何?林肯究竟如何成长?读方纳此书,不难获一清晰线索。

Doris Goodwin, *Team of Rivals*: *The Political Genius of Abraham Lincoln*, New York: Simon and Schuster Paperbacks, 2005(多丽丝·古德温:《林肯与劲敌幕僚》,尤以丁译,上海:上海人民出版社,2010年)。美国著名导演斯皮尔伯格之电影《林肯》,以葛底斯堡演讲词开头,情节围绕第13条宪法修正案的提交与通过而展开,其底本即为此书。

Drew Gilpin Faust, *This Republic of Suffering*: *Death and The American Civil War*, New York: Vintage Civil War Library, 2008(德鲁·吉尔平·福斯特:《这受难的国度:死亡与美国内战》,孙宏哲、张聚国译,南京:译林出版社,2015年)。美国内战,62万人丧生(最新统计出的数字达70余万)。这个数字相当于美国独立战争、1812年与英国的战争、美墨(墨西哥)战争、美西(西班牙)战争、美国参与第一次世界大战与第二次世界大战,以及越南战争中美国阵亡士兵的总和。除此之外,还有大量的平民死亡。生命的屠戮与消失成为美国人对内战不堪回首的记忆。这些死去的人如何被安置、如何被纪念、又如何成为一种历史记忆的符号?换言之,其死亡之意义何在?这本书给人很多启示。

王希:《原则与妥协:美国宪法的精神与实践》(增订版),北京:北京大学出版社,2014 年。中国学者所著的美国政治史著作中,它是难得一见的佳作。常备案头,可供时时翻阅。

DECLARATION OF INDEPENDENCE
美国《独立宣言》

DECLARATION OF INDEPENDENCE①

In Congress②, July 4, 1776

THE UNANIMOUS DECLARATION OF THE THIRTEEN UNITED STATES③ OF AMERICA

dissolve: to (cause sth to) come to an end

When, in the course of human events, it becomes necessary for one people to dissolve the political bands which have connected them with another, and to assume, among the powers of the earth, the separate and equal station to which the

① 文本依据美国国会图书馆所藏《独立宣言》原件抄录。

② 指第二届大陆会议(the Second Continental Congress),其存续时间长达近 14 年:1775 年 5 月 10 日始,1789 年 3 月 2 日结束。第一届与第二届大陆会议均在宾夕法尼亚费城(Philadelphia)举行。费城之名源出于两个希腊词:Philos 与 adelphos。"Philos"意为"love","adelphos"意为"brother"或"friendship"。两词相合,意指该地充满"兄弟之爱"(City of Brotherly Love)。1681 年,英王查理二世(Charles II)为偿还债务,将北美的这块土地赐予威廉·潘(William Penn)。Penn 是一名基督教公谊会(Society of Friends,别称 Quakers)信徒。该教派在 17 世纪属清教运动中极端一派,与新教正统教义不合,故而在英格兰遭受迫害。Penn 来此建立殖民地后,将之命名为 Philadelphia,寓意宗教宽容与兄弟之爱。《独立宣言》的讨论在该殖民地的议会大厦进行,其会议厅后来被称为"独立大厅"(Independence Hall)。

③ 这 13 个 states 是:特拉华(Delaware)、宾夕法尼亚(Pensylvania)、新泽西(New Jersey)、佐治亚(Georgia)、康涅狄格(Conneticut)、马萨诸塞(Massachusetts)、马里兰(Maryland)、南卡罗来纳(South Carolina)、新罕布什尔(New Hampshare)、弗吉尼亚(Virginia)、纽约(New York)、北卡罗来纳(North Carolina)、罗德岛(Rhode Island)。关于"states"的含义,需以两个时间点为界,作三种不同理解:1776 年 7 月 2 日宣布独立前,它们是英属殖民地(colonies),独立后,它们是主权国家(sovereign states)。1787~1789 年联邦宪法制订与批准前,United States of America 是由 13 个主权国家组成的相对松散的联盟;其后,United States of America 中的 states 不再拥有国家主权,而是统一于联邦政府下的各州,"美利坚合众国"——United States of America——才成为名副其实的国。"states"在不同历史时期,其政治涵义大有差异。

laws of nature and of nature's God entitle them, a decent respect to the opinions of mankind requires that they should declare the causes which impel them to the separation.①

We hold these truths to be self-evident: that all men are created equal; that they are endowed by their Creator with certain unalienable②rights; that among these are life, liberty, and the pursuit of happiness; that, to secure these rights, governments are instituted among men, deriving their just powers from the consent of the governed; that whenever any form of government becomes destructive of these ends, it is the right of the people to alter or to abolish it, and to institute new government, laying its foundation on such principles, and organizing its powers in such form, as to them shall seem most likely to effect their safety and happiness. Prudence, indeed, will dictate, that governments long established, should not be changed for light and transient causes; and accordingly all experience hath shown, that mankind are more disposed to suffer, while evils are sufferable, than to right themselves by abolishing the forms to which they are accustomed. But when a long train of abuses and usurpations, pursuing invariably the same object, evinces a design to reduce them under absolute despotism, it is their right, it is their duty, to throw off such government,

hath: archaic present of the third singular of have

usurp: to take and keep(sb's power, right and position) in a forceful or violent way and especially without the right to do so. usurpation: the act of usurp

① 何谓"宣言(declaration)"? 它有两个含义:其一,宣示众人并且说清楚(telling & making clear);其二,意在获得公众或外界广泛支持(Declarations are always meant to command broad public support)。因此这一段开宗明义说明殖民地人民意欲何为——独立,同时吁请公众与外界支持。第二个含义中又有一个衍生义,即为自己辩护。因此,从下段起,《宣言》开始陈述其独立的理由或者说正当性。

② 杰斐逊的原稿中,用的是"inalienable"一词,大陆会议讨论时也未曾加以改动,然而在正式公布出来的文本中,"inalienable"被换成了"unalienable"。据卡尔·贝克尔(Carl Becker)推测,这大概是因为"unalienable"在18世纪更为人们习用,所以负有指导打印责任的约翰·亚当斯将"inalienable"改成了"unalienable"。

and to provide new guards for their future security. Such has been the patient sufferance of these colonies; and such is now the necessity which constrains them to alter their former systems of government. The history of the present King of Great Britain①is a history of repeated injures and usurpations, all having in direct object the establishment of an absolute tyranny over these states. To prove this, let facts be submitted to a candid world.②

He has refused his assent to laws, the most wholesome and necessary for the public good.③

He has forbidden his governors to pass laws of immediate and pressing importance, unless suspended in their operation till his assent should be obtained; and when so suspended, he has utterly neglected to attend to them.

He has refused to pass other laws for the accommodation of large districts of people, unless those people would

---

① 指乔治三世(George III,1760~1820年在位)。

② 《独立宣言》常被引为言简意赅的典范之作。这一段文字简洁、流畅,没有任何铺陈,鲜明地表现出《宣言》庄重、冷静的风格,同时又显其沉郁顿挫。

③ 此句起,以下连续17次使用"He has"的句式指控英王,1次用"he is";并且列为单句。这样不仅在结构上起到了强调作用;而且用意特殊——宣言是在一而再、再而三地提醒读者注意:这是英王犯下的一连串罪行。不过,《宣言》对英王的指控并非条条都明确无疑。譬如这第一条,就显然是一个概括性的判断,缺乏具体所指。这种语焉不详以及后文中某些夸张性的措辞,让《宣言》的反对者与批判者给它贴上了"错误连篇、小题大做"(false and frivolous)、"无中生有"(imaginary grievances)的标签;或者认为它"既乏真实,亦无见地"(lack of truth and sense)。然而,从另一个角度来看,杰斐逊如此措辞,很符合其母国政论文件的传统,其实无可非议。以英国光荣革命中诞生的《权利法案》(*The Bill of Rights of 1689*)为例,其开头也是一个概括性的句子:"已退位之英王詹姆斯二世,得其数位所用之邪恶辅臣、法官与部长协助,曾力图颠覆、灭亡本王国之新教、法律与自由权;自命有权废弃与悬置法律,并可未经议会同意便执行法律"(the late King James the Second, by the assistance of divers evil counsellors, judges and ministers employed by him, did endeavour to subvert and extirpate the Protestant religion and the laws and liberties of this kingdom; By assuming and exercising a power of dispensing with and suspending of laws, and the execution of laws without consent of Parliament)。

relinquish the right of representation in the legislature; a right inestimable to them, and formidable to tyrants only.

relinquish: to give up (sth); to give (sth such as power, control or possession) to another person or group

He has called together legislative bodies at places unusual, uncomfortable, and distant from the depository of their public records, for the sole purpose of fatiguing them into compliance with his measures.①

He has dissolved representative houses repeatedly, for opposing, with manly firmness, his invasions on the rights of the people.②

He has refused for a long time, after such dissolutions, to cause others to be elected; whereby the legislative powers, incapable of annihilation, have returned to the people at large for their exercise; the state remaining, in the mean time, exposed to all the dangers of invasion from without, and convulsionswithin.

whereby: by which annihilation: complete destruction

convulsion: violent disturbance

hither: to or towards this place

He has endeavored to prevent the population of these States; for that purpose obstructing the laws for naturalization of foreigners; refusing to pass others to encourage their migrations hither, and raising the conditions of new appropriations of lands.

He has obstructed the administration of justice, by

---

① 此条指涉马萨诸塞总督曾于1768年令议会(Massachusetts Assembly)移至4英里之外的坎布里奇(Cambridge)一事。不过,议会移至坎布里奇后,那里的哈佛学院(Harvard College,即今哈佛大学)为议会提供了便利的会议场所,出席会议的代表也可借住私人居所。“unusual, uncomfortable, and distant”的说法其实不尽属实。另有一点:当时,波士顿城内天花流行。将议会移至坎布里奇,是议员们主动提出,并非总督强令。

② 指1769年以来马萨诸塞、弗吉尼亚、马里兰、南卡罗来纳、纽约等殖民地议会因反对英国议会颁布的法律而屡次被解散。

refusing his assent to laws for establishing judiciary powers.①

He has made judges dependent on his will alone, for the tenure of their offices, and the amount and payment of their salaries.

He has erected a multitude of new offices, and sent hither swarms of officers, to harass our people, and eat out their substance.②

harass: trouble or annoy (sb) continually

He has kept among us, in times of peace, standing armies, without the consent of our legislatures.③

standing army: a permanent army of paid soldiers

He has affected to render the military independent of,

① 这一条指控的写法颇值一提。1767年"汤森法案"出台之后,北美殖民地总督与当地议会的关系就紧张起来。一方面,殖民地议会拒绝承认"汤森法案"的合法性;另一方面,总督效忠于英国,必须令法律得以执行。但是,殖民地议会拒绝承认总督的权威,并且不肯为听命于总督的法官支付薪酬。因此,从客观的立场来看,这不是总督在妨碍司法,而是殖民地议会在违背法律。然而,在《宣言》中,杰斐逊对此类细节,从不提及。他只是简略而模糊地说,"英王阻碍了正义的实施"。他心中自然明白,殖民地人民的行为并非全都得理,其中自有一些不好提及之处。因此,他必须模糊处理。如此方可达到《宣言》的目的:争取人们的同情与支持,而不是让人看到殖民地人民并非天使的一面。正如美国历史学家波利娜·梅尔(Pauline Maier)所言,在这样棘手的问题上,"说得越少越好"(The less said the better)。不过,就当时《宣言》所受到的批评来看,这个策略似乎不大成功。批判者利用这一点大做文章,质问道:到底是谁让殖民地人民得不到正义?——"Who suffered the administration of justice totally to cease?"参见 Pauline Maier, *American Scripture: Making the Declaration of Independence*, New York: Vintage Books, 1997, pp.110~111.

② "swarms of officers"是用《圣经》中的蝗灾,来比喻英王向殖民地派遣海关官员、税务官、调查与巡视员等。"eat out"一词在这里颇得夸张之效。受英王之命前往殖民地的官员总数只有三四十余人,而在殖民地人民看来,这些人的目的就是要搜刮尽他们的资财。

③ 1763年2月,英法两国正签订和约时,布特(Bute)内阁决定在北美殖民地派驻常备军,乔治三世参与决策。在国王看来,向殖民地派驻常备军不仅可安置军人,还能提供可供其任命的大量职位;在议会看来,北美殖民地的边境线上,北有加拿大的法国人、西有印第安人、南方的佛罗里达又有西班牙人,殖民地臣民与他们屡屡冲突不断,只有把纪律严明的皇家军队派驻过去,才能维护殖民地的安全与稳定。因此,《驻军法》(*The Quartering Act of 1765*)两年后在议会顺利通过。一旦驻军,加于殖民地的税也就顺理成章——既然是为保护殖民地而驻军,部分驻军开支理应由殖民地人民负担。1768年、1774年,英政府两次向波士顿派驻军队,并建立军人政府,意图凌驾于殖民地自治政府之上。

and superior to the civil power.①

He has combined with others②to subject us to a jurisdiction foreign to our constitution, and unacknowledged by our laws, giving his assent to their acts of pretended legislation.③

For quartering large bodies of armed troops among us④;

For protecting them, by a mock trial⑤, from punishment for any murders which they should commit on the inhabitants of these States;

For cutting off our trade with all parts of the world;⑥

---

① 《宣言》对英王的指控至此已达 12 条,依据波利娜·梅尔的看法,它们可归入第一类指控:"国王意欲建立暴政之权威"(The King had attempted to establish a tyranny)。下文第 13 条指控,属第二类:"国王力图建立暴政之权威"(The King had endeavored to establish a tyranny)。其余 5 条,属第三类:"国王意欲牢固确立暴政之权威"(The King had attempted to erect a tyranny)。见 Pauline Maier, *American Scripture: Making the Declaration of Independence*, pp.107~119.

② "others"指英国议会议员(Members of Parliament),"a jurisdiction"指英国议会(British Parliament)。《宣言》全文未有一次使用"Parliament"一词。其意深长。它表示,到 1776 年时,北美各殖民地人民已有独立的政治共同体意识。他们不承认英帝国对其享有主权者权利,而将英国议会视为一种外国势力(foreign jurisdiction)。你是你,我是我,各有各的立法机关,也各有各的权力范围。设若英国议会在殖民地强行推行其法律,是对殖民地主权或自由权的侵犯。因为殖民地从未认可英国议会对其拥有权威,他们只向国王臣服过。因此,在宣布独立时,他们不可能向从未臣服过的英国议会宣布独立,而只向国王宣布独立。由是之故,"British Parliament"没有资格在《宣言》中出现。

③ 此条指控由后列 9 项"For"引导的"罪行"构成。这 9 项罪行的罗列,看似随意,实则经过杰斐逊的精心考虑:他要陈述冒充有权的立法机关(pretended legislation),即英国议会,强加于殖民地的各项法律(acts of pretended legislation)。正好体现梅尔所言"国王力图建立暴政之权威"的第二类指控。

④ 1775 年,英国议会继 1765 年之后再度颁布《驻军法》(*The Quartering Act*)。1775 年《驻军法》还规定:殖民地居民必须为进驻其家的英国士兵提供食宿。美国立国后,为保护公民住宅不被侵犯,制定了第 3 条宪法修正案,规定:和平时期,未经房主同意,士兵不得在民房驻扎,除非依照了法律规定的方式;战时也不允许如此。

⑤ "mock trial":有意庇护、不公正的审判;这里指 1774 年《公平行使正义法》(*The Impartial Administration of Justice Act*)。

⑥ 1775 年,议会通过《禁止法》(*The Prohibitory Act*),对殖民地实施经济制裁。

For imposing taxes on us without our consent;①

For depriving us, in many cases, of the benefits of trial by jury;②

For transporting us beyond seas to be tried for pretended offenses;③

therein: in that place

For abolishing the free system of English laws in a neighboring province④, establishing therein an arbitrary government, and enlarging its boundaries, so as to render it at once an example and fit instrument for introducing the same absolute rule into these colonies;

For taking away our charters, abolishing our most valuable laws, and altering fundamentally the forms of our governments;⑤

For suspending our own legislatures, and declaring themselves invested with power to legislate for us in all cases what-

① "未经同意,不得征税"被英国人视为最为传统、历史最为悠久的自由权。此处再度提出,提醒读者注意殖民地人民自由权一再被侵犯的事实,包括1764年《糖税法》(*The Sugar Act*)、1765年《印花税法》(*The Stamp Act*)、1767年"汤森法"(Townshend Acts)、1773年的《茶叶法》(*The Tea Act*)。

② 1764年,英国议会通过《贸易与航海法》(*The Act of Trade and Navigation*),其中规定:触犯条例者将被移送地方海事法庭审理,而地方海事法庭的审判没有陪审团的参与,这就意味着被起诉一方失去由陪审团裁决有罪与否的权利。这一项权利向来就属英国人传统的自由权。

③ 这一条指控依据《贸易与航海法》(*The Act of Trade and Navigation*)等法令从理论上推出,但实际上并无殖民地人民被运送至海外接受审判。它是又一个被《宣言》批判者引为缺乏事实依据的例子。

④ 指1774年《魁北克法》(*The Quebec Act*)。

⑤ "charter"(特许状),是英政府授予北美殖民地用以自治的文书。各殖民地都有自己的政府,由总督和议会组成,总督由英王指派,议会有上、下两院,主要权力在下院。下院由殖民地人民选举产生,在内部事务上,有充分的自治权。拥有特许状的殖民地称之为自治殖民地,如罗德岛与康涅狄格;宾夕法尼亚、马里兰、特拉华则属于业主殖民地,拥有英王颁发的业主文书(patent);其他8个殖民地属英王直辖(colonies under instruction of Crown)。1774年,英国议会通过《马萨诸塞规制法》(*The Massachusetts Regulatory Act*),剥夺了马萨诸塞殖民地政府的自治权。

soever.①

He has abdicated government here②, by declaring us out of his protection③, and waging war against us.

He has plundered our seas, ravaged our coasts, burnt our towns, and destroyed the lives of our people.

He is at this time transporting large armies of foreign mercenaries to complete the works of death, desolation, and tyranny, already begun with circumstances of cruelty and perfidy, scarcely paralleled in the most barbarous ages, and totally unworthy the head of a civilized nation.

perfidy: treachery

He has constrained our fellow-citizens, taken captive on the high seas, to bear arms against their country, to become the executioners of their friends and brethren, or to fall themselves by their hands.④

high seas: the open seas beyond the legal control of any one country

brethren: brothers

He has excited domestic insurrections amongst us, and has endeavored to bring on the inhabitants of our frontiers the merciless Indian savages, whose known rule of warfare is an undistinguished destruction of all ages, sexes, and conditions.

insurrection: a usually violent attempted to take control of a government

---

① 这里指 1766 年《宣告法》(*The Declaratory Act*)与 1767 年《纽约议会暂停法》(*The New York Assembly Suspend Act*)。"in all cases whatsoever"是一个无论在什么情况下都不能忽略的词语。因为这是英国政府一再向殖民地强调的立场:任何情况下,英国议会都保留对殖民地的权威;任何情况下,殖民地人民都必须服从大英帝国的法律与英王意旨。《宣言》反其意而用之,强调:任何情况下,殖民地人民都拥有不容任何人侵犯的自由权。

② 不知是巧合还是有意,"He has abdicated government"与《1689 年英国权利法案》中的"King James the second having abdicated the Government"用词相似,似乎是在说明:乔治三世与詹姆斯二世一样,放弃了他对政府的责任,因此也就无权得到人民的效忠。此条起至下文"He has excited……"一句,属梅尔所说"国王意欲牢固确立暴政之权威"的指控,共 5 条。

③ 1775 年 12 月,英国议会通过《禁止法》,宣布不再保护北美殖民地,并禁止与其贸易,劫夺殖民地在海上航行的船只。

④ "to become the executioners of their friends and brethren"这一条指控只是依据《禁止法》在理论上推出,实际上并未发生过。

redress：to correct (sth that is unfair or wrong)

jurisdiction：limits within which legal authority maybe exercised

magnanimity：the quality of being generous and kind nature

conjure：appeal solemnly to (sb)

kindred：family relationship

In every stage of these oppressions we have petitioned for redress in the most humble terms. Our repeated petitions have been answered only by repeated injury①. A prince, whose character is thus marked by every act which may define a tyrant, is unfit to be the ruler of a free people②.

Nor have we been wanting in attentions to our British brethren③. We have warned④ them, from time to time, of attempts by their legislature to extend an unwarrantable jurisdiction over us. We have reminded them of the circumstances of our emigration and settlement here⑤. We have appealed to their native justice and magnanimity, and we have conjured them by the ties of our common kindred to disavow these usurpations, which would inevitably interrupt our connections and correspondence. They, too, have been deaf to the voice of

---

① 指第一届与第二届大陆会议(Continental Congress)3次向英王递交请愿书,吁请国王废除在殖民地人民看来不公正的法案,给予殖民地人民与英国本土臣民平等的权利。这里"injury"本当作"injuries",然而,大陆会议定稿如此。不过,杰斐逊在他自己保存的草本中,把这个单数表达改成了复数。可见他在大陆会议通过《宣言》后,还在修改其文稿,显示出渴求完美的气质。

② "unfit to be a ruler of a free people"说明了英国政治的传统:国王必须尊重英国人民传统的自由权,不得施行暴政,否则,会被国民认为其不宜为王而赶下王位。英国历史上,不乏此例。1327~1485年,有五位在位君主被终止王权;17世纪,复有两位。见 Pauline Maier, *American Scripture: Making the Declaration of Independence*, New York: Vintage Books, 1997, p.51.

③ 北美殖民地人民曾数次致信英格兰、爱尔兰与加拿大魁北克的英国人,向其陈述苦情,争取声援。

④ 从此处起,《宣言》连用几个动词:warned(告诫)—reminded(提醒)—appealed(呼吁)—conjured(恳请),辞气渐趋加重,委屈、不忿中连带哀恳之意,显示殖民地人民是在万般无奈、求告无门的情势下,方决定与大不列颠解除政治关系。

⑤ 这里的提醒是说:殖民地人民的祖先离开英国、征服与移居北美,正与英国人民的祖先撒克逊人离开北欧、占有大不列颠岛,并在那里建立拥有全部主权的国家一样,北美殖民地人民享有同样独立与不受干预的主权者权利。他们只是与英国人民拥戴同一位国王,除此之外,二者在政治上没有任何联系。美洲的征服、北美殖民地的建立乃至国家体制的创立,英国政府未曾为之出过一分钱。因此,殖民地人民与英国人民一样,享有与任何一个主权国家的居民同等的自由权;英国议会没有资格对殖民地称王称霸。这番提醒,杰斐逊在他1774年撰写的《英属美利坚权利概观》中就说得非常清楚。

justice and of consanguinity. We must, therefore, acquiesce in the necessity which denounces our separation, and hold them, as we hold the rest of mankind, enemies in war, in peace friends.

We, therefore, the representatives of the UNITED STATES OF AMERICA, in General Congress assembled, appealing to the Supreme Judge of the world for the rectitude of our intentions, do, in the name, and by authority of the good people of these colonies, solemnly publish and declare, that these United States Colonies are, and of right ought to be, FREE AND INDEPENDENT STATES; that they are absolved from all allegiance to the British crown, and that all political connection between them and the state of Great Britain is, and ought to be, totally dissolved; and that, as FREE and INDEPENDENT STATES, they have full power to levy war, conclude peace, contract alliances, establish commerce, and to do all other acts and things which INDEPENDENT STATES may of right do. And for the support of this Declaration, with a firm reliance on the protection of DIVINE PROVIDENCE, we mutually pledge to each other our lives, our fortunes, and our sacred honor.

consanguinity: relationship be being descended from the same family

acquiesce (in sth): accept sth without protest

rectitude: the quality of being honest and morally correct

of right: justly, correctly

allegiance: loyalty to a person, country, group, etc

levy: to wage; to carry on

DIVINE PROVIDENCE: the way God cares for and protects all creatures

译 文

美国《独立宣言》[①]

第二届大陆会议 1776 年 7 月 4 日

人类事务进程中，当一个民族必须解除其与另一个民族相联系的政治纽带，并在世界各国中取得由自然法和造物主赋予其独立与平等的地位时，出于对人类意见的适当尊重，有必要将促使其分离的原因公之于众。

我们认为下述真理是不言自明的：一切人生而平等；造物主赋予他们某些不可剥夺的权利，其中包括生命、自由和追求幸福；为了保障这些权利，政府在人们中建立起来，经由被统治者的同意获得其正当权利；任何形式的政府一旦破坏了这些目的，人民就有权加以变更或废除而另设新政府，新政府所依据的原则以及组织权力的方式在人们看来最可能实现其安全和幸福。诚然，为慎重起见，久已设立的政府不应该由于一些微小和短暂的原因而被改变；一切的经验也都表明，当弊端尚可忍受时，人们宁愿忍受也不愿废除他们所习惯的政府，以恢复其权利。但是，当一连串的、总以同一目标为方向的权力滥用与篡夺已昭示其意图置人民于绝对专制之下时，人民就有权利，也有义务，推翻这样的政府，并为他们将来的安全提供新的保障。这些殖民地过去正是这样耐心忍受的，而现在，他们也正是出于这样的原因，不得不改变他们原有的政府。当今大不列颠国王的历史是一部反复的伤害与篡夺的历史，全都以对这些殖民地实施绝对的暴政为直接目的。为了证明这点，我们把事实陈述于公正的世界。

他拒不同意一些对公众福利最有益和必要的法律。

---

① 译文参考了朱曾汶译《杰斐逊选集》（2012 年商务版）与《不列颠百科全书》（2002 年中文版）卷 8“独立宣言”词条。

他不许他的总督们通过一些紧急和情属迫切的重要法律,除非它们暂不执行,直到他许可为止;而这些法律暂不执行之后,他又对它们完全置之不理。

他拒不通过其他一些有利于某广大地区人民的法律,除非那里的人民放弃在立法机关中的代表权。这种权利对人民万分宝贵,只有对暴君才是极其可怕的。

他让立法会议在不平常、不舒服且远离档案库的地方召开,唯一目的是使议员们疲于奔命,不得不唯他的命是从。

他一再地解散代议机关,因为它们以男子汉的坚定气概反对他对人民权利的侵犯。

他在解散议会之后,久久不让选举新的议会。但立法权是不能消亡的,它又回到人民手中,由他们行使。在这同时,殖民地始终处于危险中:既有外侵之虞,又有内乱之患。

他竭力阻止殖民地增加人口;为此目的,他阻挠外国人归化法的通过,拒绝批准其他鼓励外国人移居殖民地的法律,并提高新拨土地的条件。

他阻挠司法工作,办法是拒不批准确立司法权力的法律。

他使法官完全服从于他一个人的意志,因为他们的任期、薪酬与支付都取决于他。

他设立了许多新的官职,并向这里派遣大批官员,骚扰我们的人民,搜刮尽他们的资财。

他在和平时期未经我们立法机关同意就在我们中间维持常备军。

他使军权独立于民权,并凌驾于民权之上。

他与别人联合迫使我们屈从于一种不与我们的宪法相合、不为我们的法律所承认的势力管辖之下;准许他们通过各种伪称有效的立法:

在我们中间驻扎大批武装部队;

对于他们在殖民地犯下的所有谋杀罪行,通过一种不公正的审讯使其免于惩罚。

切断我们与世界各地的贸易;

未经我们同意便向我们征税;

在许多案件中剥夺我们享有经陪审团裁决的权益;

以莫须有的罪名把我们押送海外受审；

在一邻省废除英国法律的自由体制，在那里建立一个专断政府，并扩大该省疆域，企图使其成为一个先例和称手的工具，以便将同样的专制统治引入这里的殖民地；

取消我们的自治特许状，废除我们最宝贵的法律，从根本上改变我们的政府体制；

中止我们自己的立法机关，宣称他们自己有权在任何情况下为我们制定法律。

他宣布我们不受他保护，并对我们发起战争，从而放弃了他在这里的政府。

他劫夺我们的海洋资源，骚扰我们的海岸，焚烧我们的城镇，并且杀害我们的人民。

他目前正在运送大批外国雇佣兵来完成其屠杀、破坏与倒行逆施的勾当。这些勾当已经开始。其残忍与卑劣，就连最野蛮的时代也难以与之相比，同一个文明国家的元首完全不相称。

他强迫我们在公海上被掳获的同胞拿起武器反对自己的国家，使他们成为残杀亲人和朋友的刽子手，或是自己死于亲人和朋友的手下。

他在我们中间煽动内乱，竭力挑动我们边境上的居民——残酷无情的印第安蛮族；众所周知，印第安人的战争准则是不分年龄、性别与生存状态，一律斩尽杀绝。

在遭受这些压迫的每一阶段，我们都曾以最谦恭的辞气上书请愿，请求他予以纠正；然而我们一再的请愿所得到的答复是一再的伤害。这样一个君主，其一言一行都显示出暴君的性格，是不配做一个自由民族的统治者的。

我们对于我们的英国兄弟也同样请求过关照。我们曾屡次劝请他们注意，他们的立法机构企图把没有法律依据的管辖权强加于我们身上；也曾提请他们回想，我们来此迁居的情形。我们曾向其天然的正义感与仁爱心呼吁，恳请他们看在同胞之情，谴责这些势必破坏我们之间关系与友谊的篡权行为。然而，他们对正义之声，对血亲之吁，同样置若罔闻。因此，我们必须承认宣布分离的必要性，并像对待其余的人类一样对待他们：战时是敌，和时是友。

因此,我们美利坚合众国大陆会议的代表们集会,祈求世上最高裁判者明鉴我们意图的正义性,以这些殖民地的善良人民的名义与权威庄严地发表和宣布:这些联合起来的殖民地是且理所当然是自由而独立之邦;他们从此取消对英国国王的一切忠诚,完全解除且理当解除与英国的一切政治关系;作为独立而自由之邦,它们有全权宣战、媾和、结盟、通商,并从事独立诸邦有权从事的一切行动与事宜。

为拥护本宣言,秉持着坚定地信赖上天护佑的信念,我们彼此以我们的生命、我们的财产、我们的神圣的荣誉互誓不渝。

解　　析

托马斯·杰斐逊（Thomas Jefferson，1743.4.13—1826.7.4）——《独立宣言》的起草者。

托马斯·杰斐逊是美国历史上最具神话色彩的人物之一。美国历史学家理查德·霍夫斯塔特（Richard Hofstadter）曾评论，“在美国历史上，围绕托马斯·杰斐逊而形成的神话，数量之多、给人印象之深刻，堪与任何神话相比”（The mythology that has grown up around Thomas Jefferson is as massive and imposing as any in American history）①。

神话的形成往往源于主人公多方面的才华与成就。杰斐逊正是这样。

他有着高贵的政治地位。美国立国后，他先后担任弗吉尼亚州州长（Governor of Virginia，1779～1784）；接替本杰明·富兰克林（Benjamin Franklin），出任驻法国宫廷全权公使（Commissioner and U.S. Minister to France，1784～1789）；被美国第1任总统乔治·华盛顿（George Washington）任命为国务卿（Secretary of State）；1796年，他与约翰·亚当斯（John Adams）竞选美国第2任总统，以3票之差输于亚当斯，屈居副总统（Vice-president）；最后于1800年当选美国第3任总统，连任两届（1801～1809）。但在杰斐逊本人看来，这些似乎都不值得提起。

他又有着骄人的政治成就。他在美国独立革命（The American Revolution）中扮演了重要角色。年仅33岁，他就被推为美国《独立宣言》主要起草人，为美国人民奉献了平等、自由、独立、民主等重要的政治理念。假如说，“美国人源生于一种‘理念’，那么，杰斐逊就是这理念之父”（If American had

① Richard Hofstadter, *The American Political Tradition and the Men Who Made It*, New York: Vintage Book, 1989, p.48.

originated in an "idea", then Jefferson was father to the thought)①。因此之故，1776 年的《独立宣言》与 1777 年的《邦联条例》(*The Articles of Confederation*)、1787 年的《联邦宪法》(*The Constitution of the United States*, or, *The Federal Constitution*)共同成为美利坚合众国最重要的开国文献。他虽然没有直接参与 1787 年《联邦宪法》的制订(当时他正出任驻法公使)，然而制宪会议一结束，他就与詹姆斯·麦迪逊(James Madison，美国第 4 任总统)等一起提出，应该在宪法中补入《权利法案》(*Bill of Rights*)，以保障美国民众的自由权，并推动它终于在 1791 年成为联邦宪法第 1~10 条修正案②。因为这些，他和乔治·华盛顿、本杰明·富兰克林、约翰·亚当斯、詹姆斯·麦迪逊、约翰·马歇尔(John Marshall，1801~1835 年美国联邦最高法院大法官)等，一起被尊为美国建国之父(Founding Fathers, or Founders)。

不止如此，他还为美国社会的政教分开、宗教与思想自由作出了创造性贡献。美国在立国之初，其政治延续了母国政教不分的传统：政府可以强迫人民参加安立甘国教的宗教仪式，拒不服从者，罚款处置；安立甘教会则仿佛是政府的另一只手臂，负责训练人民服从政府；其教义与教职人员享有高人一等的地位。非安立甘国教信徒虽然可以公开举行宗教仪式，但是歧视让他们感到受压迫。贵格会教徒(Quakers)、天主教徒、犹太教徒等被禁止担任政府公职。在弗吉尼亚，信仰异端(heresy)还是一种死刑罪③。这些，对于不信奉安立甘教的教众来说，无异于"精神上的暴政"(spiritual tyranny，杰斐逊语)④；而对于杰斐逊、詹姆斯·麦迪逊等自由主义安立甘教徒看来，是亟须加以改革的现状。因为它背离美国革命所树立的自由与平等原则。1776 年，就在殖民地人

---

① Thomas Jefferson, *Political Writings*, Cambridge: Cambridge University Press, 1999, p.xxx.

② 1789 年 6 月 8 日，《权利法案》由 James Madison 正式起草，一共 9 条，经国会两院辩论、增减，通过了 12 条，但最终经由各州批准者为第 3~12 条，共 10 条。未经批准的第 1、2 条分别涉及众议院议员数在各州的分配与国会议员的工资增减。1992 年 5 月，美国第 27 条宪法修正案获得批准，其内容正是 1789 年提出的第 2 条。

③ Merrill D.Peterson, *Thomas Jefferson and the New Nation: A Biography*, London: Oxford University Press, 1975, p.133.

④ Kevin J.Hayes, *The Road to Monticello: The Life and Mind of Thomas Jefferson*, Oxford: Oxford University Press, 2008, p.203.

民为反抗英国政府、争取政治上的自由与独立时,众多非安立甘教徒发起请愿,要求不同教义的信众享受彻底的宗教自由,废除政治上的不公平或歧视政策。杰弗逊是这些请愿者们的支持者。在他看来,宗教不宽容不止妨碍人的心灵自由,且"只会导致虚伪与卑鄙的恶习(tend only to beget habits of hypocrisy and meanness)"①;政治与宗教不仅应当而且必须分开。因此,他把异教徒的请愿当作自己的事业。1777 年,杰斐逊起草《一项建立宗教自由的议案》(*A Bill for Establishing Religious Freedom*),并于 1779 年向弗吉尼亚议会提出。他在议案中强调,"一切借助世俗的惩罚或靠剥夺公民资格来影响心灵的企图,都背离神圣的宗教创造者的愿望"(that all attempts to influence it by temporal punishments, or by civil incapacitations, are a departure from the plan of the holy author of our religion)②。这是一种毁灭宗教自由的做法。若要以追求真理与自由为原则,就应该立法规定:"一切人均可自由表明并通过说理坚持其对宗教事务的见解,决不可因此而缩小、扩大或影响其公民权"(that all men shall be free to profess, and by argument to maintain, their opinions in matters of religion, and that the same shall in no wise diminish, enlarge, or affect their civil capacities)③。这项议案历经 10 年挫折,终于在 1786 年初获得通过④,成为影响深远的《弗吉尼亚宗教自由法案》(*The Statute of Virginia for Religious Freedom*)。杰斐逊毕生为此成就骄傲不已,视之为"他对人性的最真诚的贡献"⑤。美国学者也将这份宗教自由法案誉为"出版史上最卓越、最犀利、为思想自由而呼吁的篇章之一"(one of the most brilliant and trenchant pleas for free thought in the history of literature)⑥。

他还是学问渊博、卓有建树的学者与弗吉尼亚大学(University of Virginia)创建人。杰斐逊出身于美国南方庄园主家庭,自幼接受良好的教育。他 5

---

① Thomas Jefferson, *Political Writings*, p.390.

② Thomas Jefferson, *Political Writings*, p.390.

③ Thomas Jefferson, *Political Writings*, p.391.

④ 杰斐逊的好友詹姆斯·麦迪逊在其中起了很大作用。正是他于 1785 年在弗吉尼亚议会重新提起该议案,并立促议案获得通过。其时,杰斐逊正出使法国。

⑤ 托马斯·杰斐逊:《杰斐逊选集》,朱曾汶译,北京:商务印书馆,2012 年,第 291 页。

⑥ Richard Hofstadter, *The American Political Tradition and the Men Who Made It*, p.49.

岁入学,青年时便掌握了拉丁语、希腊语、法语、意大利语、西班牙语[①]。尤其令人赞叹的是,他一生好学不倦,视野广阔,知识上的兴趣涉及哲学、法学、文学、历史学、建筑学、数学乃至于植物学、古生物学、地理学,机械学等。既拥有擅长深思的天赋,又有实际动手的才能;更难得的是,他还有着"宁愿为知识受苦"的勤奋。这一切,使他很早就获得文学与科学的名声。

1768 年,杰斐逊当选弗吉尼亚议会议员,从此步入政坛。很快,他就崭露出惊人的政治写作才华。1774 年,他以一篇充满激情的论文《英属美利坚权利概观》(*A Summary View of the Rights of British America*)震动政坛。这篇论文是杰斐逊提供给弗吉尼亚代表参与第一届大陆会议的文稿,以便他们向大会提出建议,并希望获得大会支持。它阐述了与两年后的《独立宣言》一以贯之的思想。文章指出,殖民地人民从来到北美大陆的第一天起,就是自由的;他们拥有与英国人民完全同等的权利;而英国政府自英法战争结束以来却一直在处心积虑地使殖民地人民沦为奴隶。因此,殖民地人民有权通过抗议声明并主张自己的权利。文章还列举了英国议会与英王乔治三世对殖民地一连串的篡权与伤害行为[②]。毫无疑问,这篇《英属美利坚权利概观》就是《独立宣言》的底本。不过,杰斐逊的观点被许多参会代表认为过于激进,他的论文也就被压了下来。但这篇文章很快就在欧洲得以发表。它那雄辩而充满力量的语言,为杰斐逊赢得了广泛的读者。文中有言,"上帝赋予我们生命的同时也赋予我们自由,暴力可以将它们摧毁,却不能拆散它们"(The God who gave us life gave us liberty at the same time;the hand of force may destroy,but cannot disjoin them)[③]。这种强烈的尊严、自信以及宁为自由而毁灭的精神使他声名远播。从那以后,弗吉尼亚"重要的政治写作任务就几乎理所当然地落在杰斐逊一人身上"[④]。《独立宣言》起草委员会之所以请杰斐逊主笔,原因就在于

① 杰斐逊专门阐述过学习西班牙语的重要性:"它对于一个美国人来说是最重要的。我们同西班牙的关系已经很重要,而且重要性还会与日俱增。此外,美洲早期的历史主要是用西班牙文写的"。引自托马斯·杰斐逊:《杰斐逊选集》,第 419 页。

② 《英属美利坚权利概观》美国历史上第一篇直接对英王提出尖锐批评的政论文章。其知名度虽远逊《独立宣言》,然其重要性不容忽略。

③ Thomas Jefferson,*Political Writings*,p.80.

④ 托马斯·杰斐逊:《杰斐逊选集》,第 5 页。

此。

杰斐逊一生,把知识的获得作为人生目的;把知识的享受视为人的福分。他曾经写信给自己的外甥,告诉他要充分享受获得知识的快乐。由是之故,当他从政治生涯的顶峰退下来之后,又在晚年创造了新的人生顶峰:弗吉尼亚大学的创办①——他心中"神圣的事业"(holy cause)。这所大学被杰斐逊自豪而亲切地呼为"小小的学术村"(an academical village),吸引了美国各州的学生"来此畅饮知识的甘醇"(to come and drink the cup of knowledge)。它不仅是美国南部第一所规模宏伟的综合性、现代性大学,课程设置涵盖自然与人文、社会科学,完全突破了以古典学为重心的传统;也是美国第一所不与教会发生关联的大学,尽管它也设置了神学科目。建校伊始,杰斐逊宣称,"这所大学将建立在人类心灵不受限制的自由基础上。因为在这里,我们不会畏惧真理将把我们导向何方,也不会容忍任何只要理性尚可自由与之抗辩的错误"(This institution will be based on the illimitable freedom of human mind. For here we are not afraid to follow truth where ever it may lead, nor to tolerate any error so long as reason is left free to combat it)。他用毕生信奉的信条——"真理使人们获得自由"——为这所大学带来了卓越的声誉。②

1826 年 7 月 4 日,也就是《独立宣言》诞辰 50 周年的那一天,杰斐逊离世,享年 83 岁。同日,他的老朋友、同样也为《独立宣言》作出了贡献的约翰·亚当斯去世。这大概也在相当程度上增加了杰斐逊在美国历史中的神话色彩。不过,杰斐逊本人未见得会接受人们加在他身上的各种神话光环。他一生功绩无数,可是他自己最珍视的只有 3 件:《独立宣言》的撰写、《弗吉尼亚宗教自由法规》的制定、弗吉尼亚大学的创建。这 3 件事情贯穿着一个统一的精神,充分体现出杰斐逊作为启蒙时代的思想家所坚持的最高原则:自由。《独立宣言》是为自由而战斗的姿态;《宗教自由法规》是将自由贯彻至人

① 弗吉尼亚大学建校获得许可是在 1819 年。不过,早在 1817 年 10 月 6 日,其奠基仪式便已举行。参与仪式者除了杰斐逊,还有美国第 4 任总统詹姆斯·麦迪逊、第 5 任总统詹姆斯·门罗(James Monroe)。1825 年,弗吉尼亚大学正式招生。

② Merrill D.Peterson, *Thomas Jefferson and the New Nation: A Biography*, London: Oxford University Press, 1975, pp.962~968, pp.986~987;托马斯·杰斐逊:《杰斐逊选集》,第 28 页。

类的心灵;大学是培育自由之思想的摇篮。无怪乎杰斐逊要在自撰的墓志铭中这样写道:“这里埋葬着托马斯·杰斐逊,美国《独立宣言》的作者,《弗吉尼亚宗教自由法规》的制定者和弗吉尼亚大学之父”(HERE WAS BURIED THOMAS JEFFERSON/AUTHOR OF THE DECLARATION OF AMERICAN INDEPENDENCE/OF THE STATUTE OF VIRGINIA FOR RELIGIOUS FREEDOM/AND FATHER OF THE UNIVERSITY OF VIRGINIA)①。

《独立宣言》是杰斐逊受第二届大陆会议(The Second Continental Congress)“五人委员会”(Committee of five)②的委托,在17天内完成的(1776年6月11日~6月28日)。草稿完成,提交大陆会议讨论通过时,其名称并不叫《独立宣言》,而叫《美利坚联盟在大会集会代表之宣言》(*A Declaration by the Representatives of the United States of America, in General Congress assembled*)。宣言经讨论、修改、通过并发表后,于7月19日被正式誊写在羊皮纸上(engrossed on the parchment),羊皮纸稿上改成了《美利坚联合十三邦一致宣言》(*The Unanimous Declaration of the Thirteen United States of America*)。《独立宣言》(*The Declaration of Independence*)是它随后才有的叫法。

杰斐逊受命起草宣言,并非为了正式宣布与大不列颠脱离。那项使命在《独立宣言》讨论通过之前,已在7月2日由大陆会议通过的一项决议完成。无疑,杰斐逊对之也有贡献。不过,杰斐逊更大的贡献在于完成了另一项使命——通过《独立宣言》这份文件陈述与母国大不列颠脱离的理由(to declare the causes which impel them to the separation),为事实上的反叛提供道德与法律上的正当性,以此赢得国际上的支持。

杰斐逊成功地完成了这项使命。他在起草宣言的时候,虽然没有翻看任何书籍或小册子,也没有过多运用玄思,只是把那个时代的“常识摆在人们面前”,表达出“与那一时代相和谐的情感”与“美国人的思想”,但是他那“朴实

① 杰斐逊葬在蒙蒂塞洛(Monticello)脚下,墓碑上对于担任两届美国总统的经历只字未提。

② “五人委员会”除杰斐逊外,其他四人是约翰·亚当斯(John Adams),本杰明·富兰克林(Benjamin Franklin),罗伯特·列文斯顿(Robert Livingston),罗杰·舍尔曼(Roger Sherman)。杰斐逊起草毕,提交大会讨论前,亚当斯与富兰克林对草稿作了少量修改(前者2处,后者5处)。

而坚定的言辞"赢得了"美国人的赞许"①。正是因为这一点，《独立宣言》通过并发表的那一天——1776 年 7 月 4 日，而不是北美 13 个殖民地(American colonies)正式宣布独立的那一天——7 月 2 日，被美国人认定为他们国家的独立日(Independence Day)。庄重典雅的文风、铿锵有力的语言、抑扬顿挫的节奏、言简意赅的行文，或者如杰斐逊的朋友约翰·亚当斯所说，"遣词造句的独具匠心"(peculiar felicity of expression)②，还使它同时成了文学经典。

不过，《独立宣言》并非没有给人留下遗憾。杰斐逊提交的文本中，有一段谴责奴隶制的文字：

他发动一场灭绝人性的残酷战争，侵犯一个遥远的、从未冒犯过他的民族的最神圣的生命与自由权利，将他们捉住并运往另一个半球为奴，有的在其运送途中悲惨的死去。这种海盗式的战争、臭名昭著的异教徒强权，是信奉基督教的英国国王所发起的。他一意坚持：继续开放买卖人类的市场；滥用其否决权，扼杀一切试图禁止或限制此种罪恶贸易的立法(He has waged cruel war against human nature itself, violating it's most sacred rights of life and liberty in the persons of a distant people who never offended him, captivating & carrying them into slavery in another hemisphere, or to incur miserable death in their transportation thither. This piratical warfare, the opprobrium of INFIDEL powers, is the warfare of the CHRISTIAN king of Great Britain. Determined to keep open a market where MEN should be bought & sold, he has prostituted his negative for suppressing every

① 1825 年 5 月，杰斐逊在写给亨利·李(Henry Lee)的一封信中，解释了他起草《独立宣言》时的想法与资料来源，相关文字如下："Not to find out new principles, or new arguments, never before thought of, not merely to say things which had never been said before; but to place before mankind the common sense of the subject, in terms so plain and firm as to command their assent, and to justify ourselves in the independent stand we are compelled to take. Neither aiming at originality of principle or sentiment, nor yet copied from any particular and previous writing, it was intended to be an expression of the American mind, and to give to that expression the proper tone and spirit called for by the occasion. All its authority rests then on the harmonizing sentiments of the day."引自 Thomas Jefferson, *Political Writings*, p.148.

② Carl Becker, *Declaration of Independence: A Study in the History of Political Ideas*, New York: Harcourt, Brace and Company, 1922, p.194.

legislative attempt to prohibit or to restrain this execrable commerce)。[①]

这段文字在大会讨论时以其辞气过盛被删除。杰斐逊对此颇为不悦,他用"糟践(depredations)"一词形容大会对原稿的修改[②]。他也想必有一定程度的挫折感。1769 年,杰斐逊任职弗吉尼亚下议院议员。他的第一个政治行动就是拿出一个解放奴隶的法案。法案没有通过,他失败了。数年后,他再次利用机会,在《独立宣言》中谴责奴隶制,又一次失败。

这是否意味着杰斐逊是坚定的废奴主义者?不能说是。杰斐逊出生于弗吉尼亚,其父彼得·杰斐逊(Peter Jefferson)是当地有名的庄园主,拥有奴隶 60 余名。杰斐逊 14 岁从父亲那里继承了他出生地的财产,当然也包括奴隶。30 岁时,他又从岳父那里继承了 135 名奴隶。加上他前后从奴隶市场上购置来的黑奴,他一共拥有 200 来名奴隶,是弗吉尼亚蓄奴最多的庄园主之一。依靠这些除了劳动再无任何权利的人类牲口,他一生过着富足、舒适的生活,从未萌生过主动解放其奴隶的想法,哪怕临死也是这样。"他的遗嘱只写明解放 5 名奴隶,剩下的大部分被卖去抵债"(In his will Jefferson freed only five of approximately two hundred slaves, most of them were sold to pay his enormous debts)[③]。尽管他未曾放弃解放奴隶的设想(见 1781 年《弗吉尼亚笔记》),并且一直在尽力阻止奴隶制的扩张:1784 年,他向大陆会议提出《关于西部土地组建的报告》,其中建议:禁止奴隶制向西北扩张。这个建议为 1787 年大陆会议通过的《西北土地法令》(*The Northwest Ordinance*)采纳。1808 年,他又敦促国会通过了《禁止奴隶贸易法案》,禁止美国参与非洲奴隶贸易。但这都不能说,他配得上废奴主义者的名号;也不能说,他对于奴隶制的反对,是基于彻底

---

① Thomas Jefferson, *Political Writings*, p.99.

② 宽厚的富兰克林为了宽慰他,给他讲了一个故事。他说:我有一个规矩——尽量不为将由公众审议的文件起草文稿。我做印刷工的时候,有一个伙伴是帽店的学徒,学徒期满想要自己开一家店。他首先要做的就是弄一个漂亮的招牌,写些字在上面。他草拟的文字是这样的:"约翰·汤普森,制帽匠,制作并出售帽子,现金交易",上面画了一顶帽子。拿给朋友们一讨论,结果只剩下了"约翰·汤普森"和那顶帽子。朋友们分别给出的理由是"制帽匠"这一身份说明纯属多余;顾客只是来购帽,不关心帽子的制作,因此"制作"应去除;本地从无赊账习惯,无须声明"现金交易";"出售"一词无用,没人要求白给,随着"出售"二字的删除,后面跟着的"帽子"也得去除,因为已经画了一顶帽子。

③ Thomas Jefferson, *Political Writings*, p.xxx.

的一切人生来平等的思想。他所设想的解放奴隶计划，以黑人移出白人社会为补充，即希望黑人“在获得自由后，被迁送到不至于发生混血的地方”。在他看来，“黑人，不管生来就是一个独特的人种，抑或由于时间和环境使然而成为一个独特的人种，其肉体与精神上的天赋都比白人差”①；这种天赋上的差异既为黑人的解放造成了巨大的障碍，也使其不可能被白人社会平等地接纳（这在事实上构成了美国内战后种族隔离的思想渊源）。而在奴隶制经济为美国人带来了特殊利益，一旦出于人人生而平等的考虑就必须损害自身利益的时候，杰斐逊和当时大多数厌恶奴隶制的美国人一样，选择了退让，且将奴隶制的结束放在了将来——希望它逐渐地萎缩。显而易见，他这个人，就和美国的立国原则一样，善于用抽象的言辞表达其实际行为达不到的境界。也正是因为他在奴隶制问题上从未彻底贯彻平等理念，将一切人生来平等的原则无条件地运用于一切人，“颇有些言行不一”（Where slavery was concerned, Jefferson's deeds did not match his magnificent words）②，杰斐逊招致了许多人的批评，甚至有学者说他是“不折不扣的种族主义者”（Jefferson was an out-an-out racist）③。即便是较为客观的评价也认为，“他始终远离民众，如果说他声称人人平等，不是因为他觉得人人生而平等，而是因为他的理性让他推想：人人必须平等（He remains always aloof from the masses, and if he claims equality for all men, it is not because he feels that men are equal, but because he reasons that they must be so）”④。与华盛顿总统相比，在这一点上，他逊色许多。当然，这也并不说明他格外虚伪。建国之父中，唯有华盛顿最终解放了他所有的奴隶。

此外，《独立宣言》也反映出杰斐逊乃至于所有大陆会议代表对印第安人的轻蔑与敌视，他们被称为“残酷无情的野人”（merciless Indian savages）。妇女似乎也未曾进入宣言者的视野。在陈述殖民地人民遭受的苦痛时，他们只诉与“英国的兄弟们”（British brethren）听。

---

① 托马斯·杰斐逊：《杰斐逊选集》，第262~263页。

② Richard Hofstadter, *The American Political Tradition and the Men Who Made It*, p.48.

③ Joseph Ellis, *American Sphinx: The Character of Thomas Jefferson*, , New York: Vintage Books, 1996, p.xv.

④ Richard Hofstadter, *The American Political Tradition and the Men Who Made It*, p.48.

不言自明的真理（Self-evident truths）——《独立宣言》的人权与政府理论

杰斐逊虽未给《独立宣言》各部分另行标题，然其结构清晰可辨。第一部分，即第一段，开章明义说明全文意旨：一个民族——殖民地人民——为什么不得不与另一个民族——大不列颠——脱离，解除双方间的政治关系（Why it becomes necessary for one people to dissolve the political bands which have connected them with another）；第二部分，即第二段，指出不言自明的真理（self-evident truths）以及依此真理而展开的政府理论——政府的形成与目的、人民对自身以及政府的权利与义务；第三部分为苦情陈述①——控诉乔治三世对殖民地人民的长久伤害与强取豪夺（The history of the present King of Great Britain is a history of repeated injures and usurpations）、英国人民对殖民地人民遭受苦情、请求伸张正义的冷漠（They，too，have been deaf to the voice of justice and consanguinity）；第四部分，即最后一段，宣布殖民地将联合起来争取自由与独立（these United Colonies，are，and of right ought to be，FREE AND INDEPENDENT STATES）；他们将不再向英王效忠（they are absolved from all allegiance to the British crown）；殖民地与大不列颠的一切政治联系都将完全解除（all political connection between them and the state of Great Britain is，and ought to be，totally dissolved）：殖民地人民从此有权宣战、缔和、结盟、通商和采取独立国家有权采取的一切行动（they have full power to levy war，conclude peace，contract alliances，establish commerce，and to do all other acts and things which independent states may of right do）。

不言而喻，宣言的主体在第二和第三部分——陈述迫使一个民族与另一个民族分离的原因（the causes which impel them to the separation）②。第一部

---

① 《独立宣言》的苦情陈述似取法于英国《大宪章》，细致入微；亦似模仿《圣经》。

② 此时，以富兰克林、杰斐逊、塞穆尔·亚当斯（Samuel Adams）为代表的政治家已改变了过去以英国臣民的身份向英王吁请同等权利的策略，而以一个独立的民族主张其自然权利。这是体现在《独立宣言》中很重要的一点。

分只是个导言(Introduction);第四部分,即通常所说的结论(Conclusion),也只是对7月2日通过的独立决议案的重申,其底本来自弗吉尼亚代表团成员理查德·李(Richard Henry Lee of Virginia)所撰写的独立决议案①。

原因陈述分两步:先述原则(principles),再陈事实(facts)。"原则"一段虽简短如序言(preamble),其作用也如序言,然则铿锵有力、掷地有声。它首先陈述了在当时那个时代为人们所普遍熟悉的人的权利理论与政府理论,然后颇有先见性地回答了人们在读到《宣言》时所可能想到的问题:

1.人们是否有权利推翻政府?又是否可以不加限制地推翻政府?

2.在哪些条件下人们可以行使其推翻政府的权利与义务?

3.北美殖民地人民提出独立,是否满足这些条件?

4.殖民地人民是否能够提供权利受伤害的事实?

所有这些,杰斐逊都想到了,并且用非常有力的语言一层一层铺叙开来;其中所表现的殖民地人民的委屈、无奈乃至遗憾,令读者不得不同意:他们的反抗与独立是有理的、必要的、值得同情与声援的。其感染力是如此之强,以至于"原则"一段长久地留在人类记忆中,成为人类政治哲学的重要遗产。而占全文篇幅五分之三的"事实"陈述,虽在当时引起无数人共鸣,现今大多被人遗忘。

这些具有如此长久之生命力的原则是什么?《独立宣言》言道:1.人人生而平等(All men are created equal);2.所有人享有不可剥夺的某些权利(They are endowed by their Creator with certain unalienable rights);3.这些权利是生命、自由与追求幸福(the right of life,liberty and the pursuit of happiness);4.为了保障这些权利,人们组成政府;政府是经过被统治者的同意而获得统治权的(To secure these rights,governments are instituted among men,deriving their just powers from the consent of the governed)。换言之,政府有保障这些权利的义务;5.如果政府拒绝履行其义务、对人民的安全与幸福构成伤害,人民就有权推翻

① 比较决议案的下列文字:"That these United Colonies are,and of right ought to be,free and independent states,that they are absolved from all allegiance to the British Crown,and that all political connection between them and the State of Great Britain is,and ought to be,totally dissolved."(引自Thomas Jefferson,*Political Writings*,p.xv)。一目了然。它与《独立宣言》末尾宣布独立的一段完全相同。而杰斐逊的原稿并非如此。这说明,大陆会议在《独立宣言》的这一部分重复了决议案。《独立宣言》与独立决议案之间的关系亦因此显而易见。

它,并建立新政府(Whenever any form of government becomes destructive of these ends, it is the right of the people to alter or to abolish it, and to institute new government);6.尽管人民不应也不愿因某些微小与一时的原因更替政府,但在持续受到迫害,以至于竟如生活在绝对专制的政府之下时,人民就有权利和义务推翻那专制政府(Governments long established should not be changed for light and transient causes, but when a long trains of abuses and usurpation evinces a design to reduce people under absolute despotism, it is their right, it is their duty, to throw off such government)。在宣言撰写者与55位签名者①看来,上述原则是不言而喻的真理(We hold these truths to be self-evident)。

显然,这是一组来源于社会契约论(Social Contract)的人权理论与政府理论。确如杰斐逊所言,《独立宣言》的目的不是创建新的原则或新论点,它只不过是要把关于这些问题的常识摆在人们面前而已(the object of the Declaration of Independence was not to find out new principles, or new argument, but to place before mankind the common sense of the subject)。一切人生来平等,享有不可剥夺的生命、自由与财产权等②;政府经人民的同意而建立,其目的是为了保障人民的福利;当政府超出其权力范围之外,实施暴政时,人民就有摆脱暴政、防止暴政的权利。所有这些,都由17世纪的英国哲学家约翰·洛克(John Locke, 1632~1704)在其自然法理论、天赋权利论与政府理论中阐述明白③。洛克的政治理论在北美殖民地与牛顿的自然科学理论一样受欢迎。它被殖民地人民"当作一种政治福音来领受"(Most Americans had absorbed

① 在《独立宣言》羊皮书上第一个签下大名的是当时正担任大陆会议主席的约翰·汉考克(John Hancock)。由于这一重大历史事件,John Hancock自此在美国人的字典中成为"signature(签名)"的代用词。

② 《独立宣言》未写"财产权",而代之以"追求幸福的权利"。

③ 洛克的自然法理论、天赋权利论、有限政府论是为环环相生的成体系理论。言人类在组成政治社会之前,处于自然状态。自然状态中,人人独立而平等,享有造物主赋予的生命、健康、财产、自由等权利,这是由自然法即人的理性所规定的。此等由自然法所规定的人人生来平等并享有不可剥夺的权利论谓天赋权利论或自然权利论。然因自然状态中有种种不便,未能充分保证人的安全与福利,于是人们契约组成政府。此政府是在经人同意并授权,旨在保障、增进人的安全与福利而成立。若政府超越其权力范围,行使暴政,便违背了与人民立的约。此时,人民有推翻暴政,建立新的政府的权利。

Locke's works as a kind of political gospel)[1]。到18世纪六七十年代时，北美殖民地的政治理论家已经在普遍地运用洛克的理论。他们懂得如何定义自然权利，如何发现暴政与强权以及如何抵制。大约在1770年，宾夕法尼亚的詹姆斯·威尔逊（James Wilson，他后来成为美国联邦最高法院大法官）在他的一本小册子《论英国议会立法权的性质和范围》（*Considerations on the Nature and Extent of the legislative Authority of the British Parliament*）中写道：

人人生而平等自由；没有人有权未经某人同意对其行使权力；一切合法的政府都以服从于被统治者的同意为基础；被统治者之所以同意受其统治，是因为他们认为这能保证与增进其幸福，获得比在独立而互不相干的自然状态下更多的幸福。由是之故，社会的幸福是一切政府的首要原则。[2]

这段话几乎就是对洛克《政府论》（下册）（*Second Treatise of Government*）观点的摘抄。不妨择取洛克《政府论》原文作一比较：

第8章“论政治社会的开端”（*Of the Beginning of Political Societies*）首段（即全文第95节）：“如前所述，人类天生都自由、平等与独立；不得本人同意，任何人不能将其置于此种状态之外，使其屈服于另一人的政治权力。使任何人放弃其自然自由、受公民社会之种种限制的唯一办法，是与其他人协议：加入并联合成为一个共同体，以谋求彼此间舒适、安全与和平的生活、安稳地享受其财产，更稳妥地防范共同体之外任何人对其安全的侵犯”（Men Being, as has been said, by Nature, all free, equal and independent, no one can be put out this Estate, and subjected to the Political Power of another, without his own *Consent*. The only way whereby any one divests himself of his Natural Liberty, and puts on the bonds of Civil Society is by agreeing with other Men to join and unite into a community, for their comfortable, safe and peaceable living one amongst another, in a secure Enjoyment of their Properties, and a greater Security against any that are not of it）。[3]

---

① Carl Becker, *Declaration of Independence*: *A Study in the History of Political Ideas*, p.27.

② Carl Becker, *Declaration of Independence*: *A Study in the History of Political Ideas*, p.108.

③ John Locke, *Two Treatises of Government*, Cambridge: Cambridge University Press, 1960, pp 330~331.

第8章第10段(第104节):“人类是天生自由的,历史实例亦证明:世界上的政府,凡于和平中创建,都以上述基础为开端,并且基于人民的同意而建立”(that Men are naturally free, and the Examples of History showing, that the Governments of the World, that were begun in Peace, had their beginning laid on that foundation, and were made by the Consent of the People)。[①]

第19章“论政府的解体(*Dissolution of Government*)”第10段(第220节):“……如果人们在彻底处于暴政控制之前,没有任何方法以逃避暴政,他们就不能免遭暴政的迫害。因此而言,他们不仅有摆脱暴政的权利,还有防止暴政的权利”(and Men can never be secure from Tyranny, if there be no means to escape it, till they are perfectly under it: And therefore it is, that they have not only a Right to get out of it but to prevent it)。[②]

第19章第12段(第222节):“因此,一旦立法机关侵犯了这个基本的社会准则,并因野心、恐惧、愚蠢或腐败,力图使自己握有或给予任何其他人一种绝对权力,以支配人民的生命、权利和产业时,他们就由于这种背弃委托的行为而丧失了权力。这种权力原是人民为了正相反的目的而交予他们的。当权力回归人民时,他们就有了恢复原来的自由的权利;并且通过建立他们认为合适的新的立法机关,为自己提供保障与安全。而这正是他们之所以加入社会的目的”(Whensoever therefore the Legislative shall transgress this fundamental Rule of Society; and either by Ambition, Fear, Folly or Corruption, endeavour to grasp themselves, or put into the hands of any other an Absolute Power over the Lives, Liberties, and Estate of the People; By this breach of Trust they forfeit the Power, the People had put into their hands, for quite contrary ends, and it devolves to the People, who have a Right to resume their original Liberty, and, by the Establishment of a new Legislative (such as they shall think fit) provide for their own Safety and Security, which is the end for which they are in society)。[③]

---

① John Locke, *Two Treatises of Government*, p.336.

② John Locke, *Two Treatises of Government*, p.411.

③ John Locke, *Two Treatises of Government*, pp.412~413.

显而易见,无论是威尔逊还是杰斐逊,二人都继承了洛克的政治思想。其间的传承关系毋庸多言。

1772 年,塞穆尔·亚当斯(Samuel Adams)为他所发起的波士顿通讯委员会(Boston Committee of Correspondence)起草了一份宣言,同样诉诸洛克的理论。到 1774 年英国政府与北美殖民地人民关系越发紧张时,洛克的学说在北美已为政治家和学者耳熟能详。1774 年第一届大陆会议与 1775 年起开始的第二届大陆会议所发表的宣言,以及不少北美殖民地的权利法案或独立宣言①,譬如 1776 年 6 月通过的《弗吉尼亚权利法案》(*Virginia Bill of Rights*)②,均以洛克的自然法理论为依据阐述其权利。1774 年 10 月 14 日通过的《第一届大陆会议宣言与决议》(*The Declaration and Resolves of the First Continental Congress*)声言:"英属北美殖民地的人民,依据不可更易的自然法、英国宪法之原则、若干权利许可状或协约,拥有下述权利:1.他们理应享有生命、自由与财产权;这些权利他们从未让与任何最高权威,也从未在未经其同意时授予任何权威以处置权"(That the inhabitants of the English Colonies in North America, by the immutable laws of nature, the principles of the English Constitution, and the several charters or compacts, have the following rights: I. That they are entitled to life, liberty, and property, and they have never ceded to any sovereign power whatever, a right to dispose of either without their consent);《弗吉尼亚权利法案》第一款如是写道:"所有人生来同等地自由与独立,并拥有某些固有的权利;当人们进入社会状态时,这些权利不能通过任何约定从其子孙后裔身上剥夺或削夺。它们是:享受生命与自由的权利、享有获得与拥有财产的手段、追求与得享幸福与安全的权利"(That all men are by nature equally free and independent, and have certain inherent rights, of which, when they enter into a state of society, they cannot by any compact deprive or divest their posterity; namely, the enjoy-

① 据美国历史学家 Pauline Maier 的研究,1776 年 4~7 月间,这类的宣言式文件至少出现了 90 余份,只不过因为《独立宣言》的光芒而大多被遗忘。见 Pauline Maier, *American Scripture: Making the Declaration of Independence*, New York: Vintage Books, 1997, p.48.

② 亦称《弗吉尼亚权利宣言》(Virginia Declaration of Rights),由乔治·梅森起草(drafted by George Mason)。

ment of life and liberty, with the means of acquiring and possessing property, and pursuing and obtaining happiness and safety)。[1]

惟因其已属常识,它能够成为殖民地人民争取自由、平等乃至独立的便利武器,杰斐逊将之写入《独立宣言》,作为陈述殖民地人民不得不与母国脱离的理论依据。它也的确如他和他的战友所期望的那样,为北美殖民地事实上的反叛行为提供了强大的道德与法律支持。当人们普遍相信,依据自然法则(laws of nature),人人都享有不可剥夺的权利时,谁能说当这些权利受到侵害,受侵害的人主张恢复其权利时,它不具有正当性？当人们普遍相信,政府的目的是为了保护被统治者的安全与自由,一旦政府反其道而行之,一再伤害人民的权利与自由,人民就有权利和义务推翻它并另行组建政府时,谁能说殖民地人民的“反叛”不具有正当和正义性？因此当美国《独立宣言》传到欧洲大陆,法国政治家拉法叶特(Lafayette, 1757 ~ 1834)把它贴在家中墙上,还特意在它旁边留出一块地方,说法国人也应该有这样一份宣言。《独立宣言》那简要明朗的原则声明,比洛克的学院式论述更加广泛地传播开来。

当然,真正令宣言具有长久的生命力,奠定其政治思想经典地位的原因,还在于美国独立革命本身。倘若这场事业归于失败,洛克的政府理论未经美国人转变为现代共和政府与宪政的实践,《独立宣言》湮没于一场反叛的平定,也并非没有可能。至少,它不能如同现在这样熠熠生辉。因为它在当时乃至后世一直遭到很多人的批评——有人说它陈词滥调、了无新意;有人说它言辞夸张,辞藻华丽;还有人说它歪曲事实,颠倒是非。

幸运的是,独立革命成功了,《独立宣言》成了美国的开国文献,获得了它作为人类政治思想史杰作的地位。美国人珍视它,把它视为“联邦宪法的奠基石(a part of the nation's organic law and the inspiration for America's Constitution);作为构成美国法律与政治体系的哲学基础(it anchors the American legal

---

[1] Samuel Eliot Morrison, *Sources and Documents Illustrating the American Revolution*: 1764 ~ 1788, *and the Formation of the Federal Constitution*, New York: Oxford University Press, 1965, pp.118 ~ 119, p.149.

and political system on a firm philosophical ground）"①，并且依据宣言所申明的自然法原则，提出了《权利法案》（*The Bill of Rights*）。美国第16任总统亚伯拉罕·林肯（Abraham Lincoln）将它奉为自由宪章，说他"在政治上的感情没有一种不是来自《独立宣言》所蕴含的情感（I have never had a feeling, politically, that did not spring from the sentiments embodied in the Declaration of Independence）"②。

世界人民珍视它。尽管它的作者并无为黑人、奴隶、妇女等群体的权利鼓与呼的意图，但它一旦成为历史文献，就超越了自身的狭隘，为诸多受歧视、压迫的族群、民族、个体争取权利与自由的正义事业贡献了战斗的武器、政治哲学的力量。1848年，美国女权运动奠基人伊丽莎白·斯坦顿（Elizabeth Cady Stanton）仿效它写出《美国妇女独立宣言》（*The Declaration of Sentiments*）③，声明人人生来平等，男人和女人都一样。黑人自由运动的领袖一再呼吁，人人生而平等，白人与黑人都一样。受歧视的个体恳请人注意：人人生而平等，无论高低贵贱，你我都一样。被压迫、被凌辱的殖民地人民坚持，人人生而平等，并都享有不可剥夺、不可让渡的权利，没有一个民族有权利凌驾于另一个民族之上。

革命者尤其珍视它。《独立宣言》一出，便为法国大革命创造了造势的典范。1789年，法国人撰写了《人权与公民权利宣言》（*The Declaration of the Rights of Man and of Citizen*），就像拉法叶特希望的那样。

---

① Timothy Sandefur, *The Conscience of the Constitution: Declaration of Independence and the Right to Liberty*, Mast: Cato Institute, 2014, p.14.

② Philip V.D.Stern, ed., *The Life and Writings of Abraham Lincoln*, New York: The Modern Library, 2000, p.485.

③ Declaration of Sentiments 又名 Declaration of Rights and Sentiments。1848年7月20日，100名参加第一次妇女权利大会即"赛尼卡福尔斯会议"（Seneca Falls Convention）的代表在此文件上签名。其中，女性68名、男性32名。

逼出来的革命[①]——《独立宣言》之苦情陈述

从1607年英国人渡海而来,在詹姆斯敦(Jamestown,James意指当时的英国斯图亚特王朝的詹姆斯一世James I)建立第一个永久居住地(Permanent Settlement),直到1763年英法战争[②](Seven Years War was called in America)结束,这一百多年间,北美殖民地与其母国(mother country)的关系大体上是令双方满意的。英国政府对于北美殖民地的统治取放任政策,仿佛任其处于地方自治的无政府状态。虽然各殖民地的总督(governor)由英王指派,但其内部事务主要由殖民地人民自主决定,英政府对殖民地的征税也很少。因此,在很大程度上说,殖民地是一个长期以来享受惯了特权的地区。殖民地与英国之间主要是一种情感上的依恋与庇护关系。对殖民地来说,不列颠是母国;对国王,各殖民地是她的孩子、臣民、依附者与受庇护者。但这种情感从英法战争即将结束时开始发生变化。因为英国政府为了多从殖民地征得税款,以补偿战时巨额支出与欠款[③]、改善国内经济衰退造成的财政紧张,开始加大对殖民地的干预。与此同时,英国这让久已形成自治传统的殖民地人民感到空前的不舒服,对于母国的不满情绪逐渐滋长起来。

---

① 此处必须作个说明。美国早期史著名史学家戈登·伍德在其成名作《美利坚共和国的缔造:1776—1787》一开篇就指出,"美利坚革命中,没有历史传说中常常把绝望的人民逼上梁山的暴君。殖民地人民比18世纪其他任何地方的人或许都更加自由。因此对于英国托利党人(即保王党人——译者注)而言,这场革命是难以理解的"(参见Gordon S.Wood,*The Creation of the American Republic:1776~1787*,New York:W.W.Nordon & Company,1993,p.3)也就是说,依据史学家的客观判断,将这场革命形容为被暴君"逼出来的革命"并不妥当。在戈登·伍德看来,美国革命乃是殖民地人民依据他们对自由与权利的理解,在对现实感到不满时,基于理性而创造的结果。笔者完全认同伍德的看法,但依然用"逼出来的革命"作小标题,其目的是为了说明殖民地人民对英国政府的不满与失望心理。在笔者看来,这场革命是在双方都被误解很深的背景下被"逼出来"的。

② 七年战争开始于1756年,由奥地利企图收回普鲁士所占领的西里西亚所引起,也是英法两国争夺欧洲霸权和殖民地的延续。奥地利与法国、俄国、萨克森、瑞典结成反普联盟,普鲁士与英国、汉诺威联合。法国战败,1763年2月,《巴黎和约》签订,承认法国在美洲、西印度群岛、印度的部分殖民地转归英国。

③ 1763年英政府与法国缔结和约时,借债数额已达1.3亿英镑(130,000,000),见Robert Middlekauff,*The Glorious Cause:The American Revolution*,Oxford University Press,2005,p.24.

英国政府首先从打击久已盛行于殖民地的海上走私（maritime smuggling）开始。1763 年 7 月，首相格伦威尔（George Greenville）命令海关官员报告其在殖民地的工作，否则解除其职务。这让殖民地一向松弛的海关管理骤然严格起来，靠走私盈利的殖民地商人大感不便与恼火。

1764 年 4 月起，格伦威尔接连颁布《糖税法》（*The Revenue Act*，or *Sugar Act* as it was popularly called）与《贸易与航海法》（*The Act of Trade and Navigation*）。这些条例除了利于英国政府增加税收外（例如殖民地的木材只许出口至英国），还设置了对殖民地人民不公平的惩罚措施。凡违反条例者，均可被起诉至地方海事法庭（local vice admiralty）。在地方海事法庭，没有陪审团，法官往往带着有罪推定的心理审理案件，这让被起诉的殖民地人民很难有胜诉机会（即《宣言》所述："depriving us in many cases，of the benefits of trial by jury"）；而且无论胜诉与否，诉讼费用都由被起诉一方承担。

对于这些措施，殖民地人民的办法是联合起来，妨碍海关与效忠于英王的殖民地官员执行公务，甚至有官员因严格执法而被陷害入狱者；抵制英国货，以期迫使议会撤销《糖税法》。与此同时，他们还批评英国议会超越权限，在殖民地没有代表在议会的情形下通过向殖民地征税的法案①。

但是，殖民地人民的不满，英政府并未放在心上。他们对议会权威的挑战，还令首相与议员们不悦。1765 年 3 月，议会在不顾殖民地反对的情况下又通过了《印花税法案》（*The Bill of Stamp Act*）②。议案三读过程中，殖民地派出的代表向议会递呈了多份请愿书，然而议会拒绝接受。

《印花税法》的通过，引发了一场前所未有的"印花税危机"（The Stamp Act Crisis）。5 月末，弗吉尼亚议会率先通过决议谴责《印花税法》，重申："殖

---

① "无代表不得征税"的抗议，体现的也正是殖民地人民与其母国英国议会对于代表权的理解的不同。19 世纪的英国人，尤其是托利党人，已经将议会中的议员代表理解为全体人民的代表，而非某个地区的代表。英国议会对于殖民地的抗议，也正是这样答复的。然而，北美殖民地人民关于代表权的理解还停留在中世纪，即由某地区选出的代表仅代表某地区的利益，他们否认非殖民地的议员有代表殖民地利益的权利。美国早期史史学家伯纳德·柏林对于这一点，有深入细致地分析。参见 Bernard Bailyn，*The Ideological Origins of the American Revolution*（Enlarged Edition），Cambridge：The Belknap Press of Harvard University Press，1992，pp.161～175.

② 该法规定：北美殖民地的印刷品包括报纸、书刊、契据、执照、文凭、纸牌、入场券等均需加贴印花税票，税额自 2 便士到几英镑不等，违者罚款或监禁；11 月 1 日起生效。

民地人民无代表在议会,议会没有权力向其征税”(Parliament,a body to which they sent no representatives,had no authority to tax them)①。其他殖民地纷纷效仿。8 月间,在波士顿等地,一些自称为“自由之子”(Sons of Liberty)、由手工艺者、店主……组成的群体,发起暴力抗议。他们把发放印花税官员的肖像吊在树上,羞辱它,再将它烧毁,拆毁将要执行《印花税法》的官员的房屋。抗议风暴之下,发放印花税的官员要么辞职,要么逃离,《印花税法》眼看无法实施。

消息传到英国,舆论哗然。“叛国”(treason)、“无政府”(anarchy)、“反叛”(rebellion),议员们如是谴责殖民地人民。1766 年 2 月,《宣告法》(*The Declaratory Act*)通过,宣布:“殖民地的暴力行为违反了法律(The riots in America violated the law);当地的立法机关支持了他们(the legislative assemblies in America had countenanced them);凡是因遵行印花税法而受到身体伤害与财产损失者应该由殖民地予以赔偿(those persons who suffered injury or damage on account of their desire to comply with the law should be compensated by their colonies);这些人受到议会下院的保护(such persons would have the protection of the House of Commons);任何因得不到印花税票而被罚者应该得到赔偿(anyone suffered penalties because stamped paper was unavailable ought to be compensated)”②。

殖民地人民听到这样的宣告,第一反应就是英国政府在施行“暴政”(tyranny)。他们开始怀疑和担心,觉得英国政府正在筹划一个阴谋,要把殖民地置于绝对专制之下(即《宣言》所言:“to reduce them under absolute despotism”),“剥夺其自由、把他们变成奴隶(a conspiracy existed to deprive Americans of their liberties and to reduce them to slavery),印花税法只是将其奴隶制锁链永远上紧的第一步(and the Stamp Act was merely the first step to rivet the chains of slavery upon us forever)”③。尽管英国政府并无此等邪恶用心,但殖民地人民的感觉并非没有道理。英法战争刚结束,英国就向殖民地派驻了常

① Robert Middlekauff,*The Glorious Cause*,p.81.

② Robert Middlekauff,*The Glorious Cause*,p.118.

③ Robert Middlekauff,*The Glorious Cause*,p.130.

备军。其意图一方面是安置参与英法战争的大量军人，免得他们因为失去收入与职位而不再支持国王；另一方面是为了防卫殖民地边境安全，并借此理由向殖民地征税——保护殖民地的支出，殖民地理当承担一部分。可是殖民地人民不这样看，他们不能理解为什么和平时期要在殖民地驻军，只觉得这是压迫，是强制他们服从的工具（即《宣言》所言："He has kept among us, in times of peace, standing armies, without the consent of our legislatures"）。驻军之后，又来了各种各样的税。而印花税的购买还必须用银币（sterling silver），这就意味着很多人将因支付印花税陷入困境，因为殖民地的硬币非常短缺。

不过，《印花税法》很快就被撤销了。其原因并非出于北美殖民地的抗议被英国议会采纳，而主要是因为英国本土的商人发起了强烈的请愿。他们的利益由于殖民地的贸易抵制大大受损。不过，无论如何，《印花税法》的撤销还是令殖民地人民感受到了胜利。他们欢天喜地地庆祝。然而，惧怕英国人剥夺其自由的阴谋论，依旧仿佛一个幽灵，时常隐现于殖民地人民心头，挥之不去。

1767 年 5 月，英国首相汤森（Charles Townshend）拿出一系列所谓的"汤森法"（Townshend Acts），再次引爆了殖民地的害怕与憎恨情绪。其中的《岁入法》（The Revenue Act）规定，殖民地向英国进口的铅、茶、玻璃、纸、印刷颜料等，均需缴纳税金。国王打算用这笔收入支付殖民地皇家官吏的报酬。此举不仅在殖民地人民的钱袋上戳了一个窟窿，还使英政府对殖民地的所谓保护成为一种讽刺——不请自来的官吏还要为其支付报酬。

更令殖民地人民愤怒的是，"汤森法"中的《纽约议会暂停法》（*The Suspend Act*）将纽约议会（New York Assembly）的立法权剥夺。其起因在于两年前纽约议会的一次行动：1765 年，英政府出台《驻营法》（*The Quartering Act*），要求殖民地人民为驻扎在纽约、阿尔伯里（Albany）等城市的英军提供啤酒、盐、醋、苹果酒、蜡烛等供给，纽约议会未肯承认其效力。两年后，为惩罚纽约议会抗命不遵，《暂停法》规定：除非纽约议会同意遵行《驻营法》，否则它所通过的一切法令均归于无效。这就让殖民地人民更有理由相信阴谋论的存在。

就英政府来说，"汤森法案"的意图是令殖民地明白其臣属地位，任何时候都必须在帝国控制之下；然而它所表现出来的父母对不听话的孩子的恼怒与约束之意,无疑只会激惹殖民地人民。遗憾的是,汤森内阁中,无人对汤森的不智表示反对,或者以亲善、友好的态度提出另一种建设性意见。诚然,令孩子为母国承担一部分负担似乎有理。但在孩子如此憎恨强制收税的心理下,再加之以新税只能令殖民地人民更加抵制与英国的贸易,其结果必然使帝国利益受损。

这年11月起,一位自称"宾夕法尼亚农民"的人——约翰·迪金森(John Dickinson)[①],开始连续发表《一个宾夕法尼亚农民的来信》(*Letters from a Farmer in Pennsylvania*),信中批评:"'汤森法'如同《印花税法》一样,从根本上侵犯了殖民地的自由权"(an act of parliament, as injurious in its principle to the liberties of these colonies, as the Stamp Act was),因此他呼吁殖民地人民"万众一致,团结一心"(Let us all be united with one spirit, in one cause),一边向国王请愿,恳请他纠正议会的错误,恢复殖民地的自由权;一边勤俭节约、自力更生,减少对英国货的消费,抵制"汤森法"。他还宣称,殖民地人民是一个"自由的民族"(A FREE PEOPLE),他们"之依赖于大不列颠,正如一个完完全全自由的民族依赖于另一个自由民族"(we are as much dependent on Great Britain, as a perfectly free people can be on another)[②]。这个重要的平等民族概念马上就由马萨诸塞的塞穆尔·亚当斯(Samuel Adams)加以发挥。他说,"殖民地只是在地位上'次于'而不是'臣服于'英国议会"(colonies were 'subordinate' but not to 'subject' to the British Parliament)[③]。所谓殖民地人民是英国

---

① John Dickinson 实际上既非宾夕法尼亚人,也非农民。他于1732年出生于马里兰(Maryland),10岁时移居特拉华(Delaware),并在那里接受完整的教育(1742~1753),学习古典学与历史。1753~1757年,他在伦敦修习法律。回到北美后,在宾夕法尼亚从事法律工作,很快声名远播。1760年,他投身政治,当选为特拉华议会(Assembly of Delaware)议员;2年后,当选为宾夕法尼亚议会(Assembly of Pennsylvania)议员(当时,特拉华与宾夕法尼亚尚未完全分立,虽然各自拥有自己的立法机关,却在同一个总督辖下)。《一个宾夕法尼亚农民的来信》(*Letters from a Farmer in Pennsylvania*)总共12封,每周连载于宾夕法尼亚的一份周刊(*Pennsylvania Chronic and Universal Advertiser*)。它被誉为是美国独立革命前夕仅次于托马斯·潘恩(Thomas Paine)《常识》(*Common Sense*)的重要作品。

② Forrest McDonald, ed., *Empire and Nation: Letters from a Farmer in Pennsylvania* (*John Dickinson*) & *Letters from the Federal Farmer* (*Richard Henry Lee*), Indianapolis: Liberty Fund (E-book), 1999, p.14, 25, 17.

③ Carl Becker, *Declaration of Independence: A Study in the History of Political Ideas*, p.98.

臣民的概念被颠覆了。

马萨诸塞议会(House of representatives in Massachusetts)议员詹姆斯·欧提思(James Otis)支持亚当斯的理论。他们联合采取了行动，并在1768年2月成功地使议会通过了一封向各殖民地立法机关发出的吁请信(Circular Letter，或译“通函”、“通讯”)，敦促其形成统一的立场，反对“汤森法”。立即作出回应的殖民地并不多。然而又一轮类似印花税法案的危机由此在波士顿引发。这一次，英政府的压制措施走得更远——马萨诸塞议会被英王任命的总督解散、英军开进了城。

波士顿议会的解散、英军的开入，当然是为彰显帝国的权威，但是殖民地人民对这种耀武扬威的做法益发地不满起来。很快，各殖民地的立法机关也都直接或委婉地接受了马萨诸塞的吁请。代表英王权威的总督对此不肯退让。马里兰、南卡罗来纳、纽约、弗吉尼亚的议会均被解散。

议会可以解散，殖民地人民的愤怒难以压制。到1770年，各殖民地的商人自发地签署了不进口英国货的约定，家庭主妇拒绝购买来自英国的茶叶，人们以身着自制的粗布衣裳为豪。一切来自英国的奢侈品——丝绸、洋酒、礼服等，均已失去昔日的荣光。殖民地人民不缺乏卓绝的吃苦精神，他们大多是新教徒。

抵制的过程中，严重的对抗发生了。1770年，驻扎于纽约和波士顿两地的英军与当地民众发生流血冲突。后者造成多人伤亡，立刻被殖民地人民称之为屠杀，视之为英政府迫使其变成奴隶的险恶用心的表现。尽管此后的两三年，以诺斯勋爵(Lord North)为首的英内阁对殖民地的政策趋于温和，但维护其权威的态度没有变。他们坚持“无论在什么情况下，殖民地都应该受其约束”(Parliament asserted that it possessed the authority to bind the colonies in all cases whatsoever as did in the Declaratory Act)①。而殖民地虽未与英帝国发生大的冲突，却从未停止质疑其用心与权力来源的合法性，并向英政府请愿，使令殖民地不满的总督离职。反复的摩擦与冲突终因“波士顿倾茶”案导致双方都不能容忍的局面。

---

① Robert Middlekauff, *The Glorious Cause*, p.222.

1773年5月,英政府为帮助英属东印度公司解决财政困难,促使议会通过《茶叶法》(*The Tea Act*),一面使东印度公司垄断殖民地的茶叶贸易,一面从中获取茶叶税。此举被殖民地人民再度视为对其权利的侵犯,于是就在当年的12月,波士顿倾茶案发生,价值1万英镑的茶叶被倒入波士顿港口。

英国议会对此反应强烈,即便是对殖民地向来温和的议员如厄金汉姆(Rockingham)也表示,波士顿的倾茶行为"绝不可说是正义的"(There was no way it could be justified),更多人认为"它近乎犯罪"(It was criminal)①,应该予以惩罚。1774年3月,议会首先通过《波士顿港口法》(*The Boston Port Act*),关闭波士顿港口,规定:除非当地人民向东印度公司支付了足够的赔偿,它才可能重新开放。随后的三个月里,议会连续通过四项法案,前三项均属惩罚性质,其意明了:殖民地必须安于从属地位。《马萨诸塞规制法》(*The Massachusetts Regulatory Act*, or *Massachusetts Government Act*)规定:马萨诸塞的议会不再由当地人民选举而由国王提名;大多数官员得由总督任免;没有国王许可,各镇不许集会;陪审团成员的挑选不再由持有土地的自由民(freeholders)决定,此权力交给地方治安官(sheriff)。简言之,马萨诸塞的自治特许状被取消,其政府事务直接置于英王控制之下。《公平行使正义法》(*The Impartial Administration of Justice Act*)规定,凡在北美殖民地被指控犯有死刑罪的官员得移送英国或其他英属殖民地审判。《驻营法》(*The Quartering Act*)赋予英军的权利比1765年《驻营法》赋予的更多。英军不但有权要求殖民地人民提供军需、有权住进旅店、酒馆与空房,现在还可以住入当地居民的家庭。最后一项——《魁北克法》(*The Quebec Act*),虽无明显惩罚之意,但将北美殖民地以西的俄亥俄河流域和伊利诺伊地区划入加拿大新建的魁北克省的管辖范围,实质上限制了殖民地西部边境的扩张。

这五项法案激起殖民地人民极大愤怒。在他们看来,这无疑是对其自由的剥夺,是为"不可容忍的法案"(The Intolerable Acts)。马萨诸塞人民呼吁停止与英国的一切贸易。弗吉尼亚议会作出决议,谴责波士顿港口的关闭是一种"敌意的入侵"(hostile invasion),并决定对英国议会关闭港口的法令置之一

---

① Robert Middlekauff, *The Glorious Cause*, p.234.

旁。作为弗吉尼亚下院议员的托马斯·杰斐逊发表《英属美利坚权利概观》。文中指出，“英国议会无权对殖民地行使权力”（British parliament has no right to exercise its authority over us）；它所做的一切都是“篡权”（parliamentary usurpation）；哪怕是“英王也无权令一兵一卒登上殖民地的海岸”（But his majesty has no right to land a single armed man on our shores）；“国王是人民的公仆，而非人民的主人”（Kings are the servants, not the proprietors of the people）①。

不消说，弗吉尼亚议会又一次被总督解散。殖民地人民则于当年9月召集大陆会议（Continental Congress），一个表示各殖民地人民已接近绝望，不得已联合起来以捍卫其自由与自治传统的集体行动。捍卫的手段主要有三：1. 发表《权利宣言》（*The Declaration of Rights*, Oct. 4），表示殖民地人民决不放弃依据自然法、英国宪法、殖民地特许状赋予的权利；2. 达成《大陆联合协议》（*The Continental Association*, Oct. 20），中止与英国及英属西印度群岛的贸易：不进口、不出口、不消费，直至“不可容忍法案”撤销为止；3. 向英王递呈请愿书，并致信英国人民、殖民地人民与魁北克居民，陈述其苦情。此外，不少乡镇开始自发地组织民兵，进行训练。

乔治三世接到请愿，丝毫未有同情与退让之意。他表示，如果殖民地不与英国贸易，“大不列颠就应该不让其与别国贸易”（Great Britain, would take care they should trade on where else）②。英政府因而对殖民地采取了不只是惩罚而属镇压的措施：规定新英格兰（New England）地区③只能与英国贸易（即《宣言》所言，“cutting off colonies trade with all parts of the world”）；向殖民地增派部队与巡逻船只；不允许殖民地训练民兵；“倘有暴力发生，必须予以弹压”（Force should be repelled by force）④。英政府还传递出一个在它看来是为橄榄枝，而殖民地人民绝无可能接受的信息，即，如果殖民地同意供给英政府在殖民地的军需与民政所费，可暂停对其征税，但议会仍保有对殖民地的征税

---

① Thomas Jefferson, *Political Writings*, p.69, 70, 78, 79.

② Robert Middlekauff, *The Glorious Cause*, p.267.

③ 新英格兰地区由6个殖民地组成，由北至南分别为：缅因（Maine）、新罕布什尔（New Hampshire）、佛蒙特（Vermont）、马萨诸塞（Massachusetts）、罗得岛（Rhode Island）、康涅狄格（Connecticut）。该地区濒临大西洋、毗邻加拿大，进出口贸易发达。

④ Robert Middlekauff, *The Glorious Cause*, p.272.

权。显然,英政府对殖民地人民的情绪并无透彻了解。殖民地人民早已认定,议会无权在未获其同意时对殖民地征税,而英政府还在坚持议会有权对其征税。

1775 年 4 月 19 日,就在双方都不肯退让的僵局中,英军与殖民地民兵在列克星敦与康科德(Lexington and Concord,some twenty miles north and west of Boston,Massachusetts)交火①,英军伤亡 236 人,殖民地 95 人。它后来被视为美国独立战争的开端,但在当时并不是殖民地人民要求独立的行动,只是一种激烈的反压制的对抗。当时的殖民地对其母国的情感,正如美国历史学家卡尔·贝克尔(Carl Becker)所言,"长期以来,他们以大英帝国的成就与其在世界上的声名自豪;大英帝国也是他们的帝国;他们担了它的名,分享着她的荣光"(They had long been proud of the British empire,of its achievement,of its name and fame in the world;its was their empire too;they bore the name and shared the fame)②。一旦放弃了与母国的名分,他们就放弃了曾经的荣耀与自豪感,放弃了情感上的归属。这是令人不安、不愿,甚至有几分恐惧的。因此,他们无意完全独立,而希望和解。虽然他们组织民兵与英军对抗,但这是其坚持权利与自由的表现,并非独立意愿的表达。其中情感之苦涩,一名宾夕法尼亚议会议员,亦即前文提到的约翰·迪金森(John Dickinson)一语道尽:"正当我们崇敬、热爱母国的时候,她用剑刺破了我们的血管"(While we revere and love our mother country,her sword is opening our veins)③。

正因为不愿与母国分离,激烈的对抗发生后,殖民地人民依然不肯放弃与母国和解的努力。第二届大陆会议于 5 月 10 日召开后,先后于 5 月底、7 月初两次向英王递呈请愿书。第二封请愿书即通常所说的"橄榄枝请愿书"(Olive Branch Petition)。与此同时,又因不甘压制,各殖民地纷纷武装起来。大陆会议决定大规模地招募军队,并任命乔治·华盛顿为总司令。7 月 6 日,

① 1775 年 4 月 19 日,一支英军骑兵进入列克星敦,遇到民兵抵抗,随即在康科德发生激战,独立战争爆发。战争持续 6 年。1781 年 10 月 19 日,英军在约克镇(Yorktown)投降,战争结束。1783 年 9 月,《巴黎和约》签订,英国承认北美殖民地独立。

② Carl Becker, *Declaration of Independence:A Study in the History of Political Ideas*, p.128.

③ Robert Middlekauff, *The Glorious Cause*, p.285.

大陆会议还通过了《拿起武器之原因与必要性宣言》(*Declaration of the Causes and Necessity for Taking Up Arms*)①。

然而一面祈求和平，一面为战争做准备；一面向国王恳请和解，一面坚持其自由不可放弃；一面向国王表示敬意，一面向国王派出的军队宣布其有死而无生，这种似乎显得矛盾的心态和行为不可能得到英王、英政府与议会的理解。

8月末，乔治三世表示，"橄榄枝请愿"不值得答复，殖民地"已在公然与公开的叛乱中"(The colonies were in open and avowed rebellion)。10月末，他又在议会上说，叛乱的原因在于"殖民地阴谋策划独立，其意图显然是要建立一个独立的帝国"(a desperate conspiracy existed in America to make a rebellious war which is manifestly carried on for the purpose of establishing an independent empire)②。

为了征服叛乱，英政府招募外国雇佣军，派往殖民地。弗吉尼亚总督邓默尔爵士(Lord Dunmore)则于11月煽动当地的奴隶反叛，允诺他们只要加入英军，就可获得自由；并于1776年1月下令海军炮轰弗吉尼亚小镇诺福克(Norfolk, Virginia)，将之毁于火海。

议会与英王、政府官员行动一致。12月22日，《禁止法》(*The American Prohibitory Act*)通过，宣布北美殖民地人民不再受英帝国保护，并规定：停止与殖民地的一切贸易；殖民地在海上航行的船只及其装载的货物均为英国海军截获的对象；所有与殖民地贸易的船只都将视如敌人被没收，并受军事法庭审判。

这一切令和解难以达成的言论与行动，将北美殖民地推上了不得不独立的方向。1776年1月，一位来自英国的政治思想家托马斯·潘恩(Thomas Paine)③在宾夕法尼亚发表他的小册子《常识》(*Common Sense*)。《常识》原名

---

① 这篇宣言的起草者是托马斯·杰斐逊与新泽西的约翰·迪金森(John Dickinson of New Jersey)。

② Robert Middlekauff, *The Glorious Cause*, p.321.

③ Thomas Paine(1837~1809)，生于英国，死于美国(纽约)，且曾亲身参与法国大革命。他出身下层阶级，前半生行藏少为人知，然多失意；后半生虽获声名，却常在漂泊之中。1774年11月，首度从英国来到北美殖民地费城。1775~76年，任《宾夕法尼亚杂志》(*The Pennsylvania Magazine*)编辑，撰文鼓动殖民地人民与英国政府脱离。1776年1月，《常识》发表。当年7月，他加入美国军队，献身于美国独立革命事业。其思想以坚定的反君主制、支持共和制而著称。他的笔锋辛辣、不留情，为所有保守政治党派所痛恨与畏惧。

《真相》(*The Truth*),其目的是为揭示北美殖民地人民在英国君主制度下无可摆脱的奴役命运。他首先指出,"对绝对权力的渴求是君主制与生俱来的一种病"(a thirst for absolute power is the natural disease of monarchy);只要其君主世袭产生,"它就内含着压迫的天性"(It has in it the nature of oppression);无论英国的立宪君主制显得多么复杂,都不能改变这一专制与压迫的实质。就北美殖民地而言,再与母国维持政治上的联系,不仅于其经济、贸易有害,且将沦为被英国政府与军队任意劫掠与破坏的囚徒。所谓的"和解现在是一个虚妄的梦"(Reconciliation is now a fallacious dream)①。殖民地人民若要保全自由,必须独立。舍此别无选择。因为殖民地被奴役的阴谋内在地存在于英国的君主制度中。再者,殖民地与不列颠的对抗已使英政府视其如敌人、叛徒,充满敌意;而殖民地人民在英军枪炮下流出的鲜血,也将他们对母国的依恋之情早已荡涤干净,双方要回到1763年前的友好与和谐关系已完全没有可能。

和解既无希望,那就只有独立。1776年3月起,南卡罗来纳、佐治亚、北卡罗来纳、罗德岛、弗吉尼亚等殖民地纷纷表示,支持大陆会议的独立决议。6月7日,弗吉尼亚的理查德·李提交动议:联合起来的殖民地应与不列颠彻底解除政治关系。《独立宣言》起草委员会就此成立,一份伟大的宣言问世,大陆会议最著名的宁馨儿诞生。

① Thomas Paine, *Political Writings*, Cambridge: University of Cambridge Press, 1989, pp.6~22.

延伸阅读

Carl Becker, *Declaration of Independence: A Study in the History of Political Ideas*, New York: Harcourt, Brace and Company, 1922（卡尔·贝克尔：《论〈独立宣言〉：政治思想史研究》，彭刚译，南京：江苏教育出版社，2004年）。研究《独立宣言》的经典之作，虽显过时，但其中关于《独立宣言》思想史的追溯颇多洞见；对《宣言》文学特色的评论既显个人风格，亦常得读者会心。

Pauline Maier, *American Scripture: Making the Declaration of Independence*, New York: Vintage Books, 1997. 杰斐逊常被视为"美国民族的化身（an incarnation of the American nation）"，原因之一就在于，他是美国人心中的政治经文——《独立宣言》——起草人。Maier的这部著作细致地呈现了《独立宣言》从其诞生到在美国人心中圣化的过程，一丝不苟的描述中揭示出不少常人所未见之处。

Merrill D.Peterson, *Thomas Jefferson and the New Nation: A Biography*, London: Oxford University Press, 1975; Thomas Jefferson, *Political Writings*, Cambridge: Cambridge University Press, 1999（托马斯·杰斐逊：《杰斐逊选集》，朱曾汶译，北京：商务印书馆，2011年）。读其作，先读其传，了解其一生事业与生涯；转而知其相关著述，体会作者思想体系之形成与特色。Peterson所著《杰斐逊传》是众多杰斐逊传记中忠实可靠的一种；剑桥大学出版社所编撰《杰斐逊政治著作选》（*Political Writings*）以及商务版《杰斐逊选集》则是中国一般读者较易获得的读本。两书均收录《英属美利坚权利概观》（*A Summary View of the Rights of British America*），此作对于理解《独立宣言》具有重要意义。宜作比较阅读，由此深入体会美国革命前夕殖民地人民政治心理，以及两者之间的联系。

John Locke, *Two Treatises of Government*, Cambridge: Cambridge University

Press,1960(约翰·洛克:《政府论》(下),叶启方、瞿菊农译,北京:商务印书馆,2005年)。理解《独立宣言》的政府理论,需从自然法理论开始。《独立宣言》撰写人受洛克影响颇深,读其作须知其源。

Robert Middlekauff, *The Glorious Cause: The American Revolution, 1763 ~ 1789*, Oxford University Press, 2005; Joseph J. Ellis, *Revolutionary Summer: The Birth of American Independence*, New York: Vintage Books, 2013; 两书篇幅一大一小,时间跨度一长一短。前者是为美国革命与共和国诞生的全景式描述,从英法战争结束写到联邦宪法批准;文字朴实而生动,问题分析透彻入理,被誉为与美国革命一样光辉的著作。后者专述1776年美国革命之夏,侧重政治与军事史,笔调风趣。两书互作补充或延伸阅读,尤为有益。

Thomas Paine, *Political Writings*, Cambridge: University of Cambridge Press, 1989.本书收入了《常识》(*Common Sense*)这一推动了美国革命与《独立宣言》诞生的作品;读之可了解当时人对北美殖民地与英国政府关系的看法,同时也可获得对托马斯·潘恩政治思想的理解。

John Chester Miller, *The Wolf by the Ears: Thomas Jefferson and Slavery*, New York: Free Press, 1977; Joseph J. Ellis, *American Sphinx: The Character of Thomas Jefferson*, New York: Vintage Books, 1997.杰斐逊与《独立宣言》在奴隶制问题上的保留态度,是人们经常感兴趣和讨论的。杰斐逊的思想,也令许多人困惑、着迷。他的性格,沉稳而复杂,仿佛静水流深,难以见底。美国历史学家 Joseph J.Ellis 曾如是言说:"如果杰斐逊是一尊雕像,他应该是斯芬克斯;如果杰斐逊是一幅画,他应该是蒙娜丽莎;如果杰斐逊是一个戏剧中的主人公,他应该是哈姆雷特"。读此两书,或可对当时的时代以及人性本身的复杂多一分认识。

Bernard Bailyn, *The Ideological Origins of the American Revolution* (Enlarged Edition), Cambridge: The Belknap Press of Harvard University Press, 1992(伯纳德·贝林:《美国革命的意识形态渊源》,涂永前译,北京:中国政法大学出版社,2007年)。美国革命发生于何时? 是1775年4月19日列克星敦的第一声枪响? 还是1776年7月2日第二届大陆会议宣布独立之日? 革命的亲历者 John Adams 在1815年写给 Thomas Jefferson 的一封信中说,早在1760年,

革命就在殖民地人民的思想上发生了。然而美国历史学家 Bailyn 将美国革命在观念上的起源推至更早，早至革命实际发生前半个世纪。他还指出，美利坚人思想上的革命虽在 1770 年之前只如涓涓细流，静静流淌，却于 1770 年后汇成一股强大的浪潮，最终推动了独立革命的爆发；此种思想上的革命虽在当时人看来顺理成章，实则相当激进。作为美国早期史研究的经典名作，Bailyn 这本书初版于 1967 年，1992 年予以扩充，其思想与学术价值为学界所公认。

Gordon S. Wood, *The Creation of the American Republic: 1776 ~ 1787*, New York: W.W.Nordon & Company, 1993（戈登·S·伍德：《美利坚共和国的缔造：1776~1787》，朱妍兰译，南京：译林出版社，2016 年）。《独立宣言》只是美国革命的一个开端，若要理解美利坚人民何以构筑起一个共和主义的国家？其思想渊源何在？那就必须读一读这本书。其作者 Wood 师承 Bernard Bailyn，这本书也是他在 Bailyn 指导下完成的博士论文，其内容与《美国革命的意识形态渊源》一脉相承。《渊源》一作探求殖民地人民反英意识的缘起与发展，《缔造》则论述美利坚人如何从英国君主制的魅影中脱魅而出，而建立起共和政体。当然，在读《缔造》之前，如果先读一读 Wood 后来所写的《美国革命的激进主义》（Gordon S, Wood, *The Radicalism of the American Revolution*, New York: Alfred A.Knopf, 1991.有中译本，傅国英译，商务印书馆 2011 年出），预先对美国 18 世纪的政治文化与社会生活有清晰认识会更好。另外，美国早期史研究专家李剑鸣教授为《缔造》中文版所作的“序”也颇值一读，其中涉及 20 世纪美国早期史研究领域的学术动态与学术流派，对于初入美国史研究领域的学子，颇具引导价值。

Film: Ken Burns 制作的 2 集纪录片“Jefferson”较为可靠。

DECLARATION OF THE RIGHTS OF MAN AND OF CITIZEN

法国《人权与公民权宣言》

DECLARATION OF THE RIGHTS OF MAN AND OF CITIZEN[①]

August 26,1789[②]

The representatives of the French people, constituted as a National Assembly[③], and considering that ignorance, neglect, or contempt of the rights of man are the sole causes of public misfortunes and governmental corruption, have resolved to set forth in a solemn declaration the natural, inalienable and sacred rights of man: so that by being constantly present to all the members of the social body this declaration may always remind them of their rights and duties; so that by being liable at every moment to comparison with the aim of any and all po-

liable: subject to sth

① 原文标题为 *Déclaration des Droits de l'Homme et du Citoyen*.本文文本取自 Lynn Hunt ed., *The French Revolution and Human Rights: A Brief Documentary History*, Boston: Bedford Books, 1996, pp.77~79.

② 《人权及公民权宣言》通过时间有两种说法:一说 8 月 27 日,譬如法国革命史学家亚尔培·马迪厄在其《法国革命史》便如是记载;《大英不列颠百科全书》第 9 卷"拉法耶特侯爵"词条也指明,宣言于 8 月 27 日通过。另一说 8 月 26 日,见《大英不列颠百科全书》第 14 卷"人权与公民权宣言"词条。不过,大多数法国大革命史学家如乔治·勒费弗尔、阿尔贝·索布尔等,均采 8 月 26 日一说。

③ "National Assembly"(国民议会)诞生于 1789 年 6 月 17 日。是年 5 月,路易十六召集三级会议(Estates General)。第三等级(Third Estate, made up of every one who was not a noble or a cleric, ie., commoners)不同意与教士(clergy)、贵族(nobility)组成的第一、第二等级分厅议事,并要求按人头而非按等级投票(vote by "head" but not by "order")。三方僵持不下。6 月 17 日,第三等级宣布:自己就是国民议会,代表全部国民。6 月 20 日国民议会在网球场宣誓:"绝不解散,直到宪法制定出来"。7 月 9 日,国民议会宣布,它也是制宪议会(Constitutional Assembly)。

litical institutions the acts of the legislative and executive powers may be the more fully respected; and so that by being founded henceforward on simple and incontestable principles the demands of the citizens may always tend toward maintaining the constitution and the general welfare.

In consequence, the National Assembly recognizes and declares, in the presence and under the auspices of the Supreme Being, the following rights of man and the citizen:

Supreme Being: God; the supernatural being conceived as perfect and omnipotent

1. Men are born and remain free and equal in rights. Social distinctions may be based only on common utility.

2. The purpose of all political association is the preservation of the natural and imprescriptible rights of man. These rights are liberty, property, security, and resistance to oppression.

imprescriptible: inalienable

3. The principle of all sovereignty rests essentially in the nation. No body and no individual may exercise authority which does not emanate expressly from the nation.

emanate from: come or flow from sth

4. Liberty consists in the ability to do whatever does not harm another; hence the exercise of the natural rights of each man has no other limits than those which assure to other members of society the enjoyment of the same rights. These limits can only be determined by the law.

5. The law only has the right to prohibit those actions which are injurious to society. No hindrance should be put in the way of anything not prohibited by the law, nor may any one be forced to do what the law does not require.

hindrance: the act of making it difficult for someone to act or for sth to be done

6.The law is the expression of the general will[1].All citizens have the right to take part, in person or by their representatives, in its formation. It must be the same for everyone whether it protects or penalizes. All citizens being equal in its eyes are equally admissible to all public dignities, offices, and employments, according to their ability, and with no other distinction than that of their virtues and talents.

admissible: able to be admitted or allowed

7.No man may be indicted, arrested, or detained except in cases determined by the law and according to the forms which it has prescribed. Those who seek, expedite, execute, or cause to be executed arbitrary orders should be punished; but citizens summoned or seized by virtue of the law should obey instantly, and render themselves guilty by resistance.

indict: accuse sb officially (of sth)

expedite: hasten or speed up

8.Only strictly and obviously necessary punishments may be established by the law, and no one may be punished except by virtue of a law established and promulgated before the time of the offense, and legally applied.

promulgate: make sth widely known

9. Every man being presumed innocent until judged guilty, if it is deemed indispensable to arrest him, all rigor unnecessary to securing his person should be severely repressed by the law.

10.No one should be disturbed for his opinions, even in religion, provided that their manifestation does not trouble public order as established by law.

① "general will"（公意）不是"will of all"（众意）。二者之间有质的差异。卢梭在其《社会契约论》中，着意指出："公意只着眼于公共的利益，众意则着眼于私人的利益，众意只是个别意志的总和（There is often a considerate difference between the will of all and the general will; the latter looks only to the common interest, and the former looks to private interest, and is nothing but a sum of particular will）"。Rousseau, *The Social Contract and other Later Political Writings*, Cambridge: Cambridge University Press, 1997, p.60.

11.The free communication of thoughts and opinions is one of the most precious of the rights of man. Every citizen may therefore speak, write, and print freely, if he accepts his own responsibility for any abuse of this liberty in the cases set by the law.

12.The safeguard of the rights of man and the citizen requires public powers.These powers are therefore instituted for the advantage of all, and not for the private benefit of those to whom they are entrusted.

13.For maintenance of public authority and for expenses of administration, common taxation is indispensable. It should be apportioned equally among all the citizens according to their capacity to pay.

apportion sth among/to sb; allot sth; give sth as a share

14. All citizens have the right, by themselves or through their representatives, to have demonstrated to them the necessity of public taxes, to consent to them freely, to follow the use made of the proceeds, and to determine the means of apportionment, assessment, and collection, and the duration of them.

15.Society has the right to hold accountable every public agent of the administration.

accountable: responsible

16.Any society in which the guarantee of rights is not assured or the separation of powers not settled has no constitution.

17.Property being an inviolable and sacred right, no one may be deprived of it except when public necessity, certified by law, obviously requires it, and on the condition of a just compensation in advance.

译 文

法国《人权与公民权宣言》

1789 年 8 月 26 日

法国人民的代表、国民议会的组成者认为：不知人权、轻视人权、蔑视人权是致使公众不幸与政府腐败的唯一原因，因而决定作一庄严的宣言，阐明自然的、不可剥夺的、神圣的人权，以便它可经常呈之于全体社会成员前，使他们能时刻意识到其权利与义务；以便出之于立法与行政权的决议与决定能随时与整个政治机构之目标相比较，从而受到更充分的尊重；以便公民依据简单而无可争辩的原则所提出的要求，能时时裨益于宪法之维护与公共福祉。

因此，在主宰面前并赖其庇佑之下，国民议会确认并宣布下述人与公民之权利：

第一条　人之权利，生而且始终自由与平等。社会差别只可基于公共利益之考虑。

第二条　一切政治结合之目的，均为保全人之自然与不可摇撼的权利。这些权利是自由、财产、安全和反抗压迫。

第三条　一切主权的行使原则本质上赖于国民。任何团体、任何个人均不得行使国民未明确赋予之权威。

第四条　自由就在于能做一切无害于他人之事。因此，每一个人行使其自然权利，只以保证其他社会成员享有同样权利为限制。这些限制只能由法律决定。

第五条　法律只可正当地禁止有害于社会的行为。任何未被法律禁止之事，均不可设之以障碍；也不可强制任何人做法律未予要求之事。

第六条　法律是公意的体现。所有公民均有权亲自或通过其代表参与法律的制定。无论施以保护或惩罚，法律必须对全体公民一致。因公民在法律上平等之故，他们可平等地依其能力获得政府雇佣、担任公职、占据一切高位。区分其职位之标准，唯德与才，无有其他。

第七条　除非在法律规定的情况下并遵行了法律所规定的程序，任何人不得被控告、逮捕或拘禁。发出、催促、执行或令人执行专断命令者，应受惩罚；但依据法律被传唤或拘押的公民应立即服从，抗拒则构成犯罪。

第八条　法律只可规定必不可少的惩罚，除非法律已规定某种行为属违法，并已公之于众，任何人不得因此种行为而受处罚。

第九条　如确属必要将某人逮捕，任何人在被判有罪前均应推定为无罪；一切为扣留其人身所不必要的残酷行为均应受到法律的严厉制裁。

第十条　意见的发表只要不扰乱已为法律所建立的公共秩序，任何人不可因其意见，即使是宗教上的看法，而受干涉。

第十一条　思想与看法的自由交流是人类最宝贵的权利之一。因此，每一位公民都可自由地发表言论、著述并出版，然在已由法律所规定的范围内，公民应为其滥用自由承担责任。

第十二条　人权与公民权利的保障需要公共武装力量的存在。因此，武装力量的设立是为了全体的利益，而非为被委以权力者的私人利益。

第十三条　为了公共武装力量的维持与行政管理开支，共同承担税收是必要的。它应依据公民的支付能力在全体公民间作平等地分摊。

第十四条　所有公民都有权亲自或通过其代表了解公共税收的必要性，按其自由意志表示同意，追问其用途，决定所应分摊的份额、征税标准、征税方式与持续时间。

第十五条　社会有权要求所有公共行政机构承担其责任。

第十六条　凡权利无保障和分权未确立的社会，就没有宪法。

第十七条　财产权神圣而不可侵犯，除非情属公共之需，且得法律所许可，并预先获得了公平的赔偿，否则，任何人的财产权不得被剥夺。

解　　析

《人权与公民权宣言》的理论渊源与诞生土壤

林木生于根苗。任何理论都有其近亲远祖。《人权与公民权宣言》(以下简称《人权宣言》)在法国大革命(The French Revolution)中诞生,但是它的思想在大革命之前就已产生。不少学者认为,它反映了让·雅克·卢梭(Jean Jacques Rousseau)的人民主权(popular sovereignty)理论。尽管有人不同意这种看法,譬如德国公法学家格奥尔格·耶里内克(Georg Jellinek)。他认为法国《人权宣言》只是在表述上与卢梭的《社会契约论》(*Of the Social Contract*,1762)有些相似,而在"原则上与后者冲突"(The principles of the *Social Contract* are at enmity with every declaration of rights)。在他看来,《人权宣言》是为了保证个人的权利,而《社会契约论》的宗旨并非如此,它是为了保障公意(general will)①。

耶里内克的看法是否有理?颇难令人信服。首先,无论二者目的为何,都不能否认,卢梭在《社会契约论》中所阐述的主权在民、公意与平等理论渗入了《人权宣言》。虽然宣言起草人究竟属于谁,史学界向来有争议。有说由著名的拉法耶特侯爵(Marquis de Lafayette)起草②;亦有说大革命的领袖埃马努

① 参见 Georg Jellinek, *The Declaration of Man and of Citizens: A Contribution to Modern Constitutional History*, New York: Henry Holt and Company, 1901, pp.8~12。这部 1895 年发表的作品(英译本发表于 1901 年)受到了很多批评。其中最为有力者,是布特米(Boutmy)在《政治科学年鉴》17 卷上发表的论文。

② 据《大英不列颠百科全书》"拉法耶特侯爵"词条,《人权宣言》草案由拉法耶特侯爵于 7 月 11 日提交国民议会,经国民议会修改后通过(《大英不列颠百科全书》第 9 卷,北京:中国大百科全书出版社,2007 年,第 445 页)。拉法耶特侯爵的朋友、大革命爆发时正在巴黎担任美利坚合众国驻法公使的托马斯·杰斐逊(Thomas Jefferson)也在 1789 年 7 月 19 日写给朋友约翰·杰伊的信中说明,宣言由拉法耶特侯爵起草(托马斯·杰斐逊:《杰斐逊文集》,朱曾汶译,北京:商务印书馆,2012 年,第 473 页)。

埃尔·西耶斯(Emmanuel Joseph Sieyès)贡献了最重要的草案;还有说最终由国民议会投票采纳的宣言草案出自"一个不那么知名的人物,甚至没有署上起草者的姓名"(which bore no author's name)①。由此,我们无法确知起草者是否读过卢梭的《社会契约论》并深受其影响。但是我们知道,宣言经过了国民议会(General Assembly)的讨论,是一份得到集体修改与认可的作品。参与讨论的人中有不少熟读《社会契约论》,并且同意其学说,他们之所以愿意通过《人权宣言》,无疑是因其包含了他们所认同的理论。再者,以二者间的抵牾或冲突为据否认其理论渊源,表面看似乎有理,实则不然。因为参与讨论的国民议会成员并非个个都是卓越的理论家,能清晰地看出二者矛盾所在。何况,一份由众人制订出的文件存在矛盾与抵触之处,没有什么可奇怪的。最后,或者说最重要的是,《人权宣言》第 1 条"人是生而且始终自由与平等";第 2 条"一切政治结合之目的,均为保全人之自然与不可摇撼的权利";第 3 条"一切主权的行使原则在本质上赖之于国民";第 4 条"自由就在于能做一切无害于他人之事";第 6 条"法律是公意的体现"等等,使用的几乎都是卢梭的语言。焉能说它未体现卢梭的理论实质?

还有很多人认为,《人权宣言》与美国《独立宣言》构成姊妹篇,后者是前者的模板。关于这一点,也有人反对。譬如美国历史学家卡尔·贝克尔(Carl Becker)。在贝克尔看来,美国《独立宣言》启发了法国人想要有一份权利宣言的愿望,但这不等于说,《人权宣言》的思想来自《独立宣言》。因为《独立宣言》所表达的政治哲学在法国人那里,早已是老生常谈。他认为,"对法国的历史进程造成深远影响的是美国革命这一事件本身,而不是这一事件的标志"(It was the event itself, the American Revolution, rather than the symbol of the event, which exerted a profound influence upon the course of French history)②。

不能不说,贝克尔的看法颇有道理。即便换个角度,人们也不难发现《人

---

① John Acton, *Lectures on the French Revolution*, Kitchener: Batoche Books, 1999, pp.88~89。阿克顿勋爵同时说明:"国民议会拒绝了由大人物提交的所有方案(The Assembly rejected all the plans which were submitted by the celebrities)"。

② Carl Becker, *Declaration of Independence: A Study in the History of Political Ideas*, New York: Harcout, Brance and Company, Inc., 1922, p, 232;卡尔·贝克尔《论〈独立宣言〉——政治思想史研究》,彭刚译,南京:江苏教育出版社,2004 年,第 152 页。

权宣言》与《独立宣言》的相异。《独立宣言》篇幅颇长，原则叙述审慎周全，事实举例不厌其烦；《人权宣言》短小简练，权利要求直截了当。无怪乎耶里内克评论，“与美国人的漫无边际相比，法国人的语言简洁得多”（In contrast to the diffuseness of the Americans, the French are distinguished by a brevity characteristic of their languages）①。这种风格上的差异不见得必然由两种不同的语言所致，其中包含着两国革命背景与两国人民政治思想的不同。再就内容来看，《人权宣言》所包含的政治哲学远较《独立宣言》丰富。《独立宣言》仅仅在不长的前两段中列出了自然法；人人生而平等并享有不可剥夺的生命、自由与追求幸福的权利；政府建立的原则与目的；人民有推翻和另行组建政府的权利等。其他权利均从“苦情陈述”中推导而出。《人权宣言》则通篇都在列举人民所享有的权利，而且比《独立宣言》显得清晰。

但是尽管如此，依然不能否认，《人权宣言》与《独立宣言》有切不断的联系。将《人权宣言》与北美各殖民地宣布独立后发表的《权利法案》（Bill of Rights）逐一比较，不难看出，《人权宣言》凡17条与弗吉尼亚、马萨诸塞、马里兰、北卡罗来纳、新罕布什尔、宾夕法尼亚、佛蒙特等州《权利法案》的诸多条款相近似②，以至于耶里内克断言，“法国大革命的《人权宣言》绝大部分都是从美国各种各样的‘权利宣言’里抄来的”（The French Declaration of Rights is for the most part copied from the American Declarations of ‘Bill of Rights’）③。而这些权利法案与《独立宣言》在思想上一脉相承，弗吉尼亚的《权利法案》对《独立宣言》还起到了示范作用。《独立宣言》起草者托马斯·杰斐逊（Thomas Jefferson）正是弗吉尼亚的公民。当然，与其说法国《人权宣言》与美国《独立宣言》关系密切，不如说它与美国立国前后各州的权利法案关系更直接。

不过，认定《人权宣言》是法国人依样画葫芦，从美国各州权利法案“抄来”，未免贬低了法国人的创造力，于事实也不符。且不说《人权宣言》对于人

① Georg Jellinek, *The Declaration of Man and of Citizens: A Contribution to Modern Constitutional History*, p.43.

② Georg Jellinek, *The Declaration of Man and of Citizens: A Contribution to Modern Constitutional History*, pp.13～42.

③ Georg Jellinek, *The Declaration of Man and of Citizens: A Contribution to Modern Constitutional History*, p.20.

之理性的乐观与自信得益于启蒙运动,也不论其中诸多重要原则早已由法兰西启蒙运动的领袖如孟德斯鸠(Montesquieu,1689~1755年)、伏尔泰(Voltaire,1694~1778年)、狄德罗(Denis Diderot,1713~1784年)等论述明白(后文还要谈到),只要读一读大革命的领袖西耶斯于大革命前夕发表的两篇影响深远的作品——《论特权》(*An Essay on Privileges*,November of 1788)与《第三等级是什么?》(*What is the Third Estate*,January of 1789),就能很清楚地看出,这两部著作中的不少主张,如政治的结合是为保障人的自然权利、法律是公意的体现、未被法律禁止之事不可设之以障碍、平等承担赋税等,被直接写入了《人权宣言》。这都足以说明,《人权宣言》诞生之前,其思想已在法国人头脑中生根。法国学者布特米(Emile Boutmy)认为宣言体现了18世纪法国人的政治观念,实有充分依据。无论如何也不能说《人权宣言》是抄来的!恰当的说法只能是:《人权宣言》与美国各州权利法案的作者政治理想接近,政治主张相似,对于人权与公民权尤具共识;在此基础上,法国人可能引用或借鉴了美国人的措辞。

好奇心重的学者不会满足于肤浅的涉猎。他们往往将探询的目光投向更久远的年代。西耶斯以及其同时代人——弗吉尼亚《权利法案》的起草人乔治·梅森(George Mason)、《独立宣言》的起草者托马斯·杰斐逊、在国民议会上提议制订一部《人权宣言》的拉法叶特侯爵、为宣言奉献了前三条的让·穆尼埃(Jean Mounier)等,熟读17世纪英国哲学家约翰·洛克(John Locke)的《政府论》等著作,了解英国的诸多由近到远的权利法案与相关文献:1689年《权利法案》(*The Bill of Rights of* 1689)、1679年《人身保护法》(*The Habeas Corpus Act of 1679*)、1628年《权利请愿书》(*The Petition of Rights of 1628*)、1215年《大宪章》(*The Magna Carta of 1215*)。因此又有人提出,洛克的自然法理论、自然权利学说、政府契约论,以及上述权利法案与文献都是《人权宣言》的祖父或先祖。如此推论不无道理,毕竟思想的影响力无处不在,《人权宣言》中确也留有洛克的思想印记和英国诸权利法案乃至《大宪章》的影子。不过,我们不能因为理论源头的追问而忽略了催生《人权宣言》的现实土壤。不能忘了,《人权宣言》的作者生活并感受在18世纪的法国,置身于革命的风暴。他们所拿出的《人权宣言》必然反映法国社会最现实的方面,是对现实的修正,也是对理想的表达。这也正是《人权宣言》与美国《独立宣言》以及其他权利法案存有差异的原因所在。

大革命前的法国,是为旧制度(Ancien Regime,or Old Regime)下的社会。旧制度是什么?是波旁君主专制统治下由三个等级——教士[①]、贵族与平民——构成的社会与政治体系。这个社会的本质,正如英国历史学家阿克顿勋爵(Lord Acton)所言,“不是建立在正当与正义的基础上的”(rested on no foundation of right and justice)[②];而是一个基于门第与财富特权盛行的社会,到处都是不平等。教士中的高级僧侣与贵族等级构成享有特权的贵族阶级,他们“仅凭出身便有权获得荣誉,仅因生存便有权享受人民奉献中的一份”(They have acquired,by birth alone,a right to public honors;and,by the continuance of their existence,a claim to a portion of homage from the people)[③]。法律给予他们特别的优免。相同大小的一块地,“贵族只用交 3 法郎的税,平民要交 14 法郎,只因一个是贵族,另一个不是”(A patrician's land paid three francs where the plebeian's fourteen,because one was noble and the other not)[④]。

经济上的税务减免之外,贵族阶级在宗教、司法、军役等方面同样受到优待。教堂有专座、狩猎有专权、被处死不受绞刑而施以体面的斩刑、被起诉也给予充分的保护,允许长时间辩论和监护性的公开审理;农民却不断被逮捕,而且往往由法官即席判决,不准上诉。所谓特权,是指独占他人想望而不可得的位置与好处,且不承担其他人承担的义务。因此,养路、徭役、乃至军役税等国家义务,一体不落在贵族阶级的头上;这些义务由“负荷这个社会重负的牲畜”——农民——来负担。虽则农民们生活困苦,“唯有过节时才能吃点肉,

① 作为第一等级的教士,仅包括高级僧侣,如主教、修道院长和大部分议事司铎。诸如本堂神甫与修士等下层僧侣,大都出身庶民,其社会地位属于第三等级。另需注意:高级僧侣都属于贵族阶级。

② John Acton,*Lectures on the French Revolution*, Kitchener:Batoche Books,1999,p.6.

③ Emmanuel Sieyès,*Political Writings*,Indianapolis:Hackett Publishing Company,2003,p.81;中译文见西耶斯:《论特权 第三等级是什么?》,冯棠译,北京:商务印书馆,1991 年,第 10 页。

④ John Acton,*Lectures on the French Revolution*, p.51.

生病时才可以尝点儿糖"①；但最穷的人反而纳税最多：军役税、人头税、念一税②、力役、现金与实物地租，一样样都由他们奉献给这个旧制度下的国家。其中的军役税还随着农民收入的增长而增长。

贵族阶级的特权因何而来？乃因其垄断了国家权力。1774～1789年，执掌政府中枢要职的大臣中，只有1人不是贵族。他们私心隆盛、贪婪无边，不仅独揽军队、教会、司法与行政部门的高官显爵，还令国家官职成为其家族世袭的权利。路易十六当政时，负责各省行政责任的巡按使全都属于贵族家庭，有的已然持续几代③。1781年，国王发布敕令：能证实自己为三代贵族出身者方可成为军官④。也是从这一年起，只要证明四代封爵，不问有无资历，均可充当司法行政官吏。任何时候，最显赫的姓氏，即寡头贵族，都占据了最重要的政府职位；所有的主教，也都由贵族出任。虽然贵族阶级在法国人口中所占比例极低，依据西耶斯的测算：1788年，法国总人口为2650万，其中教士与贵族总数不到20万⑤，仅占总人口比例0.75%（当代法国史学家给出的比例略高，阿尔贝·索贝尔在其《法国大革命史》中指出，"贵族的人数估计有35万左右，占全国人口的1.3%"）⑥，可是他们"充斥宫廷，包围大臣，独占了所有的恩赐、所有的年金、所有的带薪神职"（They fill the Court, besiege ministers, monopolize all favors, pensions, church-preferments）⑦。如此情形，令国王时而也有所不满。

不满的情绪不止发自国王，还有在法国工商业发展与繁荣中壮大起来的资产阶级。他们为社会贡献了大量的财富，然因身属第三等级，被集体排斥在国家权力圈之外，政治上毫无地位。他们希望与教士、贵族享有同等的社会地

---

① 马迪厄：《法国革命史》，杨人楩译，北京：商务印书馆，2003年，第18页。

② 念一税课自1749年，课及不动产、商业、地租甚至封建捐税的收入。僧侣以定期"自由赠礼"的方式赎清此税，贵族往往得到豁免。

③ 马迪厄：《法国革命史》，第11～12页。

④ 阿尔贝·索贝尔：《法国大革命史》，马胜利、高毅、王庭荣译，北京：北京师范大学出版社，2015年，第10页。

⑤ 西耶斯：《论特权 第三等级是什么?》，第36～38页。

⑥ 阿尔贝·索贝尔：《法国大革命史》，第8页。

⑦ Emmanuel Sieyès, *Political Writings*, p.84；西耶斯：《论特权 第三等级是什么?》，第13页。

位，并且要求在国家权力体系中至少“拥有与特权等级相等的影响”（The Third Estate's modest aim is to have an influence *equal* to that of the privileged orders）①。然而，特权等级最典型的特色即为贪婪。贪婪的心从来不肯将已然垄断的权力拱手让出，只想拥有更多；也只有少数自由派贵族懂得，让出一部分权力给资产阶级对他们有好处。如此一来，资产阶级，或者说第三等级的中上层，与特权等级中的大多数，即僵化、顽固、保守的贵族阶级，产生着不可避免的矛盾与难以协调的冲突。二者间的互不妥协，为法国大革命埋下了点燃火药的导线。法国革命史学家马迪厄因而有此一评：“社会的激变往往起于阶级间的不平衡”②。

身居社会下层的城市工人，当然也卷入了“阶级间的不平衡”。波旁王朝以来，法国在经济上迅速发展，进入历史上前所未有的繁荣与辉煌时期。国家日见富裕，人口日渐增多。到路易十六统治时，总体来看，法国人民的生活比当时欧洲其他国家都好。然而，各阶级所享受到的实际收益是不平衡的。贵族阶级坐享其成，不劳而获；中上层资产阶级的生活，或则舒适，或则优渥；小资产阶级由于资本的匮乏，往往在生产竞争与物价上涨的过程中，逐渐沦为仆役、帮工、搬运夫等雇佣劳动者；至于那些主要依靠工资为生的工人，“物价与工资之间日渐扩大的差距使他们深受其害。尽管名义上工资上升了，购买力却下降了。……旧制度末期，一个一般的工人，每日工资收入够其购买 10 磅面包（1 磅面包 2 个苏）”。虽在一般情况下，“每天 15 个苏可以使一个工人生活得蛮好”；然而一旦面包价格上涨，其生活就艰难异常③。1789 年前，面包在法国下层人民生活中的开支“已占 58%”。到 1789 年，由于法国农村连年歉收，“面包的开支比重上升至 88%”。正如法国大革命史学家索贝尔所言，尽管“物价上涨对富裕的社会阶层显得宽容；对穷人来说却是难以忍受的”（The price rise treated those who were already well-to-do with a certain respect, but for the poor it proved an overwhelming disaster）④。它意味着饥饿时刻会来

---

① Emmanuel Sieyès, *Political Writings*, p.104.

② 马迪厄：《法国革命史》，第 12 页。

③ 面包是法国平民的主食，每人每天平均消费一磅半，重体力劳动者需要两至三磅。

④ 阿尔贝·索贝尔：《法国大革命史》，第 18～26 页；英译本第 55 页。

临,生存也可能面临危机。当工人们看到,自己的收入仅可糊口;贵族们生活奢侈,挥霍无度,不惜倾家荡产;路易十六的王后玛丽·安托瓦内特于奢华之外,还滥赌娱乐,其内心何以会不愤?旧制度下的两极对比,恰正是仇恨与暴动滋生的土壤。

农民,作为法国社会的主要人口,承受着比工人更重的压迫。“他们生来就要供养统治阶级,向国库提供比别人更多的钱财和养活城市居民”①。旧制度下的法国,保留着封建社会的特征。乡村社会要服从领主的权威,农民须承担种种封建义务。无论自由农与农奴,均要向领主缴纳年金、领地附加捐与土地转让捐等封建捐税。国王作为最大的领主,向全体国民征收人头税、念一税、军役税、盐税以及徭役等。这些税务,贵族与教士往往得到豁免,或只缴纳很少的一部分,绝大部分由农民负担。教会作为地产的拥有者,如同领主一样向农民征收什一税,要求他们把农作物(主要是小麦、黑麦、燕麦、大麦)和牲畜的一部分上缴给主教、教堂与修道院。征收上去的什一税却很少用于宗教活动、救济教区穷人,完全成了僧侣们的私产。设若农民有所不满或抗拒,领主则通过其封建司法权,在其领地上肆行其权利,迫害其附庸。

非天主教徒更易成为迫害的对象。路易十六曾经对其财政大臣、新教徒雅各·奈克尔(Finance Minister Jacques Necker,a protestant,also a supporter of the Third Estate)说,“你已经是个新教徒了,我宣布你是个犹太人”(Now you have been a Protestant,and I declare you a Jew)。这番话是他为显示对犹太人的宽免所说,恰好反映出犹太民族在这个国家低下的社会地位。由于宗教信仰与种族,犹太人在旧制度下的法国备受歧视、身份卑微。他们大多不能住在大城市;只能从事法律所许可的行业:牲畜贸易、转手布匹、放高利贷等;而且连公民也不是,如同一群生活在这个国家的动物。他们“无论去哪里,都不得不像只猪一样交过路费”(Wherever they went,Jews were forced to pay the same toll as a pig)②。

新教徒在这个国家的命运并不好过犹太人。天主教教士与贵族随时都想

① 乔治·勒费弗尔:《法国革命史》,北京:商务印书馆,2013 年,第 52 页。

② John Acton,*Lectures on the French Revolution*, p.38.

令其“遭受最严厉的惩罚”，恨不得将他们“推至覆灭的绝境”。举国上下，对新教徒的迫害仿佛是“大围场里进行的狩猎”①。1685年，以宗教宽容而闻名的《南特敕令》(*Edict of Nantes*)②终于被取消。新教教堂被捣毁，牧师被放逐。几年之内，超过40万胡格诺教徒逃往英格兰、荷兰、普鲁士和北美。他们的财产被没收。不愿领受天主教临终圣事者，死后遗体被扔进垃圾场。灵魂无有皈依。设若要求信仰自由并诉之武力，一体受到镇压。虽则到1787年，路易十六颁布了“宗教宽容令”(*Edict of Tolerance*)，赐予了新教徒公民身份、财产权、继承权、自由选择职业等权利；但是，担任国家行政与司法官职的政治权利，他们依然不得享有。

特权与压迫之外，是政治绝对主义或君主专制的横行。国王乃为法律的化身，权力的一切来源，且不受任何限制。路易十六(Louis XVI)宣称，“凡是他愿意的，就是合法的”。他凭什么将自己视为“活的法律”？乃因其将自己视为上帝在人间的代表，其王权来自神的授予(Divine Right)。这是波旁王朝亨利四世(Henry IV)时便已成形、路易十三的时代已然确定的君权神授论。该理论宣称：法国“历代君主的统治权仅仅来源于上帝，他们不必屈从人间的任何权势，享有完全、绝对的主权，因此在王国内是至高无上的”(since our kings hold their scepters on no authority other than God's, are answerable to no authority on earth, and enjoy all the rights that can be attributed to total and absolute sovereignty, therefore they are fully sovereign within their kingdoms)③。君权神授论发展到高峰，以路易十四自封为“太阳王”为象征符号。法国人献给国王一枚太阳徽，徽上刻字：“高于一切”④。路易十四欣然领受。到路易十五，神圣王权论排斥一切分权与干涉。国王傲慢地声明：“至高无上的权力属于我一

① 伏尔泰：《路易十四时代》，吴模信等译，北京：商务印书馆，1996年，第532~534页。

② 《南特敕令》由波旁王朝的首位君主亨利四世(Henry IV)于1598年4月13日在布列塔尼的南特颁布。它在法律上结束了1572年圣巴托罗缪大屠杀以来基督教新教与天主教水火不容的局面。敕令规定：天主教为法国国教，但是信奉新教的臣民(胡格诺教徒)享有广泛的宗教自由。新教徒可以在巴黎以外的地方公开举行礼拜仪式，并享有充分的公民权。新教牧师的俸给由国家支付，并免除某些义务。

③ 阿尔贝·索贝尔：《法国大革命史》，第42页；英译本，第78页。

④ 伏尔泰：《路易十四时代》，吴模信等译，北京：商务印书馆，1996年，第127页。

人。整个立法权都归我自己,我不依赖别人,也不与他人分享它”(Sovereign power resides in my person alone. To me alone belongs all legislative power with neither any responsibility to others nor any division of that power)①。

有了这样至高无上的绝对王权论,国王便可只用一封密札(lettres de cachet)就将人投入监狱或者拘禁。他把轻视人民的生命当作维护君权的保证,他依靠恐怖压制人们抵抗专制的勇气。他还可以拿出书报审查的手段,控制人们的思想,堵塞人民的言论,阻止一切不利于专制主义的著述出版。没有任何人或者权力能与之抗衡或者对其加以限制。权力制约的想法,在专制主义的王朝,是为大逆不道。由是之故,旧制度下的法国表现出专制社会独有的特征:“被压迫者养成了沉默寡言、畏首畏尾的习惯”(The habits of silence and fear are the hallmark of the oppressed)②。对于命运之无常,厄运之到来,普通人已被训练得靠本能来服从。

不过,旧制度下的法国,又是一个准备着终结自己的社会。腐殖的土壤中孕育着新思想;法兰西启蒙运动正在为旧制度的死亡、新制度的诞生准备着理论武库。正如米涅所言,“革新的时代脱胎于哲学的时代”③。启蒙运动的哲人中,出现了擎着思想火炬的巨人:孟德斯鸠、伏尔泰、卢梭与狄德罗等,他们以自由为主题,靠着理性的光芒驱逐那专制的暗夜。

孟德斯鸠,生于英国光荣革命的那一年,先与英国政治家博林布鲁克子爵(Henry St John, Viscount Bolingbroke)相识,受其自由主义思想影响甚深;后又游历英国,被选为英国皇家学会会员,参与议会辩论,推崇英国君主立宪制度(British constitutional monarchy)。1748 年,他将一生政治思想的成熟思考付诸《论法的精神》(*The Spirit of Law*)④,并公之于众。他在书中指出,国家权力

① 阿尔贝·索贝尔:《法国大革命史》,第 45 页;英译本,第 78 页。

② Emmanuel Sieyès, *Political Writings*, p. 119;西耶斯:《论特权 第三等级是什么?》,第 45 页。

③ 米涅:《法国革命史》,第 8 页。

④ 1748 年起,18 世纪法国最伟大的著作相继问世:孟德斯鸠《论法的精神》、布丰《自然史》(1749 年)、伏尔泰《路易十四时代》(1751 年)、狄德罗主持《百科全书》第 1 卷(1751 年)、孔迪亚克《感觉论》(1754 年)、卢梭《论人类不平等的起源和基础》(1755 年)、摩莱里修士《自然法典》(1755 年)、伏尔泰《风俗论》(1756 年)、爱尔维修《论精神》(1758 年)、卢梭《爱弥儿》与《社会契约论》(1762 年)等等。

分为立法、行政、司法三权;若欲有效地抵制专制、保证自由,唯有将之分授不同人或团体;各个权力独立行使,互相制约。何以分权如此重要?因为权力若由一人专享,他就可利用行政与立法权即"一般意志去蹂躏全国";又可利用司法权,使其"个别意志毁灭每一个公民"(It can plunder the state by using its general wills;and,as it also has the power of judging,it can destroy each citizen by using its particular wills)①。孟德斯鸠警示人们:任何一个人或者一个机关同时掌控了三权中的任何两权,都可能使法律的执行变得暴虐,公民的安全失去保障,人民的自由从此消失。这一分权制衡学说(separation of powers, check and balance of power)立即风靡法国。无论贵族还是资产阶级都为其吸引。对贵族,孟德斯鸠为其提供了抵制王权专制的盾牌;对资产阶级,他为其奉上了斩断特权的刀剑。原本即为贵族出身的孟德斯鸠不仅成为整个贵族群体的律师,也充当了资产阶级的代言人。与此同时,他还像英国政治思想家洛克一样,捍卫私人财产的神圣,符合那个时代所有人对财富的敬意。

伏尔泰,与孟德斯鸠一样,既在思想上反映那个时代又超出那个时代。他一度身为皇家史官,在政体问题上显得比孟德斯鸠保守,或者说现实②,从不主张法国实行君主立宪制,而崇拜"愿意为善的专制国王"③。尽管他也曾在英国与荷兰生活,目睹自由在那里的繁荣。但是他坚持认为,专制并不意味着暴政;那种暴政式的"专制主义只是君主制的滥用"(Despotism is the abuse of monarchy)④。在他看来,只要君主智慧、宽容、遵行法律——建立在正义与理性之上的法律,暴政就可以避免。也就是说,他期待开明的君主专制制度。

---

① 孟德斯鸠:《论法的精神》(上),张雁深译,北京:商务印书馆,2002年,第153页。

② 旧制度下的法国,其政体性质与英国光荣革命前是截然不同的。它没有与英国相似的议会,也没有自由权不可侵犯的政治文化传统,缺乏培育立宪制度的土壤。若非狂风暴雨般的法国大革命,法国政体不可能自此染上不可脱落的共和色彩。

③ 伏尔泰:《路易十四时代》,第120页。

④ Voltaire, *Political Writing*, Cambridge: University of Cambridge Press, 1994, p.98.

不过,对于暴政的深恶痛绝,伏尔泰与孟德斯鸠完全一致①。他所反对的暴政,包括言论与思想的钳制、宗教的不宽容以及法律的滥用、无理与凶暴。他一生见证了暴政的凶悍,也表现出反抗暴政的勇气。1717 年,他因发表讽刺性言论而被投入巴士底狱(Bastille)。出狱后不得不流亡英国(1726~1728 年)。后又数度因著述受到官方与教会谴责。1762 年,法国西南部城市图卢兹(Toulouse)发生一起宗教与司法迫害案件。胡格诺教徒让·卡拉斯(Jean Calas)之子自缢而亡,有人污蔑其原因为卡拉斯不许其子转信天主教,卡拉斯因此被法院残害致死②。伏尔泰闻讯而怒,为其伸冤,并撰文《论宽容》(*The Treatise on Toleration*,1763),谴责宗教迫害与司法权力的滥用③。该著立刻被官方禁止。但是他坚持人们有选择信仰之自由与权利的言论传遍整个欧洲。文中指出,"己所不欲,勿施于人"(Do not to others what they would do not to you),这是人类法与自然法均须遵从的原则。在此原则下,"一个人不能对另一个人说:'信我所信,不信你所不该信,否则你就该死'"(One cannot say to another:'Believe what I believe, and what you cannot believe, or you shall perish')。言论的不宽容,在伏尔泰看来,"不仅荒唐,而且野蛮;野蛮得甚于老虎,因为老虎仅因觅食而伤生,人类却因言语而将对方撕成碎片"(The supposed right of intolerance is absurd and barbaric. It is the right of the tiger; nay, it is far worse, for tigers do but tear in order to have food, while we rend each other for paragraphs)④。朴素而生动的语言中饱含着理性与人道的力量。

---

① 孟德斯鸠在其《波斯人信札》中,语带讥讽与不屑地称法国国王与罗马教皇为魔法师,左右着法国人的思想。见孟德斯鸠:《波斯人信札》,罗大冈译,北京:人民文学出版社,2011 年,第 36~39 页。

② 卡拉斯被加以严刑拷打,车轮碾身,最后绞刑处死。

③ 狄德罗在 1762 年写给伏尔泰的一封信中,亲热地称其为"卓越的、高尚的、亲爱的'反基督'"。见阿伦·布洛克:《西方人文主义传统》,董乐山译,北京:生活·读书·新知三联书店,1997 年,第 81 页。

④ Lynn Hunt ed., *The French Revolution and Human Rights: A Brief Documentary History*, Boston: Bedford Books, 1996, p.40.

卢梭，启蒙时代的第二代哲人[①]，与第一代之翘楚孟德斯鸠、伏尔泰并为法国启蒙运动三剑侠。但是，这位出身寒微、作品被焚禁、人也被迫逃亡、几乎一生都在流浪的天才思想家，与孟德斯鸠、伏尔泰那强烈的贵族或精英取向不同，他代表平民发声[②]。

大众的统治，孟德斯鸠是反对的，伏尔泰亦然。前者推崇贵族政治，后者想让资产阶级掌权。二者都认为，除了选举代表，参与政府治理"是人民完全不能胜任的事情"[③]；民众不适合治理政府。伏尔泰甚至声明："我不能忍受给我制假发的人成为一个立法者。那样的话，我宁愿永远不戴假发"（The people are not fit for govern. I could not bear my wig-maker to be a legislator; I would prefer never to wear a wig）[④]。然而卢梭却说："人们尽可以在力量与才智上不平等，从权利来说，却是人人平等的"（While they maybe unequal in force or in genius, they all become equal by right）[⑤]。因此，"无论在什么情况下，人民都可以做主改变其法律"（A people is in any case always master to change its laws, even the best of them）[⑥]。卢梭所说的"人民"，并非排除了平民在外的贵族或有钱人群体，而是所有的公民。为什么必须包括所有的公民？因为"在立法权上，人民是不能被代表的"（the people cannot be represented in its Legislative power）。在他看来，立法权一旦被代表，公民的自由就失去了。法律不过是公意的表达，而公意作为一种意志，是绝不可能被代表的。由是之故，卢梭批评"英国人民自以为自由，其实是大错特错。英国人只有在选举议会议

① 彼得·盖伊：《启蒙时代（上）：现代异教精神的兴起》，刘北成译，上海：世纪出版集团，2014年，第14页。

② 关于这一点，英国历史学家阿伦·布洛克（Alan Bullock）曾评论："启蒙运动的对象是受过教育的阶级，不是群众。除了卢梭以外，它对群众是表现出一种既蔑视又不信任的态度的"。见阿伦·布洛克：《西方人文主义传统》，董乐山译，北京：生活·读书·新知三联书店，1997年，第124页。

③ 孟德斯鸠：《论法的精神》（上），第159页。

④ Voltaire, *Voltaire Political Writings*, p.127. 笔者注：在法国，戴假发的习俗保持到18世纪末。不过，这种习俗仅属于上层阶级，穷人和没有社会地位的平民不能戴假发。

⑤ Rousseau, *The Social Contract and other Later Political Writings*, Cambridge: Cambridge University Press, 1997, p.56.

⑥ Rousseau, *The Social Contract and other Later Political Writings*, p.80.

员的时候,才是自由的;一旦将议员选出,他们就沦为奴隶,什么也不是"(The English people think it is free;it is greatly mistaken,it is free only during the election of Members of Parliament;as soon as they are elected,it is enslaved,it is nothing)①。何以说他们沦为了奴隶? 因为他们放弃了自己的自由,放弃了自己做人的资格,乃至于自己的义务。这义务就是保全其自由。

设若人民意图恢复自由,理应如何? 卢梭为人民举出了反抗权。他说,"当人民被迫服从而服从时,他们做得对;当人民一旦可以打破桎梏而去打破它时,他们做得更对。因为他们正是依据别人剥夺其自由时所依据的那种同样的权利,而为自己恢复自由的"(as long as a People is compelled to obey and does obey,it does well;as soon as it can shake off the yoke and does shake it off;it does even better;for in recovering its freedom by the same right as the right by which it was robbed of it)②。

卢梭的理论显然相当激进,富有浪漫主义色彩。他本人也看到了这一点,并且指出,按照其严格意义的人民主权理论,"真正的民主制从来就不曾有过,而且永远也不会有"(In the strict sense of the term,a genuine Democracy never has existed,and never will exist)。但这是多么合乎理性的浪漫! 设若人类行为追随理性,以十全十美的自由为目标,完善的政府形式也许可以出现。不过这显然只有将人改造为神明才能做到。由是之故,卢梭在《社会契约论》的一开篇就指出:"人是生而自由的,但却无所不在枷锁之中"(Men is born free,and everywhere he is in chains)③。

法治,是卢梭的人民主权理论之核心,也是他向往的理想政治。1754 年,卢梭在日内瓦发表《论人类不平等的起源和基础》(*The Discourse on the Origin and Foundations of Inequality Among Mankind*)。开篇致辞献给日内瓦共和国。文中表示,他"愿意出生在一个法制健全的民主政体下;自愿地服从法律,服

① Rousseau,*The Social Contract and other Later Political Writings*, pp.114~115.

② Rousseau,*The Social Contract and other Later Political Writings*, p.41.

③ Rousseau,*The Social Contract and other Later Political Writings*, p.91,41.

从这种任何人都不可能摆脱的体面的束缚;希望国家之中无人能凌驾于法律之上"①,哪怕是君主。如何实现这样的理想?他后来在《社会契约论》中展开论述(卷二第六章"论法律")。即,依靠公意的统治。在他看来,只要"法律乃是公意的行为,人们就无须问君主是否超乎法律之上,因为君主也是国家的成员;也无须问法律是否会不公正,因为没有人会对自己不公正;更无须问何以人们既是自由的,又要服从法律,因为法律不过是其自身意志的记录"(Since laws are acts of the general will,one need no longer ask whether the Prince is above the laws,since it is a member of the State;nor whether the law can be unjust,since no man can be unjust toward himself;now how one is both free and subject to the laws,since they are merely records of our wills)②。

狄德罗,比卢梭小一岁,博学而笃行,一生以树立理性的尊严为己任。虽然他的政治哲学在体系构建与原创性上不能与卢梭比肩,但在18世纪的法国,没有人比他更加有力地推动了理性思想的传播。从1740年中期到1760年末,狄德罗不遗余力地献身于百科全书的编纂。卷帙浩繁的"百科全书之于理性时代的呈现与赞美,恰如19世纪的水晶宫献礼于工业时代"(Like a Crystal Palace built a century later to pay tribute to an age of Industry,the Encyclopedia was an assembled as an exhibition of and celebration of an age of Reason)③。其作者名单囊括了那个时代西欧诸多思想巨擘:伏尔泰、卢梭、杜尔哥(A.R.Jacques Turgor)④、霍尔巴哈(Baron d'Holbach)、贝卡里亚(Cesare di Beccaria)等。狄德罗当然也跻身其中。他在为百科全书所撰写的大量文章以及后来的部分著作中提出了他的政治哲学。

启蒙时代的法国人讨论得最热烈的主题之一是人类社会的不平等。卢梭

---

① 让·雅克·卢梭:《论人类不平等的起源和基础》,高煜译,桂林:广西师范大学出版社,2002年,第52页。

② Rousseau,*The Social Contract and other Later Political Writings*, p.67.

③ Diderot,*Political Writings*,Cambridge:Cambridge University Press,1992,p.x.

④ 杜尔哥(1727~1781),法国文学家、政治家,也是经济学家。他先后协助路易十五与路易十六管理国家财政。1774年,出任路易十六财政大臣,推行经济改革。其改革举措触及特权阶级利益,遭到宫廷大臣、贵族与教士的反对。迫于压力,路易十六于1776年5月解除杜尔哥财政大臣的职务。杜尔哥任内所施行的改革法令随即被取消。

以其锋利的笔锋不遗余力地抨击与谴责它。两相比较,狄德罗在平等观上偏于保守。他呼吁法律面前人人平等,指出“法律不可为一人所造,而为万众所立”(laws should be made for all,and not just for one)①;但亦认可社会的不平等。在他看来,经济上的适度不平等更利于创造和平有序的社会②。不过,就政府权力的来源而言,狄德罗与卢梭同声相应。他一再强调:君主的权力或权威不来自上帝的恩惠,而来自臣民的同意及授予;他们只能依据自然法和国家的法律实施其统治;设若违背臣民据以授予其权力的契约,君主就取消了自己的权力或权威。而那种“依靠暴力获得的权力只能叫僭政”(Power acquired by violence is nothing but usurpation)。何以称之为僭政?因为“没有人曾被自然赋予命令他人的权利”(No man has by nature granted the right to command others);人们是在理性的指挥之下,为了充分地享有自由,而将权力授予了君主,使他统治一个国家。由是之故,狄德罗宣布:“国家不属于君主,君主属于国家”(The state does not belong to the prince,but the prince to the state)③。

如何使君主从属于国家?狄德罗提出了他的宪政与法治主张。首先,令主权者(sovereign,这里指君主)承认:“除了国家,没有真正的主权者”(There is no true sovereign except the nation),其权威来源于民众的同意与授予;“除了人民,没有真正的立法者”(There is no true legislator except the people),制定法律的权力永远保留在人民手中。其次,令主权者与人民共同宣誓:“遵从法律,这法律将令我们得到平等裁判(We the people and we sovereign of these people swear conjointly to obey these laws by which we will be equally judged);法律如需加以改变或侵犯,唯有人民有权这样做;形势需要时,主权者可受人民劝诫、驱逐,甚至被判死刑”。复次,每隔五年,由人民选出的代表来裁决:主权者是否遵从了他宣誓遵从的法律;如若违背,是否对之加以惩罚;并决定其留任或被驱逐;如果使其留任,他应当再次宣誓遵从法律。这个代表人民的中间机构(intermediary power)必须独立,其权利不能被任何立法者或最高权力

---

① Diderot,*Political Writings*,p.20.

② Diderot,*Political Writings*,p.xxviii.

③ Diderot,*Political Writings*, pp.6~9.

(supreme power)取消[①]。如此言论,显露出狄德罗对17世纪英国光荣革命的支持与对开明专制的排斥[②]。在这一点上,他接近于孟德斯鸠。不过,他并不像后者那样认为唯有权力机构间的制衡才能保证自由。在他看来,“自由存在于民主中(Freedom exits in democracies)”[③]。只要公众与政府之间意志和谐一致,换言之,令公意来统治,自由就可实现。

至于宗教信仰,狄德罗反对一切针对异端(heresy)与异教徒(pagan)的暴力手段,而呼唤人道主义的宗教宽容[④]。他指出,心灵或信仰上的归属难以靠暴力改变。“对一个软弱的人,暴力只能使其成为一个伪君子;对一个有勇气的人,暴力只能将其变为烈士”(Violence will render a man a hypocrite, if he is weak; a martyr, if he is courageous)。无论何种形式的暴力,譬如立法强制,事实上都属于对信仰的不敬。而“在一个施行宗教不宽容的国家,其君主徒为迫害者而已”(In an intolerant state, its prince would be simply a torturer)。[⑤]

---

① Diderot, *Political Writings*, pp.81~82,93.

② 从这里看,狄德罗似乎有强烈的革命倾向。但这样理解他是不准确的。尽管他坚持人民有抵制暴政的权利,却很少公开主张以暴力革命颠覆法国的君主制度。他支持渐进的改革。而在他发表于18世纪50年代的文章中,我们还能看到更为保守的观点。譬如在1851年,他指出:“人民与君主立定契约后,就应永远向君主表示服从与忠诚。哪怕君主行事不义,致使其臣民遭受不幸,后者也只能通过向上天祈祷获得解救。设若诉之于反叛,只能加重其不幸”(参见Diderot, *Political Writings*, pp.10~11)。既如此,如何理解狄德罗的“革命”言论?笔者有两个看法。其一,狄德罗的思想发生了变化。其二,与其说,狄德罗所言是一种革命的主张,不如说,这是他对沙俄女皇的进谏。1769年,叶卡捷琳娜二世(Catherine II)所撰《圣谕》(*Nakaz*, or *Introduction of Catherine II*)在法国出版并得以广泛传播。《圣谕》一作,尽管吸收了诸多西欧启蒙思想家如孟德斯鸠的政治理论,并将人人平等的口号写入其中,却也明显透露出女皇的绝对主义或专制倾向。1773~1774年,狄德罗访问俄国,亲见女皇政治个性。回程途中,他撰写《〈圣谕〉评论》(*Observations on the Nakaz*, or *Observations on the Introduction of the Empress of Russia to the Deputies for the Making of the Laws*)。《评论》对叶卡捷琳娜二世颇多劝讽,甚至指其为专制君主。狄德罗去世后,《〈圣谕〉评论》传至圣彼得堡。女皇读之,震怒不已,禁止其传播。另外,笔者还想指出,对于法国民众,狄德罗这番话说给谁听并不重要;重要的是,他的言论给法国人的思想带来了怎样的启迪。尽管狄德罗本人未曾宣扬革命,其思想却为法国人实践革命提供了理论依据。

③ Diderot, *Political Writings*, p.91.

④ 狄德罗首先辨析了教会的不宽容(ecclesiastical intolerance)与公民的不宽容(civil intolerance)。前者仅指在思想上认为除自身信仰以外的一切宗教均为错,后者则由思想上的不宽容进一步扩展到采用一切暴力手段驱逐与自身信仰不同者。见Diderot, *Political Writings*, p.29.

⑤ Diderot, *Political Writings*, pp.29~30.

总之,尽管启蒙时代的法国思想家在政治、宗教、乃至哲学理念上各执己见,但他们有统一的思想纲领:免于专横、反对暴政、要求自由。这些在启蒙运动中集中迸发出来的思想纲领,联同旧制度下的特权、压迫与专制主义,逼出了《人权宣言》中特色鲜明的原则与主张:平等、自由、人民主权、人身保护、选举、法治、分权。所有原则的提出都有它实实在在的根基,每一条都能从现实中找到活生生的例子来证明其正当性。对于大革命的发起者,颠覆旧制度的神圣,摧毁特权、专制与压迫的根源,是他们最迫切的想法,视之为无上光荣的使命。因此,他们以毫不含糊的决断口气将其理想提了出来:要建立自由、平等、有宪法的新社会;要让权力掌握在人民手中,并由人民行使。其中所反映的浪漫精神与历史背景,与美国《独立宣言》的审慎、严谨、实际以及殖民地人民无可奈何脱离母国的心态是截然不同的。

需要强调的是,从历史上看,大革命前夕的法国,并非专制统治最为严酷时,法国人民所受的压迫也并非特为深重。相反,由于路易十六的改革与开明,大革命前夕,法国社会的专制与压迫程度比路易十四与路易十五统治时要轻。"当时的形势既非贫困时期,亦非压迫太重,而且相对于政治来说社会还有一定的自由度"①。即便是对政治、文化思想的控制,也远未达到万马齐喑的程度。拿书籍出版来说,"1731 年前后,法国每年出版 400~500 部著作,1789 年前后达到 1000~1200 部"②。著名的《百科全书》于 1772 年出齐。正是在专制与压迫出现了松动的时刻,同时由于启蒙思想的掀动,法国人抓住了争取权利的机会,革命爆发。因此就整个人类革命史看,法国"大革命是一个不平衡的新发明……这个社会是在经济生活水平提高、个人首创精神及愿望增多、文化传播日益广泛的情况下逐渐解体的"③。另外还须指出,法国大革命的爆发是多方面因素长时段积累的结果,不能仅仅归因于路易十六登基以来的财政危机、经济衰退,以及 1788 年以来主要由于农产品歉收而形成的经济危机。

---

① 弗朗索瓦·傅勒:《思考法国大革命》,孟明译,北京:三联书店,2005 年,第 37 页。

② 阿尔贝·索布尔:《法国大革命史》,第 37 页。

③ 弗朗索瓦·傅勒:《思考法国大革命》,第 165 页。

“新制度的出生证(the birth certificate of new system)”——《人权宣言》的主张

旧制度终结了①。新秩序必须迅速建立。革命者雄心勃勃。他们不仅要摧毁特权、确认权利,建立起法国历史上前所未有的自由与民主制度,还要开创一个崭新的时代,一个充满“青春、热情、自豪、慷慨、真诚的时代”(This was a time of youth, enthusiasm, and pride, of generous and sincere passions)②。从这个崭新的时代里,革命者领出了一张“新制度的出生证”——《人权宣言》。出生证上,赫然盖着两个印章:人与公民的权利、政府的义务。

宣言首先援引自然法(natural law),将它作为高于人间一切权威的最高律令,指明个体权利的神圣、自然与不可剥夺(the natural, inalienable and sacred rights);同时说明政府的存在只为保障人的权利(The aim of all political institutes or association is to preserve the natural and imprescriptible rights of man),而非其他,这是它义务所在。

人拥有哪些权利? 宣言第二条(Article 2)指出,这些权利是自由、财产、安全与抵抗压迫(These rights are liberty, property, security and resistance to oppression)。

自由包含不同领域——政治、经济、社会、宗教自由等,宣言并未全部列举,它只是强调了某些方面,一些使宣言制订者感受最深的方面:言论、著述与出版的自由(Every citizen may speak, write, and print freely)。它还提到了信仰自由(Article 10:No one may be disturbed for his opinion, even in religion)。尽管“even”一词透出宗教宽容(religious tolerance)的有限性。法国是以信奉天

---

① 旧制度特指路易十五与路易十六统治时期的封建专制制度,而非其他。它的终结以一系列事件作为标志:国民公会的成立、巴士底狱的被攻陷、“八月法令”的发布等。“八月法令”指8月4日夜教士与贵族主动放弃特权后,国民议会于4~11日连续发布的一系列废除封建特权的法令。

② Alexis de Tocqueville, *The Ancien Regime and French Revolution*, Cambridge: Cambridge University Press, 2011, p.4.

主教为主的国家,大革命前被奉为国教,新教徒与犹太教徒的宗教生活受到严厉压制。这一条的提出,使不同宗教信仰都有了合法性。言论、著述、出版与信仰的自由又都归入宣言给自由规定的总则中——自由就在于能做一切无害于他人的事(Article 4:Liberty consists in the ability to do whatever does not harm another)。这是一个关于自由的相当宽泛的定义。它表示,每一个公民都是自己的主人,只要其行为无害他人,便可自由行使自己的意志。

财产权,在第二条和第十七条中分别提出,意味深长。首先,它反映出《人权宣言》在逻辑上失于严整,用词也颇显累赘——既然前文已说明财产权是不可剥夺与神圣的(Paragraph 1:inalienable and sacred;Article 2:imprescriptible),何必又在第十七条中再度声明它是"不可侵犯与神圣的"(Article 17:Property being an inviolable and sacred rights)?无怪乎阿克顿评论它"非属于卓越心智的产物,毫无名家之手的印迹。虽有笛卡尔式的明晰,却无逻辑,也不精确,未见法国思想的彻底性"(It is not a work of superior minds, and bears no mark of the lion's claw.The stamp of Cartesian clearness is upon it, but without the logic, the precision, the thoroughness of French thought)①。其次,它透露出宣言制定与讨论过程中的意见纷繁与匆忙。当时的情形,依据两个目睹草案制定的外国人的记录,可谓"杂乱无章"、"纷乱万分,简直是女巫的安息日"②。草案提交上去,进入讨论阶段。实际讨论时间只有 6 天——8 月 20~24 日以及 8 月 26 日。经过不知多少争论才定稿。再次,它还透露出某种强有力的意志的流动。宣言第十六条明显是一个结束语,阐明宪法必须具备何种条件。这也是《人权宣言》的使命:为宪法的制订提供指导原则。可是在它之后,突然跟上一条关于财产权的补充规定,且语气强烈,"任何人的财产权不得被剥夺,即便是出于某种显然的公共需要,也必须得到法律的认定,并预先获得公平赔偿"(No one may be deprived of it except for an obvious requirement of public necessity, certified by law, and then on condition of a just compensation in advance)。这很像是依托于某种强有力的意志最后加上去的。

---

① John Acton, *Lectures on the French Revolution*, p.90.

② 马德楞:《法国大革命史:关于法国革命进程的总记录》,伍光建译,北京:人民日报出版社,2013 年,第 66 页。

是哪方面的意志如此强大？当然是有产者。在国民议会占据主导作用的是第三等级与部分自由派教士(clergy)与贵族(nobility)①。尽管国民议会的领袖、被阿克顿认定为“最早提出革命思想的政治家”(the most original of the revolutionary statesmen)②、因发表《第三等级是什么?》而声名大振的西耶斯宣称：第三等级“是被束缚被压迫的一切”(What is the Third Estate? Everything;but an everything that is fettered and oppressed)③;但它不等于无产阶级的集合，其中有大量的中产阶级和拥有大宗财产的资本家。它之所以称为第三等级，是相对于享有特权的教士(第一等级)与贵族(第二等级)而言。作为第三等级的代表参与国民议会者，是律师、各旧司法区议会成员、工商业资本家、行政官吏、医生等各行业的有产者④。对于他们来说，财产权的保障不仅是政治与经济自由主义的必要，也与其切身利益密切相关。因此，令财产权在《人权宣言》中得到强调是为其强烈的要求。这种强有力的意志表达体现出，为大革命制订原则的是有产者，而非一无所有的工人、农民、手工艺人与流浪汉等受压迫最深的阶层，他们的利益并未得到实在的关照。尽管要求财产权的保障，本身无可非议，事实上也颇为正当——它属于人的自由权的一种。然而，当它与权力相勾结，并且不惜以伤害其他人而保障某一类人的利益时，人类的私心就露出了它伤人的尖牙。大革命时期，国民公会为保障法国农村领主的权益，使之获得补偿，提高了农民的税负。1791 年，法国农民的税负与大革命前相比，增加了 15%~20%。

比财产权更受重视的是平等——权利平等(Article 1:Men are born and remain free and equal in rights)、受法律保护平等(Article 6:Law must be the same for all whether it protects or penalize)、平等参与政府职位的竞争(Article 6:All citizens being equal in law's eyes are equally admissible to all public dignities, offices and employments)、平等承担赋税(Article 13: Taxation should the

---

① “nobility”与“aristocracy”均指贵族，但前者系因出生拥有贵族身份，后者往往不是。

② John Acton, *Lectures on the French Revolution*, p.57.

③ Emmanuel Sieyès, *Political Writings*, p.96.西耶斯：《论特权 第三等级是什么?》，第 22 页。

④ 1789 年 5 月参与三级会议的第三等级代表有教士 2 人、贵族 12 人、行政官吏 18 人、各旧司法区议会成员 108 人、律师 212 人、医生 16 人、商人和农民 216 人。米涅：《法国革命史：从 1789 年到 1814 年》，北京编译社译，北京：商务印书馆，2013 年，第 18~19 页。

apportioned equall among its citizens）。可以说，平等原则的反复强调是《人权宣言》最为鲜明的特色。它即是一种政治哲学的宣示，也是一种宗教观——上帝面前，人人都是平等的，因此《人权宣言》的制订者在确认并宣布公民权利时，恭敬地表示他们是“在主宰面前并赖其庇佑之下”（in the presence and under the auspices of the Supreme Being）。条款 1 的“权利平等”是为总则，条款 6 与条款 13 的“平等”是对总则的执行。之所以在抽象的总则之后加以具体的说明，实在是对特权的抗议。人们似乎听到一个洪亮的声音响起：任何人都不可以仅凭出生便享受荣誉、仅因生存便享受人民的奉献！无异于种姓（caste）制度的贵族世袭制必须废除！

平等之外，还必须有安全的保障，最基本的是人身安全保障。因此宣言规定：法律只可正当地禁止有害于社会的行为（Article 5：Law may rightly prohibit only those actions which are injurious to society）；除非在法律规定的情况下并遵行了法律所规定的程序，任何人不得被控告、逮捕或拘禁（Article 7：No man may be indicted，arrested，or detained except in cases determined by the law and according to the forms which it has prescribed）；除非法律已规定某种行为属违法，并已公之于众，任何人不得因此种行为而受处罚（Article 8：No one may be punished except by virtue of a law established）；任何人在被判有罪前均应推定为无罪，一切为扣留其人身所不必要的残酷行为均应受到法律的严厉制裁（Article 9：Every man being presumed innocent until judged guilty，all rigor not necessary to secure his person should be severely repressed by law）。这些条款不是“空洞的哀怜”（empty pathos），就像某些学者所批评的那样①。它们相当切实地指出，公民的政治自由或者说安全再没有比受到控告或拘捕时更容易受到威胁了，良好的刑法是确保公民自由的基本条件。正如伏尔泰所说的那样：“人权，只能依靠法律而非人的意愿”（Human rights only depends on the law and not men’s whims）②。

人民有反抗压迫的权利，最典型地表现了法国大革命的颠覆精神。此种

① Georg Jellinek，*The Declaration of Man and of Citizens：A Contribution to Modern Constitutional History*，pp.1～2.

② Voltaire，*Voltaire Political Writings*，p.xxiii.

权利从何而来？源于任何政治权威都来自国民的赋予。宣言表示，倘若此权威未能执行国民的意志，不能保障人民的权利与公共福祉，甚或利用人民赋予的权力压迫国民，人民就有权加以抵制或反抗。宣言还赋予了人民组织公共武装力量的权利，并声明：这些武装力量的设立是为全体的利益，而不是为接受权力委托者的私人利益（Article 12：These forces are instituted for the advantage of all，not for the private benefit of those to whom they are entrusted）。一言以蔽之，“一切主权的行使原则在本质上赖之于国民”（Article 3：The principle of all sovereignty rests essentially in the nation）。这一条人民主权原则以及人民有反抗压迫的权利主张，再加上上述各类权利声明，使得《人权宣言》在世界宪法史上占据了重要的位置。它随即成为1791年“93宪法”的序言，“第一次以其强大的气势给实证法注入了一个概念：国民凭其个人权利可以对抗作为整体的国家。这一概念此前只在自然法中存在”（The Declaration of the Rights of Man for the first time originated in all its vigor in positive law the conception，which until then had been known only to natural law，of the personal rights of the members of the state over against the state as a whole）①。

惟因主权在民，政府便没有理由声明它自己的权利。它只有义务，保障公民享有权利的义务。这是它之所以存在的目的。从这里出发，《人权宣言》确认了责任政府的概念。宣言第十五条指出，社会有权要求所有公共行政机构承担其责任（Article 15：Society has the right to hold accountable every public agent of administration）。

责任政府当如何履行其义务？宣言为它设立了分权（separation of powers）原则。虽然宣言未予“分权”较多篇幅，只在序言与第十六条里一笔带过，留下些狮爪之痕；然而末尾一句，“凡分权未确立的社会就没有宪法”（Article 16：Any society in which the separation of powers not determined has no constitution），实如高山耸立，确立了分权原则在随后将要制订出的宪法中的地位。分权之所以如此重要，乃因“一切有权力的人都容易滥用权力，这是万

① Georg Jellinek，*The Declaration of Man and of Citizens：A Contribution to Modern Constitutional History*，p.3.

古不易的一条经验。有权力的人们使用权力一直到遇有界限的地方才休止”(It has been eternally observed that any man who has power is led to abuse it;he continues until he finds limits)。要防止权力的滥用,除非“用权力约束权力”(So that one cannot abuse power;power must check power)。如此,方可避免由“一般意志蹂躏全国”、“个别意志毁灭公民的”专权结果。① 这是孟德斯鸠在《论法的精神》里论述得明明白白的道理,也是以“太阳王”路易十四为代表的专制君主在历史与现实中反证得实实在在的道理。

至于政府如何产生,宣言确立了代议制度与选举原则。它规定,立法与行政权由公民代表行使(through their representatives);一切政府职位均由选举产生,而区分职位担当的标准惟在德与才(Article 6:according to their according to their capacity,and with no other distinction than that of their virtues and talents)。确立代议与选举原则,实为人民主权理论的重申与执行,神授王权论的呵斥与颠覆。自此,所有公民都有权亲身或委托其代表参与政府的组成(Article 6,All citizens have the right to take part,in person or by their representatives,in governments formation),决定或执行影响其生活的一切事务。法兰西国王则被拉下神坛,他只能依据法律才能要求人民服从于他,而法律由公民制订。政府必须作为人民而非国王的政府履行其义务。

旧制度的遗产(Legacy of Old Regime)——《人权宣言》的不协之音

《人权宣言》被法国历史学家阿卢瓦(Aulard)呼为“旧制度的死亡证”(death certificate’ of the Old Regime),也被英国历史学家阿克顿勋爵喻为约书亚②的战鼓(the trumpets of Joshua),催动法国人为捍卫人权与自由而战斗。他说“这印出来不足一页纸的宣言,其分量要重过所有的图书馆,其力量要强过拿破仑的所有军队”(This single page of print,which outweighs libraries,and

① Charles de Montesquieu,*The Spirit of Laws*,Cambridge:Cambridge University Press,2011,pp. 155~157.《论法的精神》中文版,第155、156页。

② 约书亚:《圣经》中人物,摩西死后,他接替摩西,带领以色列人走上上帝应许之地。

is stronger than all the armies of Napoleon, is not a work of superior minds, and bears no mark of the lion's claw)①，然而，撼世之音中亦混着些自私、怯懦、虚伪，甚至背叛者的声音。

宣言第一条，首先确认人的权利生来且永远自由、平等，随后却马上用"社会差别"一语承认人的不平等，只不过加上了一个限定词，这种"差别只可基于公共利益之考虑"(Social distinctions may be based only on common utility)。何为公共利益之考虑？宣言未予说明。此种含混与模糊，让阿克顿批评它：缺乏"法国思想的彻底性"。尽管后文提到了税收平等、法律面前平等，显而易见的因财富带来的不平等却只字未提。从这一点来看，所谓"公共利益之考虑"似有仅为保障有财者利益之嫌。

阿克顿的批评当然不会仅仅因为宣言第一条。

宣言第二条确立了反抗压迫的权利，可是第九条写道，"依据法律被传唤或拘押的公民应立即服从，抗拒则构成犯罪"。这仿佛是害怕新近建立起来的制度被人重新颠覆似的。一方面宣告反抗政府、反抗压迫的合法性，另一方面又在防范民众依据同样的理由推翻革命者的政权。1791 年 6 月，巴黎工人罢工，要求增加工资改善劳动条件。国民议会马上采取行动，通过《勒沙普利埃法》(Le Chapelier Law)，取消工人的结社与罢工权。当年 7 月，勒沙普利埃法推及农村，农民也失去了反抗压迫的权利。

同样的畏惧心态反映在宣言第十一条关于言论、著述、出版自由的陈述中。本已说明，"思想与看法的自由交流是人类最宝贵的权利之一"(Free communication of thought and opinion is one of the most precious of the rights of man)；因此，每一位公民都可自由地发表言论、著述与出版。"然而"——重要的转折出现了！这些自由需在法律所规定的范围内，凡滥用自由者均需承担责任。这一句"滥用自由"对于前文的影响，直如江河奔流忽遇大坝拦截，滔滔江水猛然被阻遏。众所周知，各种对言论、著述、出版自由的压制，都可借用"滥用自由"的指控。它近似于任意的压迫与权力的滥用。因此之故，《人权宣言》甫一问世便遭严厉讨伐。法国一名报社记者以辛辣的笔调写道，"我们

① John Acton, *Lectures on the French Revolution*, p.90.

已然迅速地从奴役状态奔向了自由;但是现在,我们正以更快的速度从自由状态退回奴役制"(We have moved quickly from a condition of slavery to one of freedom;but now we are marching still more quickly from freedom back to slavery)①。1792 年 9 月以后,革命政府以国家安全为由,恢复了旧制度下的书报审查制度,绝不容许政治异见的存在,否则予以严厉打击。笔者不认为,1793~1794 年法国革命恐怖时期的大流血与大迫害应归咎于 1789 年《人权宣言》的不彻底。那是革命的性质发生变化或者转向的结果。不过,《人权宣言》因何未能阻止大革命走向与之背离的方向,的确是一个值得深思的问题。是因为它本身用词模糊,给后来者留下了侵犯人权的空间;还是因为它理想过于高远而让激进派掌握了权力,制造了法国革命的悲剧?

自由的不彻底不止体现在言论领域,宗教领域亦如是。宣言第十条前半部分规定,人民有信仰自由(No one may be disturbed for his opinions, even in religion),后面来一句,"只要其表达不扰乱已为法律所建立的公共秩序"(provided that their manifestation does not trouble public order as established by law)。何为"已为法律所建立的公共秩序"?有学者指出,其中之一是天主教作为法国国教的地位。这无异于说,新教与犹太教徒的宗教生活虽则得到允许,但只能在私底下进行,不能进入公共领域。然而革命者对信仰自由的违背远远超出《人权宣言》纸面所书。大革命开始不久,革命政府面临财政困难,无以为计,决定没收教会财产。私利被侵,教士们强烈抵制。1790 年 4 月,国民议会拒绝承认天主教为国教。7 月,国民议会通过《教士的公民组织法》(*The Civil Constitution of the Clergy*),规定教士如同公务员由选举产生;教会组织按国家行政区划建立。大主教不再设立,每一个新教区由主教管理;降低教士收入。11 月,又要求教士宣誓效忠宪法。这一连串涉及教会财产、选举与管理自由权的措施将教士变成了革命的敌人。果然,拒绝宣誓的僧侣形成了反抗派。对于他们,"革命政府发动了有史以来最残酷、最全面的宗教迫害"②。这种迫害不能仅仅视为革命或政治的需要,它违背了信仰自由的誓言。虽然革命者

---

① Albert Soboul, *French Revolution*:*1787~1789*, New York:Vintage Books, 1974, p.179.

② 秋风:"立宪失败的个案:阿克顿论法国大革命",阿克顿:《法国大革命讲稿》,秋风译,贵阳:贵州人民出版社,2004 年,第 442 页。

有理由仇视旧制度下的宗教迫害,乃至于对宗教表示蔑视,然而,以其人之道还治其人之身的迫害行为只能使革命者的自由事业走向反面。“为什么在这个自由主义激情大爆发的时代,却没有宗教自由的一席之地?”(Why,in that immense explosion of liberal sentiment,there was no room for religious freedom)①。

自由不能及于信仰,也不能及于所有的种族。凡非高卢人后裔,都被排除在人人生而自由与平等的原则之外,黑人尤应列于被排除之列(这种人从来没有享受过人权)。虽然旧制度下的开明君主路易十四曾于1685年颁发过《黑人法典》,禁止贩卖奴隶、拆散黑人夫妻、迫使年幼的黑人与父母分离,然而奴隶制一直存在于法国。1789年底,国民议会宣布在其本土废除奴隶制。这是法国大革命值得高歌之处,绝不能否认。不过,在法国殖民地,奴隶制被保留下来。1790年3月,国民议会“殖民地委员会”(Colonial Committee)甚至提议:法国殖民地免于宪法约束;任何意欲在殖民地反抗奴隶制度者,均应予以严惩。1790年10月,圣多明各(Saint-Domingue,今海地)发生叛乱。一个富有的黑白混血儿(mulatto)文森特·奥杰(Vincent Ogé)领导350余名自由黑人,抗议法国的种族歧视政策,要求享有与法国白人公民同等的政治权利。尽管奥杰无意触动殖民地的奴隶制(他本人也是一个奴隶主),然而为有色人种要求权利依然触怒法国政府与白人种植园主。法国军队与白人民兵联合起来,将叛乱镇压。次年2月,奥杰与其他几位叛乱领导者被公开处决。牺牲者的鲜血激起不甘歧视者的斗志。5月,又一场叛乱爆发。迫于压力,国民议会作出妥协,宣布殖民地的自由黑人享有政治权利,只要其父母也是自由人。但即便是如此有限的妥协也遭到了白人殖民者的强烈抵制。法令难以执行。殖民地的黑人愤怒了。8月,一场最终导致海地独立的奴隶起义爆发。法国国民议会惊骇异常。9月24日,即“93宪法”刚刚通过不久,国民议会颁布两条法令:其一,有色人种不得拥有公民权;其二,保留加勒比海殖民地的奴隶制度。政治权利在自由黑人手中尚未握热就被收回;奴隶也还是奴隶,做不得翻身为人的指望。

---

① John Acton, *Lectures on the French Revolution*, p.141.

黑人的人权因何得不到尊重？这与不少国民议会的代表、《人权宣言》制订者在殖民地的经济利益相勾连。他们或者在那里拥有庄园或矿山，享受以奴隶制为基础的庄园制经济与采矿业的好处；或者参与奴隶贸易，直接以奴隶买卖作为收入来源。私利当前，公义退后，世态常情。再者，在当时大多数欧洲人眼中，“人”的概念中自然排除了黑奴，他们当然也就不能享受人之为人的权利。法国人如此，高呼“人人生而平等”的美国人亦如此。《独立宣言》草拟者杰斐逊，以及与他同样拥有奴隶的美国建国之父们，在制订 1787 年联邦宪法时，含蓄而尴尬地承认了奴隶制的合法性。因为这一点，《独立宣言》被后世的激进废奴派斥为“不言而喻的谎言”(self-evident lie)。

1792 年 3 月，法国革命渐趋激进，加上海地奴隶起义的推动，法国立法议会(Legislative Assembly)①通过法令，恢复自由黑人与黑白混血儿的权利。随后，主要出于国家安全的考虑(英国与西班牙意图利用法国殖民地的奴隶起义，入侵法国)，法国立法议会于 1794 年 2 月 4 日通过法令，宣布在法国所有殖民地废除奴隶制。然而好景何其短矣！1802 年，拿破仑·波拿巴(Napoleon Bonaparte)不仅恢复了奴隶制，连给予自由黑人的权利也剥夺了。

最为人诟病者，是宣言中的平等选举原则未曾得到遵循。尽管从宣言中几乎看不出这一点，然而国民议会随后制订的选举法与宪法映射出宣言制订时许多参与者的内心。从一开始，他们似乎就没打算严格按照宣言精神执行它。

宣言第六条规定，“所有公民均有权亲自或通过其代表参与法律的制定……因公民在法律上平等之故，他们可平等地依其能力获得政府雇佣、担任公职、占据一切高位。区分其职位之标准，唯德与才，无有其他”。然而，将此原则列在序言中的宪法不仅将全体妇女推置一旁，还违背“惟德与才”的标准，反而依据财产对公民的选举权与担任公职权做了资格限定。1789 年 12 月通过的选举法，将公民分成消极公民(passive citizen)、积极公民(active citizen)、选举人(elector)、代表(deputy)等不同等级的人群。旧等级于当年 7 月由国民议会宣布废除，新等级却在宪法中产生了。

---

① 立法议会于 1791 年 10 月替代了国民议会。因为宪法已然制定，国民议会的使命完成。

何谓消极公民？仆人以及缴不起相当于三日工资（约 1.5~3 里弗尔）的直接税[①]的贫困阶级。他们总人口约 300 万，占法国成年男子总数的 40%。如此众多的公民被剔除在有选举权的阶级之外，使享有选举权的人众比例尚不如旧制度时期。那时，只要纳税就有选举权。如今，这部分人既没有选举权，也没有参与国民卫队的资格。

所谓积极公民也必须经过金钱标准的再过滤，划分为最低级的积极公民、选举者、代表等不同等级，并且依据其财富多少，限定其具有何等层级（初级与省级会议）的选举权。只有每年能缴纳相当于十日工资（约 5~10 里弗尔）的直接税的人，才能在“初级会议”（primary assemblies）中被选为相当于省一级的“选举者会议”（electoral assemblies）的选举者，这部分人在所有积极公民中约占 1%；而有资格被选为国家立法机构代表的人必须有能力缴纳相当于 52 日工资（约 52 里弗尔）的直接税，并且拥有一定的地产。换言之，立法议会里坐的必须是金钱贵族（moneyed aristocracy）。这可真是一大讽刺。革命者以废除特权为使命，却在选举与被选举权上建立了另一种特权。虽然它受到了罗伯斯皮尔与马拉等人的谴责，但有产者才有资格与能力治理国家的概念占了上风。这是一个财富的权力与势力正在上升的时代。

不得不问，此种特权思想的复活，或者说平等思想的不彻底，因何而起？对此，学者们给出了多维度且都颇有解释力的答案。在托克维尔看来，这是旧制度的渗透。革命者虽“百般警惕，唯恐把过去的旧东西带进他们的新天地”（they took any number of precautions to ensure that they would carry over nothing from the past into their new condition），却依然“在不知不觉中继承了旧制度的感情、习惯和思想”（unbeknownst to themselves, they had taken from the Ancien Régime most of the feelings, habits, and ideas）[②]。也就是说，《人权宣言》在它问世之际，便沾上了旧制度的锈斑。

阿克顿的评论更深一层。他认为，这是革命者思想不成熟所致。他们未

① 直接税指纳税人为税负的直接承担者，其所承担的税负不能转嫁给他人；以归属于私人的财产为征税对象，如所得税。间接税不直接针对公众，以商品或服务为征税对象如关税。在当时的法国，直接税指军役税、人头税、收入的二十分之一税。

② Alexis de Tocqueville, *The Ancien Regime and French Revolution*, p.1.

曾意识到“自由是目标,而不是出发点”(Liberty is the goal,and not the starting point),未可因任何理由剥夺人的自由;未曾意识到“当那些排他性的、不平等的特权被废除之时,就有必要明确规定并坚持所有人都平等的原则”(When those that were exclusive and unequal were abandoned,it was necessary to define and insist on those that were equal of all)①。换言之,革命者所要确立的新制度架构对他们来说太新、太不熟悉,他们还没有能力彻底看清楚什么是不可动摇的原则。当然,对于这一点,托克维尔也有提及。他说,“要想使这种学说(指关于人的天赋权利)产生革命,人们的地位、习惯、风尚必须已经发生变化,为学说的深入人心做好精神准备”。也就是说,当平等原则不是作为一个口号,而是作为一个社会行为的实践原则时,它才可能得到彻底贯彻。

大革命史学家乔治·勒弗比尔(George Lefebvre)则指出,这是制宪者考虑到贫困阶级不够成熟,未见得能承担如此重要的公民权利,故而对其资格加以限制②。因为正是西耶斯提议(1789 年 10 月 29 日)将公民按财产分等,并创造了“消极公民”的概念。在他看来,德行若不与金钱结合,它就很容易变成诱发革命动乱的因素。因此,“没有财产的人固然有权得到保护,但没有权利积极地参与公共机构的构成”(Those who had no property rights were entitled to be protected their persons,their possessions,their liberty,but they were not to take part actively in the formation of public orders)③。

不妨再深究一步:这种精英民主理论的主张从何而来?翻一翻为西耶斯等人所敬重的思想家孟德斯鸠的著作,不难发现,他们不过是效仿了古希腊雅典与罗马的政制,追随了孟德斯鸠的思想。孟德斯鸠在谈到选举权时特意举了两个例子:古罗马的塞尔维乌斯·图里乌斯在公民中分配选举权时,把他们分成 193 个等级不同的“百人团”,有钱人在等级最高的团,不那么有钱的人在次一等的团,赤贫者归入最低级的团。雅典的梭伦虽授予所有公民选举权,

---

① John Acton,*Lectures on the French Revolution*, p.90.

② Georges Lefebvre,*The French Revolution:From its Origins to 1793*,London:Routledge,2001,p.146.

③ Albert Soboul,*French Revolution:1787~1789*,p.180.

但公民分成四个等级,官吏只能从前三个富有的等级中选出①。在孟德斯鸠看来,这种按"人口分级制"、"资产与财富"所施行的选举没什么不好。因为必须靠劳动生活的人,很可能由于担任公职而更加穷困,也可能使他们疏忽公职上的责任。"在这种情形下,为着民主政治的利益,民主政治公民间的平等是可以取消的。不过,这里所取消的只是表面上的平等而已"②。

旧制度的残留也好,新制度未有履新的能力与条件也好,都揭示出人性中常见的冲突:至善与自利原则间的挣扎。对于大多数人来说,他们总是一方面追求至善,渴望建构无私的超我;另一方面受自利或者说本我的强烈驱动,寻求自身利益的最大化。与一切人在一切方面平等,至善!但这也妨碍自身利益的最大化。由是之故,至善之理想很难得以彻底贯彻;自由与平等,也往往只是人们借以保护自身利益的口号。人们鼓吹自由,却反对别人的自由,因其于己不利;人们呼吁平等,却不喜欢有人依据平等冒犯其尊严、傲慢乃至利益。1789 年 8 月 4 日夜,人类历史上那旷世未有的一幕:教士与贵族主动放弃特权,表示"除非消除了导致暴力的不公正,否则不可能消除暴力(You cannot repress violence unless you remove the injustice which is the cause of it),那些应该交还给国家的权利,应当无条件地交出去;那些理应交还给人民的权利,亦应放弃而不求补偿"(that rights abandoned to the State should be ceded unconditionally,and that rights abandoned to the people should not be given up in return for compensation)③,实乃超我意识临时大发挥的结果。它高尚,但不能持久。一旦人们返身朝向自利原则,便会意识到,他们想要的平等不仅意味着"不让任何人高于自己",还隐含着"自己要高人一等"的意味④,因此绝不能容忍一向比其低一等的人群享有与之同等的权利。当然,精英民主理论并非无其合理之处:教育与基本生活的保障实乃行使政治权利或权力的基础。但与此同时,人类心理颇为隐秘的一面也不能忽略。法国政治心理学家古斯塔夫·勒

---

① 孟德斯鸠:《论法的精神》(上),张雁深译,北京:商务印书馆,2002 年,第 10 页。

② 孟德斯鸠:《论法的精神》(上),第 46 页。

③ John Acton,*Lectures on the French Revolution*, p.84.

④ 古斯塔夫·勒庞:《法国大革命与革命心理学》,倪复生译,北京:北京师范大学出版社,2015 年,第 103 页。

庞曾一针见血地指出:“隐藏在大革命人士对平等的渴望之下的只是一种强烈的不平等需求”①。

不过,无论《人权宣言》有多少瑕疵或矛盾,也无论思想家如何严厉地指责它,都不能使人低估其对人类思想与社会进步产生的影响。尽管埃德蒙·伯克(Edmund Burke)——法国大革命最猛烈的批判者,谴责法国国民议会罔顾历史传统,制定出与现实完全脱离的抽象原则,致使“法兰西以比任何民族都高昂的代价换来了不折不扣的灾难”(France has bought undisguised calamities at a higher price than any nation),并且认为:《人权宣言》所声明的“那种模糊不清的思辨的权利”(vague speculative right),在法国人思想中制造出一种“怪诞的神话”,激发起他们“种种虚假的观念和空洞的希望,其结果却加重、恶化了现实的不平等”(that monstrous fiction, by inspiring false ideas and vain expectation, serves only to aggravate and embitter that real inequality)②。大革命之后的人类历史记录却显示,《人权宣言》给世界人民带来的希望既不虚假,也不空洞。它是一张内含共和、民主、自由、平等、法治与人权格言的支票,是权利的福音书,非但激励全世界不同国家、族群、性别的人为独立、自由与平等而战,亦迫使政治家不敢忘怀革命的承诺,尽力朝至善的世界走得更近。正如托克维尔所指出的那样,《人权宣言》“不仅研究什么是法国公民的特殊权利,而且研究什么是人类在政治上的一般义务与权利”;它所指出的普遍原则虽未能创造一个崭新的世界,但是它“培植了革命的种子”,带来了“破晓的曙光”③。正是由于《人权宣言》以及在它之前的《独立宣言》,整个欧洲乃至世界人民发展了一个新的观念:权利的平等。

---

① 古斯塔夫·勒庞:《法国大革命与革命心理学》,第103页。

② Edmund Burke, *Reflections of the French Revolution*, London: J.M.Dent & Sons. 1951, pp.30~35.

③ 托克维尔:《旧制度与大革命》,冯棠译,北京:商务印书馆,1997年,第52、277页。

延伸阅读

Lynn Hunt ed., *The French Revolution and Human Rights: A Brief Documentary History*, Boston: Bedford Books, 1996. 这本不到 200 页的文献集为读者提供了极好的背景材料，便于其充分理解《人权与公民权宣言》的产生过程与意义。导言"人权的革命起源（The Revolutionary Origins of Human Rights）"由美国著名历史学家 Lynn Hunt 撰写，其内容丰富而深刻，既包含了人权与自然法理论的简要勾勒，又提取了若干重要历史细节进行前因后果的分析。

Georg Jellinek, *The Declaration of Man and of Citizens: A Contribution to Modern Constitutional History*, New York: Henry Holt and Company, 1901（格奥尔格·耶里内克：《人权与公民权利宣言——现代宪法史论》，李锦辉译，北京：商务印书馆，2013 年）。一本引发了关于《人权与公民权利宣言》理论渊源大讨论的著作，其中观点虽可商榷，然亦不乏启发意义。

Georges Lefebvre, *The French Revolution: From its Origins to 1793*, London: Routledge, 2001（乔治·勒费弗尔：《法国革命史》，顾良、孟湄、张慧君译，北京：商务印书馆，2013 年）有学者言，"乔治·勒费弗尔的著作具有示范与榜样的价值"，因为他开拓了"法国大革命的社会史研究"；还有学者，譬如美国历史学家 A.J.P.Taylor，特别注意到了勒费弗尔对法国革命的国际背景分析，并且称赞"其对法国社会与知识背景的介绍引人入胜"。这些，都是此书价值所在。关于《人权宣言》，勒费弗尔指出："这个文件既是自由、平等和国民主权的宣言，又是被平民革命所消灭的旧制度的'死亡证书'"（Proclaiming liberty, equality, and national sovereignty, the text was in effect the 'act of decease' of the Old Regime, which had been put to death by the popular revolution）（p.126）。

阿尔贝·索贝尔：《法国大革命史》，马胜利、高毅、王庭荣译，北京：北京师范大学出版社,2015年。索贝尔师承勒费弗尔(Lefebvre),"自其业师1951年再版《法国革命史》以来,索布尔这本书是用马克思主义观点分析法国革命进程最系统全面的著作。反马克思主义历史学家称之为无产阶级的《圣经》,也不是完全没有道理的。"(引张芝联为此书中译本序)。

路易·马德楞:《法国大革命史:关于革命进程的总记录》,伍光建译,北京:人民日报出版社,2013年。读此译本,至少有两个好处。其一,了解法国历史学家路易·马德楞何以被称道为"良史才,善属文,他人以千言叙一事,写一人者,路易·马德楞能一百言了之,尤能深印于读者心中"。其二,领略清末翻译家、有"翻译界之圣手"美誉的伍光建的翻译风格。此书中译本出于1927年,时隔九十余年,读者可与当下翻译作品作一比较。洞悉法国大革命之历史进程的同时,亦可对翻译史有一了解。

John Acton, *Lectures on the French Revolution*, Kitchener: Batoche Books, 1999(阿克顿:《法国大革命讲稿》,秋风译,贵阳:贵州人民出版社,2004年)。这是阿克顿勋爵于1895~1899年担任剑桥大学钦定近代史讲座教授时的讲课稿,尽管他自己认为它非常粗糙,因此拒绝出版,事实上却成为研究法国大革命的必读作,其评论充满智慧与思想的力量。

Alexis de Tocqueville, *The Ancien Regime and French Revolution*, Cambridge: Cambridge University Press, 2011(托克维尔:《旧制度与大革命》,冯棠译,北京:商务印书馆,1997年)。理解与研究法国大革命不可绕过的经典著作,体现了托克维尔对"这段历史的全部思考与评价"。通过将大革命的起因、特征与旧制度的性质相勾连,托克维尔这本书不仅在内容上呈现了难以超越的思考深度,还以其"历史哲学与历史本身的结合",创造了研究方法的典范。百余年来为牛津大学规定为基础教程。

米涅:《法国革命史》,北京编译社译,北京:商务印书馆,2013年。这部著作完成于1824年,距离法国大革命时间近;作者又以坚持采用原始材料为原则,可信度较高。

马迪厄:《法国革命史》,北京:商务印书馆,2011年。这本书是一部为一般读者而写的法国革命史,但不失为一部好书。作者马迪厄于20世纪初被称为"法国革命史研究中的革新者"。此书在哪些方面有所革新?读者不妨与其他法国革命史著作作一比较。

孟德斯鸠:《论法的精神》(上),张雁深译;卢梭:《社会契约论》,何兆武译;伏尔泰:《路易十四时代》,吴模信等译;西耶斯:《论特权 第三等级是什么》,冯棠译,北京:商务印书馆。回到大革命爆发前的时代,看看当时的法国思想家与革命家如何描述、评论旧制度下的法国,并提出其革新乃至革命性主张,这几本书是必须要读的。对于深入理解《人权宣言》理论与现实的根源,它们尤其不可或缺。另,读卢梭的《社会契约论》,可参考阅读李平沤先生《主权在民 Vs"朕即国家":解读卢梭〈社会契约论〉》一书(山东人民出版社,2001年版)。正如何兆武先生所言,它"是中文著作中对卢梭这部书最佳的解读"。

MAGNA CARTA OF 1215
1215 年《大宪章》

MAGNA CARTA OF 1215①

justiciar: the chief political and judicial officer of the Norman and later kings of England until the 13th century

John②, by the grace of God, king of England③, lord of Ireland, duke of Normandy and Aquitaine, and count of Anjou, to the archbishops, bishops, abbots, earls, barons④, justiciars, foresters, sheriffs⑤, stewards, servants, and to all his

① Magna Carta 又称 The Great Charter or The Charter of Liberties(自由权大宪章)。1215 年《大宪章》之谓"大"(Great),是因其非同寻常的长度与细致入微,并且与《森林宪章》(Charter of the Forest)相区别。《森林宪章》于 1217 年首次颁布;1225 年起,由于大宪章的部分内容转移至《森林宪章》,大宪章总与《森林宪章》一起重颁。1215 年《大宪章》上的署印日期为 6 月 15 日,实则国王约翰是在 6 月 19 日才正式接受宪章。24 日,王家法庭(Royal Chancery)制作了多份文本向外发出。现存 4 个文本保存于大英博物馆(2 份)、林肯大教堂与索里兹伯里大教堂(各 1 份)。其拉丁文原文共 3,655 个词;既无标题,也不分段落。1759 年,英国法学家威廉·布莱克斯通(William Blackstone)为各条款标上序号,共 63 条,自此为史家与法学家等沿用。本文本取自 Harry Rothwell ed., *English Historical Document, 1189~1327*, London: Eyre Spottiswood, 1975, pp.316~324.

② John(约翰王),1199~1216 年在位,兼领爱尔兰,又是诺曼底与阿奎坦大公、安如伯爵。《大宪章》诞生前,约翰王在与法王菲力普二世的交战中,已经丧失诺曼底以及他在法国的几乎所有领地,所谓"诺曼底与阿奎坦公爵、昂如(今译'安如'——笔者注)伯爵"实为虚名。

③ 英国国王此时的称呼为"Your Grace" or "Your Highness"。直到都铎王朝建立,亨利八世在位,对王的称呼才由"Your Majesty"取代。

④ 这里所列为僧俗两界贵族。"archbishop(大主教)、bishop(主教)、abbot(修道院院长)"等高级教士为宗教界贵族;"earl(伯爵,亦称 count)、baron(男爵)"为世俗贵族。需注意,此时在英国,尚未正式形成公、侯、伯、子、男的贵族等级体系。伯爵、公爵(亦称大公)与侯爵(marquis)的称呼来自法兰克公国,专门用来称呼在加洛林时代具有重要荣誉职位的后代,是权力与声望的象征。在 13 世纪的英国,伯爵与男爵群体均跻身于社会最上层,是国王的直属封臣。作为一种正式的封号,在英国,公爵爵位由爱德华三世于 1337 年首度封立。用的是旧日的名称,"但精神是新的",即不限于从前那些权贵的后代。开始仅封与王室成员,后延展至王室之外。侯爵爵位由理查二世于 1385 年创制。子爵的出现晚至 15 世纪。

⑤ "sheriff"(郡守),英国各郡行政长官;由国王任免,代表国王的权威,行使保护王室利益的职责。亨利二世统治时起,郡守权力大幅提升。郡守成为一个代表国王在地方上行使权力的总督,郡内所有财政、军事、司法与治安事务均在其掌控之下;他还是郡法庭的主持者,有权享有郡法庭收入的 1/3(the third penny)。不过在王室法庭作用日渐加强之后,郡法庭的地位开始下降。在爱德华一世统治结束前,郡法庭只对 40 先令以下的不涉及土地问题的诉讼和在封建领主法庭得不到公正救济的不动产诉讼享有管辖权。

bailiffs①and faithful subjects, greetings. Know that we, out of reverence for God and for the salvation of our soul and those of all our ancestors and heirs, for the honor of God and the exaltation of holy church, and for the reform of our realm, on the advice of our venerable fathers, Stephen②, archbishop of Canterbury, primate of all England and cardinal of the holy Roman Church, Henry, archbishop of Dublin, William of London, Peter of Winchester, Jocelyn of Bath and Glastonbury, Hugh of Lincoln, Walter of Worcester, William of Coventry, Benedict of Rochester, bishops; of master Pandulf, subdeacon and member of the household of the lord pope, of brother Aymeric, master of the order of Knights Templar in England, and of the noble men William Marshal earl of Pembroke③, William earl of Salisbury, William earl of Warenne, William earl of Arundel, Alan of Galloway constable of Scotland, Warin fitz Gerold, Peter fitz Herbert, Hubert de Burgh seneschal of Poitou, Hugh de Neville, Matthew fitz Herbert, Thomas Basset, Alan Basset, Philip de Aubeney, Robert of Ropsley, John Marshal, John fitz Hugh, and others, our faithful subjects:

[1] In the first place have granted to God④, and by this our present charter confirmed for us and our heirs for ever that the English church shall be free, and shall have its rights un-

reverence: honor or respect felt or shown

exaltation: glorification

primate: the highest ranking priest in the church of England

subdeacon: a cleric ranking below a deacon

deacon: a cleric ranking below a priest

fitz: a prefix in patronymic surnames of Anglo-Norman origin, originating in the 11th century; a Norman French noun meaning "son of", from Latin fillus(son), plus genitive case of the father's forename

seneschal: a steward in charge of a lord's estate in feudal times

---

① "bailiff"(执行官),由郡守指派以主持百户区法庭,负责照看国王在百户区内的事务,如征收税金、罚金、没收土地等。

② "Stephen"即 Stephen Langton,与诸男爵同盟,而未附和罗马教皇英诺森三世(Pope Innocent III)。后者左袒国王,于 1215 年 8 月 24 日宣布《大宪章》无效。

③ William Marshal 曾协助约翰登上王位,并因此而成为彭布罗克伯爵。他在 1215 年《大宪章》的制订与颁布中起了重要作用。约翰王去世、亨利三世继位后,他作为摄政使大宪章于 1216 年、1217 年以及 1225 年屡次重颁。

④ 原文如此。"have"前应有主语"we"。

diminished and its liberties unimpaired; and it is our will that it be thus observed; which is evident from the fact that, before the quarrel between us and our barons began, we willingly and spontaneously granted and by our charter confirmed the freedom of elections which is reckoned most important and very essential to the English church, and obtained confirmation of it from the lord pope Innocent III; the which we will observe and we wish our heirs to observe it in good faith for ever. We have also granted to all free men of our kingdom, for ourselves and our heirs for ever, all the liberties written below, to be had and held by them and their heirs of us and our heirs.

[2] If any of our earls or barons or others holding of us in chief by knight service① dies, and at his death his heir be of full age and owe relief② he shall have his inheritance on payment of the old relief, namely the heir or heirs of an earl £100 for a whole earl's barony③, the heir or heirs of a baron £100 for a whole barony, the heir or heirs of a knight 100s, at most, for a whole knight's fee; and he who owes less shall give less according to the ancient usage of fiefs.

£100: 100 pounds

100s: 100 shillings, shilling (until 1971): British coin worth twelve old pennies; one twentieth of a pound

[3] If, however, the heir of any such be under age and a

① "knight service"(骑士役保有)，一种土地保有方式，又称"military service(军事役)"。以该方式从国王处保有土地者，须以服军役回报国王，即向国王的军队提供至少1名全副武装、可以作战40天的骑兵。英格兰绝大部分土地是通过骑士役从国王处保有的。

② "relief"(继承金)，封臣义务之一；指保有封地的封臣去世时，其已成年的继承人应向领主支付费用，以继续保有该封地；该费用应在接收土地时支付。土地保有方式不同，继承金数额也不同。骑士役封地的继承金是100先令，但男爵领地(barony)的继承人须支付100英镑；农役地继承金为一年的地租(rent)。这一规定形成于亨利二世辅臣格兰威尔(Glanville)当政时期，大宪章予以了确认。

③ "barony"，男爵领地，或称直属封臣领地；有一种理论认为，该领地由13 $\frac{1}{3}$份骑士役领地组成。

ward, he shall have his inheritance when he comes of age without paying relief and without making fine①.

[4] The guardian of the land of such an heir who is under age shall take from the land of the heir no more than reasonable revenues, reasonable customary dues and reasonable services, and that without destruction or waste of men② or goods; and if wecommit the wardship③ of the land of any such to a sheriff, or to any other who is answerable to us for its revenues, and he destroys or wastes what he has wardship of, we will take compensation from him and the land shall be committed to two lawful and discreet men of that fief, who shall be answerable for the revenues to us or to him to whom we have assigned them; and if we give or sell to anyone the wardship of any such land and he causes destruction or waste therein, he shall lose that wardship, and it shall be transferred to two lawful and discreet men of that fief, who shall similarly be answerable to us as is aforesaid.

wardship: the fact of a child being cared by a guardian

[5] Moreover, so long as he has the wardship of the land, the guardian shall keep in repair the houses, parks, preserves, ponds, mills and other things pertaining to the land out of the revenues from it; and he shall restore to the heir when he comes of age his land fully stocked with ploughs and the

preserve: area where game or fish are preserved for private hunting or fishing

① "fine"一词在此非指罚金,而指封臣在契约变更时付给领主的一笔费用。这里所涉及的,是国王在充当监护人后,拒绝承认被监护人的领地继承权,而要求被监护人支付一笔高额费用后才恢复其领地继承权的行为。参见 William Sharp McKechnie, *Magna Carta: A Commentary on the Great Charter of King John*, Glasgow: James Maclehose & Sons, 1914, p.204.

② "waste of men"指解放农奴。农奴被视为财产,如使其自由,对主人来说,意味着财产损失。

③ "wardship"(监护权),属领主权利;指骑士役封臣的继承人男低于21岁、女低于14岁时,领主可对其人身与土地行使监护权。直至继承人成年前,领主可经营被监护人的土地,获取收益。其监护权还可任其自由买卖。

means of husbandry according to what the season of husbandry requires and the revenues of the land can reasonably bear.

disparage: to lower in rank or reputation

[6] Heirs shall be married without disparagement①, yet so that before the marriage is contracted those nearest in blood to the heir shall have notice②.

[7] A widow shall have her marriage portion and inheritance forthwith and without difficulty after the death of her husband; nor shall she pay anything to have her dower or her marriage portion or the inheritance which she and her husband held on the day of her husband's death; and she may remain in her husband's house for forty days after his death, within which time her dower shall be assigned to her③.

dower: a widow's share for life of her husband's estate

[8] No widow shall be forced to marry so long as she wishes to live without a husband, provided that she gives security not to marry without our consent if she holds of us, or without the consent of her lord of whom she holds, if she holds of another.

chattel: property (such as a slave, peace of furniture, tools, etc.) that a person owns rather than land or buildings

[9] Neither we nor our bailiffs will seize for any debt any land or rent, as long as the chattels of the debtor are sufficient to repay the debt; nor will those who have gone surety for the debtor be distrained so long as the principal debtor is himself able to pay the debt; and if the principal debtor fails to pay the debt, having nothing wherewith to pay it, then shall

distrain: to force or compel to satisfy an obligation by means of a distress

① 这里涉及的是与监护权相关联的婚姻指定权，强调婚姻的门当户对，即领主不允许被监护人跟与其地位不相称的人结婚。

② 指国王为某人指定婚姻时必须征询其最近的家属的意见。这一前提条件在1216年《大宪章》中被删除，以后也未恢复。

③ 1217年《大宪章》第7条将"her dower shall be assigned to her"说得更加清楚："There shall be assigned to her for her dower a third of all her husband's land which was his in his lifetime"。"dower"一词在大宪章中应理解为"丈夫留给寡妇的土地"，而非她从娘家带来的嫁妆，也就更加明确。

the sureties answer for the debt; and they shall, if they wish, have the lands and rents of the debtor until they are reimbursed for the debt which they have paid for him, unless the principal debtor can show that he has discharged his obligation in the matter to the said sureties.

[10]①If anyone who has borrowed from the Jews any sum, great or small, die before it is repaid, the debt shall not bear interest as long as the heir is under age②, of whomsoever he holds; and if the debt falls into our hands, we will not take anything except the principal mentioned in the bond③.

principal: money lent on which interest is paid

[11] And if anyone dies indebted to the Jews, his wife shall have her dower and pay nothing of that debt; and if the dead man leaves children who are under age, they shall be provided with necessaries befitting the holding of the deceased; and the debt shall be paid out of the residue, reserving, however, service due to lords of the land; debts owing to others than Jews shall be dealt with in like manner.

befitting: appropriate; decent

deceased: the recently dead person

[12] No scutage④ or aid⑤ shall be imposed on our

---

① 第 10~12 条不见于 1216 年《大宪章》。

② 此款是为保护未成年继承人的财产不因偿还犹太人的高利贷而被吞噬。当时,犹太人所放高利贷利息每英镑可达每周 2 到 4 便士,即每年需为 1 英镑的借贷偿付 $43\frac{1}{3}$ 到 $86\frac{2}{3}$ 便士的利息。参见 William Sharp McKechnie, *Magna Carta: A Commentary on the Great Charter of King John*, p.224。

③ 这一款是为防止国王利用其权势而以借债付息为由侵夺臣民财产。

④ "scutage"(军役税,或称代役捐),又称盾牌金(shield-money),由亨利一世于 1109 年创立。缴纳盾牌金并不意味着可免除骑士亲身服役。亨利一世创立此税,是为减少对封臣的依赖而招募雇佣兵,以便长期征战或远征。倘若封臣未经与国王协商,以缴纳盾牌金为由拒绝履行骑士役义务,将被处以罚金。

⑤ "aid"(协助金),指领主需要金钱时,可合法向封臣要求协助金;通常由封臣自愿贡奉,但若领主要求合理,则不应拒绝。自大宪章始,协助金受到限制。

ransom: obtain the release of(a captive) by paying a sum of money

levy: impose

kingdom unless by common counsel① of our kingdom, except for ransoming our person, for making our eldest son a knight, and for once marrying our eldest daughter; and for these only a reasonable aid shall not be levied. Be it done in like manner concerning aids from the city of London.②

[13] And the city of London shall have all its ancient liberties and free customs as well by land as by water. Furthermore, we will and grant that all other cities, boroughs③, towns, and ports shall have all their liberties and free customs.

cause: to compel by command authority or force

[14] And to obtain the common counsel of the kingdom about the assessing of an aid(except in the three cases aforesaid) or of a scutage, we will cause to be summoned the archbishops, bishops, abbots, earls, and greater barons④, individually by our letters⑤ and, in addition, we will cause to be summoned generally through our sheriffs and bailiffs all those holding of us in chief-for a fixed date, namely, after the

---

① "common counsel"(王国大会),由国王召集高级教士、贵族和较小的直属封臣组成的会议。

② 关于 scutage 的征收,1216 年与 1217 年《大宪章》均未提及;1225 年《大宪章》第 37 条规定,"回到亨利二世时的传统"(Scutage shall be taken in future as it used to be taken in the time of king Henry our grandfather),见 Harry Rothwell ed., *English Historical Document, 1189~1327*, p.346.

③ "borough"(自治城镇),不应理解为现代市区;中世纪时,它指具有较高自治度的城镇,享有某些司法与行政特权。这些特权来自从国王或其他领主获得的特许状。获得此种特许状得支付金钱。

④ "Greater barons"指较大的直属封臣(tenants-in-chief),区别于小的直属封臣。之所以有此区分,是因为直属封臣并不足以赋予其男爵封号,他可能从国王处直接保有土地,却只是一个骑士。用以区别大小的具体标准尚不明了。所可知者,是大、小直属封臣在三方面的区别:前者直接将赋税缴纳至国王的财政署,后者通过郡守代缴;行军作战时,前者自带扈从与麾下,后者通过郡守召集;出席王室法庭,前者由国王直接召集,后者通过郡守召集。参见梅特兰:《英格兰宪政史》,李红海译,北京:中国政法大学出版社,2010 年,第 45 页。

⑤ 这里的"letters"须与后文中的"letter"区分,二者发出者与接收者均不同。前者以国王名义直接发送至大的直属封臣,是专门向某人发出的信函;后者通过郡守或执行官向小的直属封臣发出,无特定对象,是一般性召集令。

expiry of at least forty days, and at a fixed place; and in all letters of such summons we will specify the reason for the summons. And when the summons has thus been made, the business shall proceed on the day appointed, according to the counsel of those present, though not all have come who were summoned.①

[15] We will not in future grant anyone the right to take an aid from his free men, except for ransoming his person, for making his eldest son a knight and for once marrying his eldest daughter; and for these only a reasonable aid shall be levied.

[16] No one shall be compelled to do greater service for a knight's fee or for any other free holding than is due from it.

[17] Common pleas shall not follow our court②, but shall be held in some fixed place.

[18] Recognitions of novel disseisin, of *mort d'ancestor*, and of *darrein presentment*③, shall not be held elsewhere than in the counties to which they relate, and in this manner we, or, if we should be out of the realm, our chief justiciar, will send two justices through each county four times a year, who

novel: of recent

disseisin: the state of being deprived of seisin (or possession) of land

① 第14、15条不见于1216年《大宪章》。

② "court"本意为宫廷,这里指王座法庭,强调民事诉讼的审理不得随宫驾的移动而移动,需在某一确定的地点听审。这一条显示出王座法庭与皇家民事法庭的区别。前者陪王伴驾,随国王移动;后者在威斯敏斯特坐堂问案。

③ 此处"novel disseisin"、"mort d'ancestor"、"darrein presentmen"均与土地所有权相关。"novel disseisin"指最近发生的对土地所有权的剥夺或中止,法律上称为"新近地产剥夺案"。"mort d'ancestor"指继承人尚未有机会获得祖先遗留之土地时,该土地所有权就被剥夺,又称"先人地产剥夺案"。"darrein presentme"意指某教堂出现职位空缺时,有田产者可通过向该教堂捐赠土地,获得职位举荐或任职权(the right of appointing to a vacant church)。设若不止一人为求某职位捐赠土地,解决争端的方式是依据捐赠早晚,将职位举荐权裁定给最近一次的捐赠人。此类纠纷称为"教堂职位捐赠案"。参见 William Sharp McKechnie, *Magna Carta: A Commentary on the Great Charter of King John*, pp.274~275.

with four knights of each county chosen by the county, shall hold the said assizes[①] in the county and on the day and in the place of meeting of the county court.

[19] And if the said assizes cannot all be held on the day of the county court, there shall stay behind as many of the knights and freeholders who were present at the county court on that day as are necessary for the sufficient making of judgments, according to the amount of business to be done.

amerce: punish with an arbitrary penalty, fine

[20] A free man shall not be amerced for a trivial offence except in accordance with the degree of the offence, and for a grave offence he shall be amerced in accordance with its gravity, yet saving his way of living; and a merchant in the same way, saving his stock-in-trade; and a villein shall be amerced in the same way, saving his meanings of livelihood — if they have fallen into our mercy: and none of the aforesaid amercements shall be imposed except by the oath of good men of the neighborhood.

villein: a person who is bound to the land and owned by the feudal lord

[21] Earls and barons shall not be amerced except by their peers[②], and only in accordance with the degree of the offence.

[22] No clerk shall be amerced in respect of his lay holding except after the manner of the others aforesaid and not according to the amount of his ecclesiastical benefice.

---

① "assize"首先指国王召集的贵族会议,后用来指在这些会议上制订的法令,以及经此法令而创设的制度。有时还指国王派出的巡回法庭,如此处。

② 这是封建贵族坚持权利的表现。封建社会中,作为附庸的贵族所珍视的权利之一,是由与其地位平等的贵族决定其命运。这就意味着,他们倘若犯罪也只愿意在领主法庭接受与其地位平等的其他附庸的审判。后文第39、52、56、57、59条关于同侪审判或裁决的规定,均为这种平等观的反映。

[23] No vill[①] or individual shall be compelled to make bridges at river banks, except those who from of old are legally bound to do so.

[24] No sheriff, constable, coroners, or others of our bailiffs, shall hold pleas of our crown.[②]

[25] All counties, hundred, wapentakes, and trithings[③] shall be at the old rents without any additional payment, except our demesne manors.[④]

demesne: manorial land possessed by lord and not held by tenants

manor: a large country house on a large piece of land

[26] If anyone holding a lay fief of us die and our sheriff or bailiff shows our letters patent of summons for a debt that the deceased owed us, it shall be lawful for our sheriff or bailiff to attach and make a list of chattels of the deceased found upon the lay fief to the value of that debt under the supervision of law-worthy men, provided that none of the chattels shall be removed until the debt which is manifest has been paid to us in full; and the residue shall be left to the executors for carrying out the will of the deceased. And if nothing is owing to us from him, all the chattels shall accrue to the deceased, saving to his wife and children their reasonable shares.

accrue: come as a natural increase

[27] If any free man dies without leaving a will, his chattels shall be distributed by his nearest kinsfolk and friends under supervision of the church, saving to every one the debts

kinsfolk: a person's blood relations

① "vill"即 village,村邑,有时也指市镇,因市镇往往由村邑转变而来。

② "coroner"(验尸官),设立于 1194 年,由郡选举产生。验尸官以守护国王财产为职责,负责调查突然死亡者的死因,决定是否没收死者遗产或对其加以征税。

③ "county(郡)、hundred(百户区)、wagentake(邑),trithing(小区,亦称 riding)",英格兰行政区划划分单位。不过,在英格兰东北部某些地区,如林肯和约克郡,百户区不称为 hundred,而称为 wagentake。

④ 第 25 条不见于 1216 年《大宪章》。

which the deceased owed him.①

[28] No constable or other bailiff of ours shall take anyone's corn or other chattels unless he pays on the spot in cash for them or can delay payment by arrangement with the seller.②

[29] No constable shall compel any knight to give money instead of castle-guard if he is willing to do the guard himself or through another good man, if for some good reason he cannot do it himself; and if we lead or send him on military service, he shall be excused guard in proportion to the time that because of us he has been on service.

[30] No sheriff, or bailiff of ours, or anyone else shall take the horses or carts of any free man for transport work save with agreement of that free man.

[31] Neither we nor our bailiffs shall take, for our castles or for any other work of ours, timber which is not ours, except with the agreement of him whose timber it is.

[32] We will not hold for more than a year and a day the lands of those convicted of felony, and then the lands shall be handed over to the lords of the fiefs.

felony: a grave crime formerly differing from a misdemeanor under English common law

[33] Henceforth all fish-weirs shall be cleared completely from the Thames and Medway③ and throughout all England, except along the sea coast.

weir: an enclosure of stakes set in a stream as a trap for fish

① 第27条不见于1216年《大宪章》。

② 白居易有诗《卖炭翁》："翩翩两骑来是谁？黄衣使者白衫儿。手把文书口称敕，回车叱牛牵向北。一车炭，千馀斤，宫使驱将惜不得。半疋红纱一丈绫，系向牛头充碳直。"这是对唐朝宫市的记载。英国约翰王时代，宫市亦存在。国王及其臣仆不仅在市场上享有优先购买权，且可只出最低价。至于何时付款则由买主而定，这意味着会有不付款的事情发生。

③ "Medway"，即River Medway（梅德韦河），泰晤士河的一条较大支流。河流上构筑堰坝、鱼梁（捕鱼用），可能造成河道堵塞，影响航运、贸易，故而有此一条。

[34] The writ called *Praecipe* shall not in future be issued to anyone in respect of any holding whereby a free man may lose his court①.

[35] Let there be one measure for wine throughout our kingdom, and one measure for ale; and one measure for corn, namely "the London quarter"; and one width of cloth whether dyed, russet or halberget, namely two ells within the selvedges. Let it be the same with weights as measures.

[36] Nothing shall be given or taken in future for the writ of inquisition of life or limbs; instead it shall be granted free of charge and not refused.

praecipe: a writ demanding action or an explanation of non-action

whereby: by which; according to which

russet: coarse homespun usually reddish-brown cloth

halberget: a tunic of chain mail worn as defensive armor from the 12th to the 14th century; hauberk. tunic: a loose garment, typically sleeveless and reaching to the knees, as worn in ancient Greece and Rome

ell: a former measure of length (equivalent to six hand breadths) used mainly for textiles, typically about 45 inches in England and 37 inches in Scotland

selvedge: an edge produced on woven fabric during manufacture that prevents it from unraveling

① "praecipe"(责成令),指御前大臣签署的要求某人做某事或为其不做某事陈明理由的令状。这里指的是国王无视封建领主的司法管辖权,责成御前大臣下达令状给郡长,指示郡长干涉封建法庭对土地持有案的裁决,责令被告将涉案土地退还原告,否则,该法庭须向王室法庭解释其为何不执行郡长之令。通过这种令状,原由郡法庭、百户区法庭以及封建法庭处理的自由民之间的民事纠纷纳入王室法庭的司法管辖权,实属王室法庭司法管辖权的扩张。在封建贵族们看来,此为王权对封臣权利的侵夺,因此大为不满。

[37] If anyone holds of us by fee-farm, by socage①, or by burgage, or holds land of another by knight's service, we will not, by reason of that fee-farm, socage, or burgage, have the wardship of his heir or of land of his that is of the fief of the other; nor will we have custody of the fee-farm, socage, or burgage, unless such fee-farm owes knight service. We will not have custody of anyone's heir or hand which he holds of another by knight service by reason of any petty serjeanty② which he holds of us by the service of rendering to us knives or arrows or the like.

burgage: a tenure by which real property in England was held under the king or a lord for a yearly rent or for watching and warding

[38] No bailiff shall in future put anyone to trial upon his own bare word, without reliable witnesses produced for this purposes.

[39] No free men shall be arrested or imprisoned or disseised or outlawed or exiled or in any way victimised, neither will we attack him or send anyone to attack him, except by the lawful judgment of his peers or by the law of the land.③

disseise: dispossess wrongfully, especially by force

[40] To no one will we sell, to no one will we refuse or delay right or justice.

[41] All merchants shall be go out of and come into

① "socage"(农役保有),土地保有方式;以此方式保有土地者,其义务为耕种土地、缴纳田租,但不服兵役。"socage"一词来源于"sock ",后者意为犁铧。农役保有方式之下是农奴保有(villenagium),即由农奴耕种土地、缴纳地租。它与农役保有相区别者,是后者属自由保有,保有者为自由民,其人身与权益受王室法庭保护。而农奴保有被王室法庭视仅仅为依据领主意志而保有的土地,不对保有者实施保护。以农奴保有方式保有土地者无人身自由,不能离开领主的土地;未经领主同意,禁止出卖其牛马,也不得擅自出嫁其女儿;嫁女须向领主缴纳罚金。他死时,还须将最好的牲口上交领主,弥补因其死亡给领主造成的劳动力损失。

② "serjeanty"(侍君役保有),土地保有方式;以此方式获得封土者,其向国王所尽义务不是提供能够作战的骑士,而是承担举旗、捧剑、担任官职、或提供军事器械等责任。篇首所提"steward(总管),servant(家臣),bailiff(执行官)"等,均属以侍君役方式保有土地者。

③ 第39条是1215《大宪章》最为重要的条款之一,1225年《大宪章》中将之与下文第40条合并,列为第29条。可参见 Harry Rothwell ed., *English Historical Document, 1189~1327*, p.345.

England safely and securely and stay and travel throughout England, as well by land as by water, for buying and selling by the ancient and right customs free from all evil tolls, except in time of war and if they are of the land that is at war with us. And if such are found in our land at the beginning of a war, they shall be attached, without injury to their persons or goods, until we, or our chief justiciar, know how merchants of our land are treated who were found in the land at war with us when war broke out; and if ours are safe there, the others shall be safe in our land.

toll: a charge payable to use a bridge or road

[42] It shall be lawful in future for anyone, without prejudicing the allegiance due to us, to leave our kingdom and return safely and securely by land and water, save in the public interest, for a short period in time of war—except for those imprisoned or outlawed in accordance with the law of the kingdom and natives of a land that it is at war with us and merchants (who shall be treated as aforesaid).①

allegiance: loyalty

[43] If anyone who holds of some escheat② such as the honor③ of Wallingford, Nottingham, Boulogne, Lancaster, or of other escheats which are in our hands and are baronies dies, his heir shall give no other relief and do other service to us than he would have done to the baron if that barony had been in the baron's hands; and we will hold it in the same manner in which the baron held it.

---

① 第 42 条不见于 1216 年《大宪章》。

② "escheat"(土地复归),属领主权利;指封臣去世时如无继承人,其土地复归领主,任领主任意处置。换言之,土地继承由领主而非封臣决定。这是中世纪西欧关于土地所有权的一个重要特征,即土地不能通过遗嘱而继承,未经国王允许,直属封臣不得转让土地。大宪章也没有改变这一点。

③ "honor"指男爵或其他大贵族所拥有的田地、庄园等。

implead: to sue or prosecute at law

[44] Men who live outside the forest need not henceforth come before our justices of the forest upon a general summons, unless they are impleaded or are sureties of any person or persons who are attached for forest offences.①

[45] We will not make justices, constables, sheriffs or bailiffs save of such as know the law of the kingdom and mean to observe it well.②

abbey: the monastery run by an abbot; a convent run by an abbess; a church that is connected to other buildings where monks or nuns live

[46] All barons who have founded abbeys for which they have charters of the kings of England or ancient tenure shall have the custody of them during vacancies, as they ought to have.

[47] All forests that have been made forest in our time shall be immediately disafforsted; and so be it done with riverbanks that have been made preserves by us in our time.③

inquire into (sth): to gather or collect information about sth

[48] All evil customs connected with forests and warrens, foresters and warreners, sheriffs and their officials, riverbanks and their wardens shall immediately be inquired into in each county by twelve sworn knights of the same county who are to be chosen by good men of the same county, and within forty days of the completion of the inquiry shall be abolished by them so as never to be restored, provided that we, or our

① 亨利二世曾规定，所有贵族、主教接到森林法庭首席法官召唤后，均须出席森林巡回法庭。

② 第45条不见于1216年《大宪章》。

③ 威廉征服以前，国王便有权将某处林地圈为御林，供其狩猎。为维护国王捕猎权，特派遣御林官监管。亨利一世明确规定，凡入御林捕猎赤鹿(red deer)、小鹿(fallow deer)、牝鹿(roe)、野猪等动物，将被处以罚金；附近居民仅允许在内捕猎兔子、狐狸、狼、獾(badger)、野猫(wildcat)等，且须事先禀告御林官；砍伐林木、捡取柴火、放养家畜等，皆有特定限制。亨利二世即位，又设立森林法官与森林巡回法庭(forest eyre)，以执行森林法规。12世纪下半叶，被圈为王家林苑的土地大面积扩张；森林巡回法庭由此获得的年收入约为2000磅。W.L.Warren, *The Governance of Norman and Angevin England, 1086~1272*, London: Edward Arnold, 1987, pp.160~162.

justiciar if we are not in England, know of it first.①

[49] We will immediately return all hostages and charters given to us by Englishmen, as security for peace or faithful service.

[50] We will remove completely from office the relations of Gerard de Athée so that in future they shall have no office in England, namely, Engelard de Cigogné②, Peter and Guy and Andrew de Chanceaux, Guy de Cigogné, Geoffrey de Martigny and his brothers, Philip Marc and his brothers and his nephew Geoffrey, and all their following.

[51] As soon as peace is restored, we will remove from the kingdom all foreign knights, cross-bowmen, serjeants, and mercenaries, who have come with horses and arms to the detriment of the kingdom.

crossbowmen: persons who carry crossbow which is a weapon that shoots arrows and that consists of a short bow attached to a longer piece of wood

serjeant: sergeant; an officer of low rank in the army

to the detriment of: in a way that is harmful to

[52] If anyone has been disseised of or kept out of his lands, castles, franchises or his right by us without the legal judgment of his peers, we will immediately restore them to him③; and if a dispute arises over this, then let it be decided by the judgment of the twenty-five barons who are mentioned below in the clause for securing the peace④: for all the things, however, which anyone has been disseised or kept out of without the lawful judgment of his peers by King Henry, our father, or by King Richard, our brother, which we have in our hand or are held by others, to whom we are bound to warrant

franchise: freedom or immunity from some burden or restriction vested in a person or group; a special privilege granted to an individual or group

① 第 48~53 条悉不见于 1216 年《大宪章》。

② Engelard 是 Gerard 的侄儿,当时任温莎城堡警卫长以及附近某处王家林苑的御林官,忠诚于约翰王,手段高强。反叛贵族恨之入骨,必欲除之。

③ 这里涉及的是王家法庭侵夺了地方领主在其领地上的司法权。

④ 此 25 人参见第 61 条。

them, we will have the usual period of respite of crusaders, excepting those things about which a plea was started or an inquest made by our command before we took the cross①; when however we return from our pilgrimage, or if by any chance we do not go on it, we will at once do full justice therein.

respite: a period of temporary delay

do justice: to treat or show something or someone that is as good as it should be

[53] We will have the same respite, and in the same manner, in the doing of justicein the matter of the disafforesting or retaining of the forests which Henry our father or Richard our brother afforested, and in the matter of the wardship of lands which are of the fief of another, wardships of which sort we have hitherto had by reason of a fief which anyone held of us by knight service, and in the matter of abbeys founded on the fief of another, not on a fief of our own, in which the lord of the fief claims he has a right; and when we have returned, or if we do not set out on our pilgrimage, we will at once do full justice to those who complain of these things.

amercement: an action of amercing amerce: to punish by a fine whose amount is fixed by the court

[54] No one shall be arrested or imprisoned upon the appeal of a woman for the death of anyone except her husband.

remit: to cancel

[55] All fines made with us unjustly and against the law of the land, and all amercements② imposed unjustly and against the law of the land, shall be entirely remitted, or else let them be settled by the judgment of the twenty-five barons

① "took the cross"指参加十字军东征。

② 13世纪,"fine"与"amercement"有重要区别。列亚历山大·布里尔所著《法律词汇辞典》原文如下:A fine was a certain punishment, growing expressly out of some statute, and was always imposed and assessed by the court; an amercement was imposed by the court in general terms, and was afterwards assessed or moderated, and reduced to a certain sum, by the peers or equals of the party. 见 Alexander Burrill, *A Law Dictionary and Glossary*, New York: Baker Voorhis & Co., Law Publishers, 1867, p.93.

whom are mentioned below in the clause for securing the peace, or by the judgment of the majority of the same, along with the aforesaid Stephen, archbishop of Canterbury, if he can be present, and such others as he may wish to associate with himself for this purpose, and if he cannot be present the business shall nevertheless proceed without him, provided that if any one or more of the aforesaid twenty-five barons are in a like suit, they shall be removed from the judgment of the case in question, and others chosen, sworn and put in their place by the rest of the same twenty-five for this case only.①

[56] If we have disseised or kept out Welshmen from lands or liberties or other things without the legal judgment of their peers in England or in Wales, they shall be immediately restored to them; and if a dispute arises over this, then let it be decided in the March by the judgment of their peers-for holdings in England according to the law of England, for holdings in Wales according to the law of Wales, and for holdings in the March according to the law of the March. Welshmen shall do the same to us and ours.②

march: an area of land on the border between two countries or territories, especially between England and Wales or (formerly) England and Scotland

[57] For all the things, however, which any Welshman was disseised of or kept out of without the lawful judgment of his peers by King Henry, our father, or King Richard, our brother, which we have in our hand or which are held by others, to whom we are bound to warrant them, we will have the usual period of respite of crusaders, excepting those things about which a plea was started or an inquest made by our com-

① 第55条不见于1216年《大宪章》。

② 此处涉及的"土地与自由权"系指亨利二世、理查德一世以来,英国国王从威尔士夺去者。

mand before we took the cross; when however we return, or if by any chance we do not set out to our pilgrimage, we will at once do full justice to them in accordance with the laws of the Welsh and the foresaid regions.①

[58] We will give back at once the son of Llywelyn and all the hostages from Wales and the charters that were handed over to us as security for the peace.②

hostage: a person taken by force to secure the taker's demands

[59] We will act toward Alexander, king of the Scots, concerning the return of his sisters and hostages and concerning his franchises and his right, in the same manner in which we act towards our other barons of England, unless it ought to be otherwise by the charters which we have from William his father, formerly king of the Scots, and this shall be determined by the judgment of his peers in our court.③

[60] All these aforesaid customs and liberties which we have granted to be observed in our kingdom as far as it pertains to us towards our men, all of our kingdom, clerks as well as laymen, shall observe as far as it pertains to them towards their men.

allay: to make sth less severe or strong

discord: an unpleasant combination of musical notes; lack of agreement between people, ideas, etc

[61] Since, moreover, for God and the betterment of our kingdom and for the better allaying of the discord that has arisen between us and our barons we have granted all these

① 第57~59条不见于1216年《大宪章》。

② Llywelyn，即Lywelyn ap Iorweith（卢埃林·阿普·约尔沃思）：威尔士诸侯，娶约翰王私生女为妻。1212年9月，卢埃林联盟法国，反叛约翰王，旋即被弹压。因此反叛之故，原已在约翰手中充作人质的28名贵族子弟被绞杀。叛乱平息后，卢埃林之子与其他一些威尔士贵族的子弟被约翰王拘为人质。《大宪章》制订之时，卢埃林参与其中，为威尔士人争得三项权利，即第56、57、58条。

③ 与英格兰贵族联盟而迫使约翰王署印《大宪章》者，除威尔士贵族，尚有苏格兰贵族。这一条即为苏格兰贵族参与联盟而获得的好处。

aforesaid, wishing them to enjoy the use of them unimpaired and unshaken for ever, we give and grant them the under-written security, namely, that the barons shall choose any twenty-five barons of the kingdom they wish, who must with all their might observe, hold and cause to be observed, the peace and liberties which we have granted and confirmed to them by this present charters of ours, so that if we, or our justiciar, or our bailiffs or any one of our servants offend in any way against anyone or transgress any of the articles of the peace or the security and the offense be notified to four of the aforesaid twenty-five barons, those four barons shall come to us, or to our justiciar if we are out of the kingdom, and, laying the transgression before us, shall petition us to have that transgression corrected without delay. And if we do not correct the transgression, or if we are out of the kingdom, if our justiciar does not correct it, within forty days, reckoning from the time it was brought to our notice or to that of our justiciar if we were out of the kingdom, the aforesaid four barons shall refer that case to the rest of the twenty-five barons and those twenty-five barons together with the community of the whole land shall distrain and distress us in every way they can, namely, by seizing castles, lands, possessions, and in such other ways as they can, saving our person and the persons of our queen and our children, until, in their opinion, amends have been made; and when amends have been made, they shall obey us as they did before. And let anyone in the land who wishes take an oath to obey the orders of the said twenty-five barons for the execution of all the aforesaid matters, and with them to distress us as much as he can, and we publicly and freely give

distress: to force by inflicting pain

leave: permission to do sth

of ones own accord: voluntarily; without being asked or forced

consent (to sth): give agreement of permission

procure: to get sth by effort

concession: privilege; the act of conceding; sth conceded or granted; acknowledgement

remit: to release from the guilt or penalty of

rancour, also rancor: an angry feeling of hatred; bitter deep-seated ill will

anyone leave to take the oath who wishes to take it and we will never prohibit anyone from taking it. Indeed, all those in the land who are unwilling of themselves and of their own accord to take an oath to the twenty-five barons to help them to distrain and distress us, we will make them take the oath as aforesaid at our command. And if any of the twenty-five barons dies or leaves the country or is in any other way prevented from carrying out the things aforesaid, the rest of the aforesaid twenty-five barons shall choose as they think fit another one in his place, and he shall take the oath like the rest. In all matters the execution of which is committed to these twenty-five barons, if it should happen that these twenty-five are present yet disagree among themselves about anything, or if some of those summoned will not or can not be present, that shall be held as fixed and established which the majority of those present ordained or commanded, exactly as if the twenty-five had consented to it; and the said twenty-five shall swear that they will faithfully observe all the things aforesaid and will do all they can to get them observed. And we will procure nothing from anyone, either personally or through anyone else, whereby any of these concessions and liberties might be revoked or diminished; and if any such thing is procured, let it be void and null, and we will never use it personally or through another.①

[62] And we have fully remitted and pardoned to everyone all the ill-will, indignation and rancour that have arisen

① 此条款通称“保障条款”(the form of security)，系《大宪章》中唯一关于如何执行上述所列自由权的条款。第61~63条不见于1216年《大宪章》。

between us and our men, clergy and laity, from the time of the quarrel. Furthermore, we have fully remitted to all, clergy and laity, and as far as pertains to us have completely forgiven, all trespasses occasioned by the same quarrel between Easter in the sixteenth year of our reign and the restoration of peace. And, besides, we have caused to be made for them letters testimonial patent of the lord Stephen archbishop of Canterbury, of the lord Henry archbishop of Dublin and of the aforementioned bishops and of master Pandulf about this security and the aforementioned concessions.

trespass: sin; wrongdoing

[63] Wherefore we wish and firmly enjoin that the English church shall be free, and that the men in our kingdom shall have and hold all the aforesaid liberties, rights, and concessions well and peacefully, freely and quietly, fully and completely, for themselves and their heirs from us and our heirs, in all matters and in all places for ever, as is aforesaid. An oath, moreover, has been taken, as well on our part as on the part of the barons, that all these conditions aforesaid shall be observed in good faith and without evil disposition. Witness the above-mentioned and many others. Given by our hand in the meadow which is called Runnymede between Windsor and Staines on the fifteenth day of June, in the seventeenth year of our reign①.

enjoin: to direct or impose by authoritative order or with urgent admonition

disposition: tendency to act or think in a particular way

① 1199 年,理查德去世,约翰即位。

译 文

1215年《大宪章》[①]

朕，约翰，蒙上帝恩惠之英格兰国王兼爱尔兰领主、诺曼底公爵、阿基坦公爵、安茹伯爵致意大主教、主教们、各修道院院长、诸伯爵、男爵、法官、护林官、郡守、总管、家臣以及全体执行官与忠实臣民：

朕敬天明命，为吾等灵魂之拯救与朕之先人、子嗣之灵魂拯救，为上帝之荣耀与神圣教会之隆福，以及国家之改良，听从奏议，制定宪章，咨尔臣民。

上奏请制者，有吾等敬重之神父：坎特伯雷大主教、全英首席主教与神圣罗马教会枢机主教斯蒂芬；都柏林大主教亨利；伦敦主教威廉；温切斯特主教彼得；巴斯与格拉斯顿伯里主教乔斯林；林肯主教休；伍斯特主教沃尔特；考文垂主教威廉；罗切斯特主教本尼迪克特；长老、副执事与教皇家族之成员潘道夫；修士、英格兰圣殿骑士团教会长老艾默里克。

并有吾等敬重之贵族：彭布罗克之威廉·马歇尔伯爵；索尔兹伯里之威廉伯爵；沃伦之威廉伯爵；阿伦德尔之威廉伯爵；苏格兰加洛韦之治安官阿兰；杰拉德之子瓦林·杰拉德[②]；赫伯特之子彼得·赫伯特；波伊图之总管休伯特·德·伯格；休·德·内维尔；赫伯特之子马修·赫伯特；托马斯·巴西特；阿兰·巴西特；菲利普·德·奥布尼；罗普斯莱之罗伯特；约翰·马歇尔；休之子

---

① 译文参考了3个正式版本：2002年版《不列颠百科全书》第10卷"大宪章"词条（漆国淦译）、商务印书馆2016年版《大宪章》（陈国华译）、2002年台湾若望保禄二世和平研究中心《英国大宪章今译》（雷敦龢译）。

② 对照原文，可知瓦林·杰拉德（Warin Gerold）的姓氏前有前缀"fitz"（意为"····之子"）插入其中，笔者未取其音，译为"费兹"，而取其义，译为"···之子"，目的是为说明"fitz"的原义。实则在了解原意的基础上，改译为瓦林·费兹·杰拉德，并无不可。恰如法国人、西班牙人姓名中表示有贵族血统的"de"、"don"通常被译为"德"、"堂"一样。

约翰·休;以及其他人等。

宪章诏告如下:

第1条　朕以及朕之千秋后嗣,首先向上帝允诺并经此宪章确认:英国教会应予自由,其权利仍旧不动,其自由权不得侵犯。此乃我等意愿遵行之。实则在朕与诸男爵发生争执前,英国教会所认为最重要与最必需之选举自由权,已由朕自愿同意、主动赐予,并经由宪章确认与教皇英诺森三世首肯。朕与后世诸君当永持诚意、遵从宪章。朕亦代表我等及千秋子嗣,将下列全部自由权赐予王国所有自由民,俾其得以世世享有与维护。

第2条　任何伯爵、男爵或其他以骑士役保有获朕之土地的直属臣等身故时,其继承人已达成年并欠有封地继承金者,应以缴纳旧时继承金之数额而承受其遗产,即,伯爵继承人为承受其全部领地,应缴100镑;男爵继承人缴100镑;骑士继承人缴100先令。依据采地之旧有习惯,所欠者少,所纳亦少。

第3条　然则上述继承人系未成年且受监护者,当其成年时,应直接继承其遗产,无须缴纳封地继承金或因恢复其被剥夺的继承权而缴纳金钱。

第4条　未成年继承人之土地监管人只应从该土地之岁入中收取合理份额、要求恰当之税金与劳役,且不应造成人与物的毁损。如朕将该土地监护权委托于郡守或任何负责为朕收取土地岁入者,当其使监管之物毁损,朕得要求补偿,并将该土地另交与该采邑2位端方人士,负责为朕或朕所指定之人收取土地所得。如朕等将该土地监管权授予或售予任何人,而其人使土地受损、荒废,其人将丧失该监管权。此监管权亦因转而授予该采地2位端方人士,为朕负上述相似责任。

第5条　复次,当其监管期内,监管人须从土地岁入中抽取部分费用,以维护与修缮房屋、园地、鱼塘、池沼、磨坊及其他依附于土地之物。至继承人成年,监护人应将土地、各季农务所需之锄犁与其他农具系数归于该土地继承人,该土地所可合理产出之收入亦应归于该土地继承人。

第6条　继承人须在不贬抑身份之条件下结婚,然婚约议定前,应通知该继承人之最近亲属。

第7条　寡妇应在丈夫亡故后即刻得其陪嫁之资与遗产,不受留难;且无须以任何物事报偿其所得——丈夫留给寡妇终身为用的土地、陪嫁之资或夫妻二人在丈夫去世之日所继承的遗产。夫死之后,寡妇可在夫宅居住 40 日。40 日内,应将丈夫留归其用的土地交与之。

第 8 条　寡妇情愿孀居时,不得强其改嫁。唯该寡妇持有朕之所封采邑时,应以未得朕之许可决不改嫁为担保;她若从其他领主获得领地,改嫁时亦须得其领主同意。

第 9 条　债务人之动产足以偿债时,朕与朕之执行官均不得强取其土地或租金以抵偿债务;只要首要债务人本人能偿债,不得扣押该债务人之担保人财产。如该债务人未能偿付债务且无他物用以偿债,担保人须代为偿还。担保人如愿意,可以扣押该债务人之土地与租金收入,直至其所代偿之债务得以偿还为止。然在首要债务人可以证明:其在债务上已无负于担保人时,担保人不得扣押其财产。

第 10 条　凡向犹太人借债,无论数额大小,借债人于还债前亡故而其继承人未达成年时,该债务不得负有利息,无论该继承人从何人手中持有其土地。设若债权归朕所有,朕将以收取契据上载明之本金为限。

第 11 条　凡对犹太人欠有债务者亡故时,其妻应享有丈夫留归其用的土地,无须偿还该债务。如该亡故者遗有未成年子女,须依据死者所持土地多寡而为其子女留出生活所必需,剩余部分用于偿债,然其应向领主提供劳役之义务保留不变。所欠非犹太人之债务,照相同方式办理。

第 12 条　除非经由王国大会同意,除下列 3 项外,不得在朕之王国征收军役税或协助金。

①赎回朕之人身所需者。

②朕之长子受封骑士所需者。

③朕之长女出嫁所需者。

为上述 3 项所征之数额,务求适当。向伦敦市征收相关协助金,同法办理。

第 13 条　伦敦市之古老自由权与自由通关权,悉应保有,水陆皆然。其他城市、自治城镇、乡镇、港口之自由权与自由通关权,朕亦一并承认,悉应保有。

第14条　为就征收协助金(上述三项除外)与代役税而召开王国大会,朕须逐一向各大主教、主教、修道院院长、伯爵、男爵发出诏书,并饬由各郡守、执行官统一向所有由朕处直接保有土地之臣属发出诏书,告知其开会日期(此日期须定在诏书下达至少40日之后)与开会地点。召集缘由,应于诏书内明述之。召集完毕,于议事之日,不论被召集者是否全部到会,应据与会者之意见,议决所议之事。

第15条　朕今将不许任何贵族向其自由民征收补助金,唯下列情形不在此限:

①赎回该贵族之人身所需者。

②该贵族长子受封骑士所需者。

③该贵族长女出嫁所需者。

为上述3项所征之数额,务求适当。

第16条　不得强迫持有骑士领地或其他自由保有地之人服额外之役。

第17条　普通诉讼不得向王座法院提起,但应于指定地点受理之。

第18条　"最近地产剥夺案"、"先人地产剥夺案"、"教堂职位捐赠案"之认定与审理,不可在土地所在地之外的郡法院举行。每郡须由朕派遣法官2人,每年4次,如朕不在国内,则由大法官代派,会同每郡推举之骑士4人,在该郡郡法院与开庭之日进行巡回审理与裁决。

第19条　如上述巡回审理不能于郡法院开庭之日举行,出席当日庭审之人中,须有足够人数之骑士与自由土地持有人留下,改日再行裁决,人数多少视事务多寡而定。

第20条　自由民犯轻罪,所受罚金须与其犯罪程度相当。犯重罪者,亦应视罪之轻重处以罚金,然需为其保留生计。商人与自由农被告上朕之法庭,亦须同法办理:处罚商人,留存其经营手段;处罚自由农,豁免其农具。上述处罚,未经邻里良善之人宣誓证明,不得科处。

第21条　伯爵与男爵犯罪者,须由其贵族同侪审判;科处罚金,须与其犯罪程度相当。

第22条　牧师犯罪者,须照上述之人处罚办法,对其世俗财产处以罚金,神职俸禄不得计在其内。

第 23 条　不得强迫任何村庄或个人修筑河上桥梁，唯历来负筑桥职责者，不在此限。

第 24 条　郡守、保安官、验尸官或朕之执行官中的其他官员，不得受理刑事诉讼。

第 25 条　全国各郡、百户区、小邑及小区之地租收取，依据原来标准，不得增加。朕之自有庄园不在此限。

第 26 条　凡受朕之世俗封地者亡故时，若郡守或执行官持有朕对该亡故者索要欠款之特许函件，并在公正人士监督下，扣押并登记与债务价值相当的该亡故者之动产，是为合法。然在债务完全清偿前，该动产不得转移。清偿完毕，所余之产，须交与遗嘱执行人，依照死者遗嘱处置。如死者不欠朕任何债务，其动产除酌情留与其妻室子女外，悉应归于死者。

第 27 条　自由民未立遗嘱而亡，其动产须在教会监督下，扣除所有债务后，由其最近之亲属与朋友分配。

第 28 条　朕之任何保安官或其他执行官，未经当场付与现金，不得拿取任何人之谷物或其他动产，除非卖者同意延期付款。

第 29 条　骑士如愿亲负守卫之责，或在理由正当、不能亲自守卫城堡而委托另一合格之人代行其职时，保安官不得强迫任何骑士给付金钱以替代守卫。骑士如奉召服役，其服役之天数可冲减守卫之天数。

第 30 条　郡守、朕之执行官或其他任何人，未经自由民同意，不得取其车、马以供运输。

第 31 条　朕或朕之执行官不得强取他人之木材以供建造城堡或其他私用，除非征得木材所有者同意。

第 32 条　被判重罪者，其土地被朕占有之时间，不得超过一年零一日。其后，须将土地交与封地之领主。

第 33 条　自现在起，泰晤士河、梅德韦河以及英国全境之堰坝或鱼梁将被全部拆除，沿海岸所建者除外。

第 34 条　今后，不得就土地持有案向任何人发出敕令，令之责成领主法庭判决被告退坏原告之土地，以免自由民丧失司法权利。

第 35 条　度量衡概应一律。葡萄酒、麦芽酒与谷物之计量标准，统一为伦敦夸脱。染色布、褐呢家纺布、锁子铠之尺幅,统一为织物两边间两厄尔[1]。

第36条　今后,验尸状须免费发放与获得,不得因之而索要财物;请求发给时,不得拒绝。

第37条　凡以固定地租[2]、农役保有或城区地租之方式从朕处保有土地,同时又以骑士役方式从另一领主处保有土地者,只要他缴纳固定地租、提供农役、或缴纳城区地租,朕便不再要求对其继承人的监护权;也不要求对他从另一领主处所保有之土地的监管权;除非以固定地租保有朕之土地者未为朕服骑士役,否则,朕不应要求对其保有之租地有监管权,以农役保有或以城区地租保有之土地,朕亦不应要求监管权。以侍君役方式保有朕之小块土地者,只要已为朕尽其供奉刀枪、弓箭等军械之役务,朕不得以其保有朕之土地为由,要求对其继承人的监护权;亦不得对其以骑士役方式从另一领主所保有之土地要求监管权。

第38条　今后,执行官未经提供可靠之证据,不得单凭其个人主张审判任何人。

第39条　凡自由民,除非经贵族或同侪依法判决或依照本国法律之规定,不得被扣留、监禁、剥夺财产、褫夺法律保护权、流放或以任何方式被伤害;朕亦不得对其加以攻击,或遣人攻击之。

第40条　对于任何人,朕不得出卖、拒绝或延搁权利与正义。

第41条　一切商人,皆可经水、陆两道安全出入、逗留或经过英格兰全境;依古老与正当之习惯,经商买卖,免于一切不合理之过路费。仅在战时对来自敌对国之商人例外。开战时,如有敌国商人在我境内寻获,于朕或朕之大法官知悉我国商人于战事爆发后在敌对国受何待遇之前,应扣留其人,但不得伤害其人身与货物。如本国商人在敌国安然无恙,敌国商人在我国亦安然无恙。

---

① 1伦敦夸脱指一个酒桶(ton)容量的四分之一,等于8蒲式耳(bushel),1蒲式耳等于8加仑(gallon),1加仑等于4.564升(litre)。1厄尔在英格兰相当于45英寸(inch),1英寸等于2.54厘米(centimeter),1厄尔相当于1.15米。2厄尔布幅宽度约为2.3米。

② 此处原文为"fee-farm",戚国淦先生译为"永代借地"、陈国华译为"固定费"(因"fee-farm"原意即指以每年约25%的固定租金而租赁来的土地)、雷敦龢译为"租金土地"。笔者参考陈、雷两译,译为"固定地租"。

第 42 条　今后，凡效忠于朕者，皆可经水、陆两道安全往返于本王国，唯战时短期内为公共利益计除外。然则依据我国法律被囚禁与被褫夺法律保护权者，以及敌国之侨民，不得享受此等往返安全之保证。敌对国之商人，照前述办法对待。

第 43 条　凡复归之领地，如瓦林福德、诺丁汉、布伦、兰开斯特的男爵领地，或其他在朕手中而又属于男爵领地者，其持有者亡故时，其继承人无须向朕另缴土地继承金，亦无须向朕承担役务；而须向持有该领地之男爵承担役务。朕保有该领地之方式与男爵保有之方式相同。

第 44 条　从今往后，居于御林之外者，不得由普通传票传唤，出庭森林法庭，除非其因触犯御林之规而被控告或为被控告者之担保人。

第 45 条　非为知晓本王国之法律并谨守法规者，不得被命为法官、保安官、郡守、执行官。

第 46 条　凡修造修道院并为之获英王颁与之特许状，或自先祖以来即保有该修道院之男爵，理当在其闲置时监管之。

第 47 条　凡朕登基以来由朕所圈之林地、所据之河岸，须立即解禁。

第 48 条　一切与御林及苑囿、御林官及苑长、郡守及其下属、河岸及河岸之守官相关之恶规，须立刻由该地良善之人推选 12 名本乡骑士宣誓就命后加以调查，调查结束 40 日内由其革除，务使其永不恢复。唯朕须事先得奏。若朕不在国内，须事先禀告朕之大法官。

第 49 条　国人交于朕之一切人质、特许状以为和平与忠君之担保、抵押者，须即交还。

第 50 条　杰拉德·德·阿泰亲属之职务，朕须全部解除之，务使彼等在英国永不叙用。他们是：昂基拉·德·西格涅、彼得·德·尚索、盖伊·德·尚索、安德鲁·德·尚索、盖伊·德·西格涅、杰弗里·德·马提尼及其诸兄弟、菲利普·马克与其诸兄弟以及其侄儿杰弗里、上述人等的所有追随者。

第 51 条　一俟和平恢复，所有携战马、武器而来祸害我国之外国骑士、弓箭手、随从、雇佣兵，均将由朕逐出英国。

第 52 条　任何人之未经贵族或同侪依法裁决而被朕强行收回或剥夺其土地、城堡、特许权或权利者，朕须立即予以归还或恢复。由此引发之争执，依下文和平保障之条款所载明25位男爵裁定。然则对未经贵族或同侪依法裁决而被朕之父亨利、兄理查德强行收回或剥夺之财产与权利,现由朕据有或在朕之担保下由他人据有者,朕将按十字军东征之通常期限延缓处理。唯于朕誓师东征前,诉讼已然提起或已以敕命审理者,不在此限。然则在朕远征、朝圣归来,或因故中止东征时,朕须即行妥善处置。

第53条　下列事由,朕将同样暂缓合理处置:朕之父亨利、兄理查德所圈之御林是否解禁或保留;原属他人之领地的监管权,当其因某人以骑士役方式保有朕之一块领地,从而由朕所得者;建于他人领地之上或不属于朕自有领地之上的修道院,该领地之主人声明对其所有者。俟朕东征、朝圣归来,或决定不拟东征时,朕须对此类申诉事由即行妥善处理。

第54条　任何人不得因妇人之控告其谋杀而被逮捕、监禁,除非被害死者乃该妇人之夫。

第55条　凡朕所科一切不当与违法之不定额与定额罚金,概应免除。如有争议,由下文和平保障之条款所载明25位男爵裁定解决;或由这些男爵会同坎特伯雷大主教斯蒂芬(如他能出席)及斯蒂芬所愿与共商此事者,依据大多数人意见裁决之。大主教不能出席时,此事亦应照常进行。但若上述25位男爵中有一人或多人为当事人,则应使其回避,由其余男爵另择他人宣誓就位,裁定争议。

第56条　凡威尔士人在英格兰或威尔士之土地、自由权或其他物,未经其同侪贵族合法裁决而由朕夺去者,朕须立即归还。由此引发之争执,依其同侪贵族之意见在英格兰与威尔士交界之地裁决:其地在英格兰者,依照英格兰法律;其地在威尔士者,依照威尔士法律;其地在交界之地者,依交界地法律。威尔士人持有朕以及英国人之土地、财产者,同法办理。

第57条　但是,威尔士人之未经其同侪贵族依法裁决而被朕之父王亨利、王兄理查德强行收回或剥夺之财产与权利,现由朕据有或在朕之担保下由他人据有者,朕将按十字军东征之通常期限延缓处理。唯于朕誓师东征前,诉讼已然提起或已以敕命审理者,不在此限。然则在朕远征、朝圣归来,或因故不拟东征时,朕须依据威尔士以及交界地区之法律即行妥善处置。

第58条　卢埃林之子以及威尔士人交于朕之一切人质、特许状以为和平之担保者，须即交还。

第59条　至于归还苏格兰王亚历山大之姊妹与人质、恢复其特许权与权利，朕之处理办法与朕对待英国其他男爵相同，除非其父威廉——苏格兰先王——交与朕之特许状表明需另法办理。此事须由其在朕之朝廷的同侪贵族决定。

第60条　上述一切惯例与自由权，由朕施予，颁行于国，朕与朕之直属臣属遵行之；王国之内，无论僧俗，其与其附属间的关系，亦当遵行上述一切惯例与自由权。

第61条　为归荣上帝、郅隆邦家、泯除朕与诸男爵之不和，朕因而允准上述一切，愿彼等永享不受侵犯、不受动摇之权利，并再给赐、应允彼等下述安全保证：

听便诸男爵推选本国之男爵25人，对朕所允准并经本宪章确认之和平条款与自由权，彼须竭尽所能遵守、坚持并令之得以遵行。如朕、朕之法官、执行官或任一家臣以任何方式冒犯任何人、侵越任一和平与安全条款，而此等侵犯行为由上述25位男爵中任何4人所知情，该4人须来至朕前（如朕不在国内，须来至朕之大法官前）面折朕之错误并奏请朕立刻修正。面折之日起40日内，如朕或朕不在国内时朕之大法官未曾改正错误，此4人须将此事提交其余男爵。此25位男爵须联合全国人民，以其可采用之任何方式，即夺取朕之城堡、土地、财产，或其可采用之其他此类手段（唯朕与王后、王子、公主之人身不得侵犯），束缚与压制于朕，直至在其看来朕已修正错误为止。错误修正后，彼等一如既往，服从于朕。

任何人只要愿意，均可宣誓：为执行上述之事，服从上述25位男爵之命，跟随其尽力施压于朕。对任何愿作此宣誓者，朕将公开并自愿地准予其宣誓，绝不阻挠。国民中有不情愿作此宣誓，以帮助诸男爵束缚与压制朕者，朕将令其宣誓。

25位男爵中如有人亡故、离国或因他故不能履行上述之责，其余男爵须依其意愿另选男爵以代之，被选者须如其他男爵一样宣誓。

交与25位男爵执行事务之全部过程中，如25位男爵全部到场，而相互间就某事有争议，或在有人接到通知却不愿或不能到场时，到场多数人所达成之意见或命令当被执行与确认,恰如其出之于全体一致同意者;上述 25 位男爵须宣誓竭诚谨守上述之言,并尽力使其得以遵行。

朕不得亲自或通过任何人去做可能使上述特权与自由权被取缔或消减之任何事。如有此等行为,必将归于无效。朕永不会亲自或通过他人利用之。

第 62 条　自此争议以来,朕与朕之僧俗臣民间所产生的一切恶意、怨愤、仇恨,朕已全然赦免、宽恕。自本朝十六年复活节至此和平恢复期间,所有僧俗两众以及与朕相关人等因此争议而犯下的一切过错,朕亦全然赦免。此外,朕已命人颁赐信件以证明:坎特伯雷大主教斯蒂芬爵士、都柏林大主教亨利爵士、前述诸主教、特使潘道夫见证了此项安全条款与上述权利的授予。

第 63 条　是以,朕愿决然而令:英国教会应予自由;英国人民应安然、泰然、全然享受上述一切自由权、权利与特权,近及其身,远及后嗣。凡事凡地,永保有之。朕与诸男爵均已宣誓:诚意遵行上述规定,不得欺罔。上述诸人及其他多人见证之。

本朝十七年六月十五日,温莎与斯坦恩斯间的兰尼米德之野,加盖朕之玉玺。

解　析

封君与封臣的权利与义务——《大宪章》之基础

1215年6月15日晨,泰晤士河边、距离温莎城堡不远的兰尼米德草地(Runnymede)——一个本义即为“经常开会的地方”①,三方人众会聚于此,《大宪章》在其谈判与调解中诞生。谈判双方一为英国贵族代表,共25名;一为国王,其时被讥为“失地王”的约翰(John Lackland)。居间调解人为坎特伯雷大主教斯蒂芬·兰顿(Stephen Langton, Archbishop of Canterbury)。罗马教皇使节(Papal legate)与诸多英国高级教士(prelate)做了《大宪章》的见证人。

国王降尊纡贵、几以平等身份与臣属立约并发誓谨守约定,决非帝国体制中皇帝与臣民所可想象,它是封建体制下封君与封臣关系发展至激烈程度的产物。

13世纪的英国,虽无人使用封建主义(feudalism)这个词,它是19世纪的词汇;但由领地或采邑(fief)、领主(lord)、附庸(vassals)这三个核心词所衍生出来的封君与封臣间的封建权利、义务关系,已经渐渐发展充分。

这套权利义务关系中,最基本的是土地分封与占有(seisin)权,所谓裂土以为“封”,领主将其土地一块块分封给附庸、陪臣(笔者总称为臣属)。从理论上说,英国的每一寸土地都归国王所有,因此一切臣民的土地都得出自国王的分封,或者说自国王处保有(tenure)。臣属之间的区别只在于是否直属封

---

① “Runnymede”中的“runny”从古英语“runieg”转化而来,意为regular meeting;“mede”意为mead or meadow。所以,Runnymede的本义是“a place of regular meeting”。

臣(tenants in chief)①,即其土地直接自国王处保有。直属封臣有大有小,也并非所有直属封臣都是贵族,他可能只是个骑士或自由民。

受封土地,意味着臣服与庇护关系的形成,因此凡获得封地的臣属必须向领主(最大领主是国王)行臣服礼与效忠礼②。臣服礼在先。封臣跪于地,双手合掌置于领主手中,宣誓:"从今往后,我将以无比崇敬的心情终我一生完全臣服于您,蒙您恩惠保有地产,故而对您忠贞不渝"。效忠礼在后③。臣属手按圣经,表示"永不背叛,保证完成应尽义务与责任"。④ 臣服礼与效忠礼之后,是郑重的封地仪式。领主将一件象征财产的物件交给臣属,譬如一根手杖、一块泥土、一柄长矛;假如这臣属是个首领,则授予他一面旗帜,表示他可驱使骑士⑤。

礼仪完成,封君与封臣相互间就应履行实质性的权利与义务。就封臣而言,其权利与义务,依身份而异。这一点,可从不同的土地保有方式看出。譬如自由教役保有(frankalmoign),是以宗教上的身份从领主处保有土地,臣属无须向领主尽世俗义务,只需通过祈祷等灵魂服务回报领主。不过,以这种轻巧的方式保有土地者数量稀少(尽管英国的很多土地由教会保有),英国绝大部分土地都是以骑士役(knight service, or military service)的方式从国王处保有。获得土地的封臣必须向国王承担义务,即在战时至少为国王的军队提供1 名全副武装(头盔、面罩、锁子甲、盾牌、刀剑、胫甲、战马等,以及马僮)、可以

---

① 关于封臣、领主与国王、直属封臣的英文称呼亦可作如下解释:有权依靠所保有的土地而生存并加以开垦的人叫封臣(tenant or vassal),他所有的土地来自他的领主(lord),如果该领主是国王,那么这个封臣叫 tenants-in-chief。

② 陪臣中身份低微者,不要求行臣服礼。

③ 臣服与效忠礼的先后表现二者重要程度不同。"臣服礼一次限定一个人的终生,通常不能重复进行;效忠宣誓则不同,它几乎是最平凡的事情,可以向同一人数度重复进行",可见其不可靠,而且"效忠礼是臣属单方面的承诺,领主对此难得回报以相应的誓言"。参见马克·布洛赫:《封建社会》,张绪山译,北京:商务印书馆,2012 年,第 251~252 页。

④ 封臣双手合掌置于封君手中、宣誓效忠,史学家另有一种有趣的解释:双手合掌置于他人手中,意味着"委身"于人,失去自由,而封臣是作为自由人侍奉封君的,因此往往借助效忠宣誓,声明其自由人身份,表明他在效忠的同时,也享有一定程度的自由。参见弗朗索瓦·冈绍夫:《何为封建主义》,张绪山、卢兆瑜译,北京:商务印书馆,2016 年,第 39~42 页。

⑤ 一个人被称作骑士,是因为他全副武装地骑马作战。当他以全副武装的方式为某人效劳,并以此为条件保有后者的采邑时,他被称为这个人的骑士。

作战40天的骑兵。此外还有侍君役保有(serjeanty)——封臣向国王所尽义务不是提供能够作战的骑士,而是承担举旗、捧剑、担任官职、或提供军事器械等责任。而以农役保有(socage)方式保有土地的自由民,其义务仅为耕种土地、缴纳田租,不服兵役①。

就最大的封臣而言,其权利与义务如何?他们在受封土地上拥有行政管理权、司法审判权,并享有由土地产出、行政管理、司法审判等带来的各项经济收益。其中尤值一提的是司法管辖权。它在所有封建权利中的重要性仅仅低于土地占有权。由于司法管辖权是伴随土地保有而获得的财产权,在很大程度上可归之于私人权利,因此领主可在其受封土地境内开设称自由民法庭(court baron)与庄园农奴习惯法庭(customary court),解决其臣属之间的刑民事纠纷。前者为自由民设立,后者为农役工设立。由司法裁决而产生的诉讼费、罚金、罚款、被没收的财产等等,也就归他所有。这笔收入相当可观。同时,他也有权出席其领主即国王的法庭,出任法官。当然,这既是其权利,也是其义务。倘若封臣犯罪,他尤其珍视的是由其同侪平行审判的权利,即有权要求由其同级的附庸,亦即贵族(peer),而非王室官员来审判。这种权利由封建制度下附庸之间地位平等的概念发展而来。国王属下最主要的附庸,譬如大男爵(Great Baron)、男爵(baron)、大主教、主教等,则享有应诏出席大会议(Great Council)与王国会议(Common Counsel),使国王听取其意见的权利。按照封建政府的好政府准则,"无论哪个等级的首领,没有事先的协商,都不能做出任何重大决定"②。因此,国王意欲作出任何重大决策,均须征求臣属意见,与之协商。尽管这项准则如何执行取决于国王与臣属的角力,但准则本身是一条古老的传统。另外,13世纪的英国,乃至于整个西欧,国王的封臣们已经形成了这样的封建观念:倘若国王不能公正对待他们,或者悖逆法律而行,他们就可以抗拒国王,甚至"参与发动对他的战争,而并不因此违背其效忠义务"③。换言之,他们有起义权、抵抗权。虽然1086年英国贵族曾在索里

① 从土地保有方式中,还可以看到整个社会的结构及各自功能:负责祈祷的教士、负责打仗的贵族、负责劳作的平民。

② 马克·布洛赫:《封建社会》,第655页。

③ 马克·布洛赫:《封建社会》,第713页。

兹伯里（Salisbury）发下誓言，向威廉王宣誓效忠，绝不反叛；但国王也需尊重古老的自由传统与封臣合法权利的观念，在他们心中，与索里兹伯里誓言（Salisbury Oath）并行不悖。

至于他对国王负有的义务，除了上述参与司法审判与大会议之外，最为重要的是军事上的义务，即为国王出兵打仗提供兵源、武器，以及经济上的义务：向国王缴纳他所要求的各种协助金（aid）、土地继承金（relief）、代役捐（scutage，又称盾牌金，shield-money）。简而言之，出钱出人出武器。

相应地，国王也有其义务与权利。其义务首先是保障领土与臣属安全、抵御外敌；其次，正如国王在登基加冕礼时通常所宣誓的，保护教会（因为教会也是其臣属）、主张正义与公平、维护境内的和平、支持王国的习惯与法律；再次，履行他与封臣间的其他契约。

国王的权利首先还是来源于其土地所有权。他分封给臣属的土地，从性质上说，是因臣属的效忠而给予的报酬而非奖赏。因此，当臣属不履行效忠义务时，他可以理直气壮地撤销给予后者的报酬，收回封地。而在效忠于他的臣属去世时，他也可以收回原来分封给臣属的土地。道理很简单。“采邑的授予是委身者的报酬，所以它的有效期即是这种人身依附关系的有效期”①。换言之，附庸关系不能继承。当然，其臣属的继承人可以重新向国王行臣服与效忠礼，获得其父曾经占有的那片土地，条件是缴纳一笔钱。国王为自身安全计，通常也愿意将土地继续分封给为他效劳过的封臣的后代。这样，国王对其臣属的继承人就获得了主张土地继承金的权利；否则，他有权行使土地复归权（escheat），即在臣属死亡时收回其土地。有时，老国王去世，新国王登基，新主也会以附庸关系已随旧主去世而终止的理由，要求臣属重行臣服与效忠礼，并缴纳一笔金钱，再举行一次封地仪式。这种权利主张往往会引起臣属不满，但它在理论上是成立的。因为非如此不能体现“一切土地都从国王处保有”的概念②。在国王

---

① 马克·布洛赫：《封建社会》，第 291 页。

② 依据 Robin Fleming 的研究，这一概念是《末日审判书》（*Domesday Book*）的产物。他指出，末日审判书结束了私人获得土地的方式，把每一个封臣的土地都转化成了国王的土地。自此，英格兰的所有土地均“从国王手中”持有。参见罗宾·弗莱明：《诺曼征服时期的国王与领主》，翟继光、赵锐译，北京：北京大学出版社，2008 年，第 236 页。

看来,这种表示国王恩典的仪式无论如何是不能省略的。

由于土地分封以效忠为条件,因此国王对其臣属的继承人享有监护权与婚姻指定权。监护权是指臣属继承人未及成年,亦即不能行使效忠义务时,国王可指派人作为其土地管理的监护人。在此期间,由这片土地所产出的全部经济收益归监护人所有。当然,被监护人的生活费用由监护人供给。国王所得到的回报是监护人的效忠。婚姻指定权则是为了防止其臣属与国王的敌人联姻。否则,国王自己的土地资源就可能被敌人所用。

以土地分封权为基础,国王还有权以各种名目要求其臣属为他提供金钱上的协助。譬如为其发动十字军东征,为其长子的成人礼——受封为骑士,以及长女出嫁提供资助,甚至为他自己被俘而贡献赎金①。协助金的给付是自愿的,但只要国王给出的理由恰当,臣属通常不能拒绝。不难想见,在一个以习俗和传统为基础的社会里,当自愿的奉献屡屡不能拒绝给付时,最终就会变成义务,演变为国王当然的权利。

以保护封臣的安全为理由,国王享有要求其臣属提供兵源、兵器与军费的权利。这就使他拥有了募兵权与征税权。当然,征税权,依照古老的传统和习惯,需要获得贵族同意。梅特兰曾指出,诺曼征服前,"没有哪位国王未经贤人会议同意就自行立法、征税"②。各税中有一种盾牌金(shield money),或称代役捐(scutage),由亨利一世于1109年创立。该词从字面上看容易引起误解,似乎缴纳此金,便可免除骑士亲身服役。其实不然,亨利一世创立此税,是为在一定程度上摆脱对封臣军事力量的依赖,以便利用此金招募雇佣兵,利于他长期征战或远征(因为封臣们的骑士役义务仅限于40天)。它也不意味着封臣可以缴纳此金为条件,拒绝提供骑士役义务,尽管他可以与国王进行特别协商。而国王是否同意以缴纳盾牌金代服军役,要看他认为是否有利于他,决定权完全在国王一方。未经与国王协商而以缴纳盾牌金代服骑士役者,会受

---

① 即比利时史学家冈绍夫在其《何为封建主义》中所描述的"四事援助"。参见冈绍夫:《何为封建主义》,第116页。

② 梅特兰:《英格兰宪政史》,李红海译,北京:中国政法大学出版社,2010年,第41页。

到缴纳罚金或其他严厉惩罚[①]。

与封臣设立领主法庭同理,国王也设立王室法庭,对其直属封臣行使司法裁判权,审理其直属封臣之间的民刑事纠纷。自然地,由此而产生的诉讼费、罚款、罚金等各项收益也都归他所有。与领主法庭不同的是,王室法庭的司法权还包括另外两项权力。一是为民申冤、主持公正。当国民在郡法庭和百户区法庭得不到公正对待时,可以诉诸王室法庭,对法官提出控诉,请求国王为其伸冤[②]。这是王权的表现,得到了所有臣民的承认,因为"国王天生是其臣民的最高法官"[③]。二是国王主张他自己的特别利益,即"国王之诉(Pleas of the Crown)"。可纳入"国王之诉"的,是某些可能对国王或宫廷造成伤害的罪行,以及国王认为危及王国秩序或侵犯其特殊权利的罪行。[④]

国王的土地并不全部分封出去,他自己拥有大片自领地。在其自领地上,他和其他领主一样,享有司法权、行政管理权以及摊派各种税务的权利。由此产生的经济利益当然非常高。

除了上述封建宗主权,身为一国首脑,国王还享有宽恕赦免权、颁发特许状、征收关税等王家权利。这些权利同样地给国王带来收益。国王没有免费施恩的习惯;特许状颁发给谁,取决于谁肯出更大的价钱。

作为王权象征的任命大主教、主教、修道院院长等高级圣职的权利,国王从来也未肯放弃过。这类权利与封建权利相关相连——高级教士均为国王之附庸,又与来自上帝的教会权力密不可分——国王亦需效忠于教会,因而在国

---

① William McKechnie, *Magna Carta: A Commentary of Great Charta of King John*, Glasgow: James Maclehose and Sons Publishers to the University, pp.70~71.另需指出,关于代役捐(scutage)是否替代军役,史学家有不同说法。譬如冈绍夫就曾指出,"在英格兰,从相当早的时候,至少在较低的封臣等级中,国王允许以钱款代替军役,12 世纪后半期,金雀花王朝出于财政目的,曾系统地推动以免役捐代替军役的做法,甚至及于国王的总佃臣"(参见冈绍夫:《何为封建主义》,第 115 页)。不过,在笔者看来,冈绍夫的这一说法,依然有很大解释余地。他只说国王在一定程度上允许以盾牌金代服军役,并没有说封臣(尤其是直属封臣)有权利在未经国王许可时可因缴纳盾牌金而拒服军役。

② 这不是现代意义的上诉。当事人来到国王面前不是为了修正判决上的错误,而是为了告诉国王,地方法官不行正义。

③ 马克·布洛赫:《封建社会》,第 602 页。

④ 参见梅特兰:《英格兰宪政史》,第 70~71 页。

王的这片权力与权利领域中，时时有可扩张的余地，又时时有被限制的可能。一方面，国王总想将"高级教士的职位同化为附庸采邑"①；另一方面，教会总不甘心精神领域的权威从属于世俗权威，难道不是"基督建立了教会，而王国只是他的一部分而已"②？但问题在于，国王不是纯粹的俗人。他受过涂油礼（an anointed king），王权已被圣化。他虽是教会成员，无疑应受教会约束；但在一定程度上，他又高出于为他行加冕礼的大主教，拥有控制教会的权力。

总而言之，这是一套复杂的封君与封臣间的权利、义务体系。除了国王与世俗贵族，教会也卷入其中。就世俗贵族或封臣来说，他们从这套包含丰厚收益的封建体系中、一种以分权为特色的统治方式中，培养出了强烈的权利意识。就兼属封臣的高级教士而言，他们也在效忠的同时具有强烈的教会自由理念与圣职权利观。而国王在一边尽忠于教会，一边享受臣属的效忠义务时，也因其王权与分封权而天然地膨胀其权力欲。正是这种封臣与封君间的权利保护与权力扩张意识导致了君臣间多次的摩擦、对立与冲突，乃至危机与叛乱。《大宪章》便为此种危机与叛乱的结果。

君权的扩张与封臣权利的受侵蚀——《大宪章》之缘起

造成《大宪章》的危机始于何时？源于何种具体原因？不少学者将之归于约翰（King John）继位后，尤其是1213年以来③，一系列令人失望、愤慨而痛恨的作为。如此持论有其历史依据。

1203年8月，约翰将布列塔尼大公（duke of Britanny）、侄儿阿瑟（Arthur）杀害于鲁昂城堡（Castle of Rouen）④，投尸于塞纳河，激起贵族们谴责。法王

---

① 马克·布洛赫：《封建社会》，第571页。

② 沃尔特·厄尔曼：《中世纪政治思想史》，夏洞奇译，南京：译林出版社，2011年，第130页。

③ 研究大宪章的权威 James Holt 以1212年为危机开始的时间，因为这一年由于约翰王的横征暴敛导致了贵族的反叛。当然，这次反叛没有成功。

④ 1190年，理查德一世指定其弟 Geffery 之子阿瑟为王位继承人；然因阿瑟后为法国人所俘，约翰成为英王王位继承人。1199年理查王逝世，约翰即位。1202年，阿瑟率军，进入诺曼底，为图王位。他成功夺取诸多城池，其中一个为其祖母所居之地。约翰率军来战，俘虏阿瑟。

腓力二世借此为由,向约翰发动军事讨伐①。1204年,约翰王丧失其在法国的领地诺曼底(Normandy),并于1206年向法兰西国王割让了所有海外领地。割地求和的卑弱,令尚武的贵族非但愤慨,而且开始蔑视王权权威。此后国王虽多次发起收复失地的战争,均未告捷,反而一次次的丧师弃甲。作为主权至尊与一国最大领主,约翰王未能尽到保卫国家领土安全的封建义务。

更令贵族不满者,约翰王屡屡借口远征或收复失地,加倍征敛。其父、兄亨利二世与理查德一世在45年中共征收盾牌金11次,而约翰王自登基到1214年短短15年中就征收了11次。有时一年征2次。1214年,他以每单位征收金额,即每骑士费(Knight's fee)3马克的标准,向贵族索取盾牌金(见表1),超出其父、兄原定标准(20先令)的1倍②。他还动辄征收动产税,违抗者加倍罚款,敛得财产无数。

表1 约翰王在位时盾牌金征收次数、时间与标准

盾牌金征收次数	年份	金额(每骑士领)
第1次	1198~9	2 marks
第2次	1200~1	2 m.
第3次	1201~2	2 m.
第4次	1202~3	2 m.
第5次	1203~4	2 m.
第6次	1204~5	2 m.
第7次	1205~6	20 shillings.
第8次	1209~10	2 marks
第9次	1210~11	2 m.
第10次	1210~11	20 s.
第11次	1213~14	3 marks

表1来源:William McKechnie, *Magna Carta: A Commentary of Great Charta of King John*, Glasgow: James Maclehose and Sons Publishers to the University, 1914, p.74.

① David Hume, *The History of England*, Vol.1, Indiana: Liberty Fund Inc., 1983, pp.413~414。约翰王杀其侄后,法兰西国王腓力二世召集众封臣,传唤约翰王出庭受审,约翰王未曾出席,被缺席判以重罪与弑亲罪,并要求他放弃在法国的所有封地与领主权。

② 1971年英国货币改为十进制前,1磅等于240便士,而不是今天的100便士。这240便士相当于20先令,每先令内含12便士。约翰王时代,常用的货币单位还有马克。1马克相当于2/3磅,即13先令4便士。3马克相当于40先令。

尤为甚者,他无视封建成规,不依惯例征取封地继承金,苛刻规定封地继承条件;竭力利用婚姻指定权与监护权,多方侵夺封臣财产,无论老幼孤寡。1205年,孀居的沃里克伯爵夫人爱丽丝(Alice,Countess of Warwick)为保持独身被迫向约翰支付1000磅。同年,另一名寡妇为相同原因而花费2000马克。1212年,奥梅尔伯爵夫人哈维沙(Hawisa,Countess of Aumale)不愿意改嫁给国王指定的人,向约翰王缴纳了5000马克①。国王之贪婪导致许多贵族负债,甚至倾家荡产。

财富的大肆攫取之外,约翰还因其专横、暴虐、荒淫令人愤恨。1209年,诺维奇的大执事杰弗里(Jeffery,archdeacon of Norwich),因国王被罗马教廷逐出教门而不肯为其任事。国王将其囚禁,令其头顶灌铅斗篷,加以其他残酷折磨,很快令其送命②。1212年,波佛利特的一位隐士因曾预言国王丧失王权而被约翰王施以马尾拖曳之刑,随后与其子一起被绞死③。同年,约翰欲图罗伯特·瓦尔特(Robert Walter)之女,被拒绝。国王怀恨在心,将瓦尔特的城堡摧毁,并毒死其女④。

丧失国土、凌虐人民、侵夺财产、破坏传统、横加暴力,种种均显示:约翰王违背了登基加冕时宣誓的义务——维护正义、公平、和平;支持王国的习惯与法律。

不过,所有这些也许都不及约翰王与罗马教皇争权、不和而带给英国人民的灵魂上的痛苦与国家主权奉献于罗马教廷的屈辱。

约翰王统治期间,罗马教皇英诺森三世(Pope Innocent III)⑤在位,"中世纪的教皇权力在他统治期间达到了最高峰"⑥。英诺森是教皇中有才干的理论家,他构建了一系列的理论说明皇帝或国王的权力来源,以及教皇与他们的

---

① 迈尔克·亚历山大:《英国早期历史中的三次危机》,林达丰译,北京:北京大学出版社,2008年,第76~77页。按当时的生活标准,岁入30磅,衣食无忧;300磅,堪称富豪。伯爵岁入,因地因人而异,少者数百磅,多者上万,通常在1000~2000磅之间。

② David Hume,*The History of England*,Vol.1,p.429.

③ David Hume,*The History of England*,Vol.1,p.433.

④ William McKechnie,*Magna Carta*,p.74.

⑤ Innocent III(英诺森三世)1198年1月登基,1216年6月16日离世。

⑥ Walter Ullmann,*Short History of the Papacy in the Middle Ages*, London:Routledge,2003,p.146.

上下关系。其中影响最为广泛是日与月、灵魂与身体的比喻。他指出,皇帝或国王是如月亮,教皇是如太阳,前者的权力就如同月亮的光芒得自太阳;教皇的法令如同灵魂,皇帝或国王如同身体,后者与教皇的关系就如同身体必须服从灵魂的指挥。受英诺森教义的影响,"英国教会在罗马教皇保护下,也极大地僭夺了世俗权力"①。生性狂傲的约翰王不肯相让,由此导致他与英国教会以及罗马教皇间激烈的冲突。冲突之高峰发生于坎特伯雷大主教的任命。

1205年,坎特伯雷大主教休伯特·沃尔特去世(Hubert Walter)。国王欲以诺维奇主教约翰·格雷(John de Gray,bishop of Norwich)任之,引诱修道院士按其意图选举。选举结果虽如其所愿,却不合教皇意图;坎特伯雷副主教们(suffragan bishops)亦不肯听从国王暗示,放弃其反对权。选任纠纷诉至教皇面前。借此机会,英诺森三世令修道院士重新选举斯蒂芬·兰顿为坎特伯雷大主教,而将国王本应拥有的发布选举令状的权利置之不顾;教士们亦"申辩道,没有得自国王事先发布的令状,选举将非常有违常规"(The monks present that an election,without a previous writ from the king,would be deemed highly irregular)。然而英诺森以逐出教门相威胁,迫使教士们屈服。国王因其视为最重要的一项王权(one of the most important prerogatives of the crown)被剥夺,勃然大怒,他没收了修道院的财产,侵夺了教士们的权利,并向罗马发出威胁,"若罗马人胆敢踏上英国国土一步,必将被捉,并受挖眼割鼻之刑,以示其与其他各邦人民的区别"(He threatened,that,if thenceforth he caught any Romans in his dominions,he would put out their eyes,and cut off their noses,in order to set a mark upon them,which might distinguish them from all other nations)②。

约翰王捍卫王权的言行遭到罗马教廷的报复。1207年起,英国人民受到了接近六年禁教令(interdict)的处罚——一切教堂外的宗教活动都禁止进行(The nation was of a sudden deprived of all exterior exercise of its religion)。教堂不再鸣钟,连大钟也从教堂尖顶上取下。弥撒必须关门进行,只允许少数神职人员参加。葬礼不再超度,死者也不得归葬于神圣的墓园,而抛于沟渠或田

① David Hume,*The History of England*,Vol.1,p.420.

② David Hume,*The History of England*,Vol.1,pp.423~425.

野。日常生活的各方面都受到禁教令的影响，每一天都仿佛在大斋节(Lent)那样，不得取用肉食，甚至行礼、剃须、仪容的修饰都受禁止。由于国王行为的乖张，英国人民的灵魂受到煎熬。然而国王无视于此，他命令教士们对抗教廷；凡不服从者，严加打击。屈服的教士遵循了约翰的命令，却感到背叛了原则，为世俗的利禄牺牲了良心①。

然而，国王的傲慢与强横终于在英诺森三世层层加重的强硬威胁下瓦解。教皇先是宣布将约翰逐出教门(the sentence of excommunication)，不料约翰不为所惧；继而决定褫夺其王权(the sentence of deposition)，即令国王失去王权之神圣来源：上帝的授予。约翰终于卑身屈膝，觍颜求和。1213 年 5 月，他与教皇特使潘道夫(Pandulf)会见，无条件地接受了他从前拒绝所服从的一切，承认兰顿为坎特伯雷大主教，赔偿流亡教士们的损失与财产。10 月，约翰王又献出英格兰与爱尔兰，将之作为教皇采邑而对其称臣纳贡，拜倒在教皇使节跟前，行效忠礼，以求庇护。英格兰、爱尔兰自此将各奉年贡 700、300 马克②。此举不仅令王国尊严被外来势力践踏，亦将迫使英格兰人与爱尔兰人承担奉送年贡的义务，因为约翰必将依据封建领主与国王的权利，将此负担转嫁于封臣与自由民。

不堪羞辱、压迫与重负之下，一批英国大贵族结成联盟并联合民众起而反之。反叛先在秘密酝酿中，1213 年 8 月便已形成联盟。公开与国王对抗则在 1214 年 5 月 26 日(一说 5 月 3 日)，以国王再度索取盾牌金、且高达每骑士领 3 马克为导火索，北方贵族为领导。次年 4、5 月形成烽火燎原之势，贵族们选举罗伯特·瓦尔特(Robert Fitz Walter)为军事统领(此人即前文所提被约翰王夺去并摧毁城堡、毒死其女者)，集结军队，进逼伦敦。其间(可能在 1215 年 1 月)，反叛贵族曾拿出一份宪章，即 1893 年以后才为英国历史学家所知，因而又被称之为“不为人知的权利宪章”(*The Unknown Charter of Liberties*，共 12 条)，与国王谈判，未果。5 月 17 日，伦敦市民洞开城门，贵族联盟不战而克。国王不得已与反叛贵族接触、谈和。6 月 15 日，在兰顿大主教的调停下，

① David Hume, *The History of England*, Vol.1, pp.425~427.

② Harry Rothwell ed., *English Historical Document, 1189 ~ 1327*, London: Eyre Spottiswood, 1975, pp.307~309

贵族联盟与国王在兰尼米德草地分营列阵,以一份《贵族的条款》(*The Articles of the Barons*)①为基础,开始正式谈判。6月19日,约翰王同意,遵行双方议定的协约。《大宪章》诞生(但文件所署日期仍为6月15日)。它显然是一份强迫性的宪章。尽管"在形式上,大宪章只是一份特许状,由国王自愿授予。但,实质上,它由全体主教与贵族讨论通过,将原先的法律加以修订后强加给这位暴虐的国王"②。

由上可见,以约翰王统治时期作为《大宪章》之所以诞生的起点,并将其归因于约翰王的不智、不公与残暴下的软弱,从近处来说,是没有错的。然而,"《大宪章》比它产生的时代要老得多"(Magna Carta is much elder than King John's time)③。它的出现并非偶然事件的结果;也不是说如果没有约翰王、没有他那些乖张举措,类似的文件就不会在英国历史上产生。历史从来就不乏暴虐、荒淫、无视法度的君主。与其说,它是一个偶然事件;不如说,它是自诺曼征服以来为时已久的封君与封臣间权力扩张与权利维护竞争中,一方力量形成优势,另一方力量暂居弱势,而必然导致的结果。换言之,《大宪章》的产生自有其内在逻辑,它在约翰王时代出现,实只因双方权利义务关系已至极不平衡的地步,约翰王无力维持其强势而已,其源头早发于约翰王之前。唯因如此,一位研究大宪章的权威威廉·麦基奇尼(William McKechnie)评论说,"大宪章起源深远,绝非某纯粹偶然的现象所可决定"(The origin of Magna Carta lies too deep to be determined by any purely contingent phenomena)④。

诺曼征服,带来了大陆的封建制度,同时也开启了英国君主"强大而富有进取精神的王权"⑤扩张过程。之所以如此,乃因英格兰的国家统一进程已开始于诺曼征服前。为顺应这一趋势,诺曼王朝与安茹王朝的君主们承前启后,

---

① 笔者未将"Articles of the Barons"译为《男爵的条款》,而译为《贵族的条款》,系因"Barons"在这里实代指贵族。

② 梅特兰:《英格兰宪政史》,第46页。

③ Samuel Johnson, *A History and Defense of Magna Carta*, London: Printed for J.Bells at His Circulating Library, 1772, p.3.

④ William McKechnie, *Magna Carta*, p.3.

⑤ J.H.Round, Feudal England, p.317;迈尔克·亚历山大:《英国早期历史中的三次危机》,第38页。

代际不断地强化王权或者说中央政府权力。

威廉一世（William the Conqueror，1066～1087 在位）雄才大略，目光敏锐。他看到了封建制的核心——土地保有制（land tenure）——作为一种社会经济制度对巩固国家控制力的好处，因此他鼓励封建制度在英格兰发展；同时亦看到了封建制作为一种政治制度对王权乃至国家的统一、有序可能形成的威胁，深知封臣权利过多将弱化他作为最高封建领主的权利，因此他又以多种方法遏制封建势力。

他利用英吉利传统的法律与规制，譬如令状、封印（writ and seal），消减诺曼封建制的强势，使其充分为己所用；通过召开郡与百户区会议对贵族的司法权行使形成掣肘，乃至剥夺；令治安官而非贵族作为王权在地方的代表，削弱贵族在地方上的影响力，使其“徒有虚名”（The great nobles obtained only an ornamental position in the state）①。贵族们非但“不允许有超过其受封头衔所应拥有的土地”（No earl was allowed to hold too large an estate within his titular shire）；他们在其领地所拥有的权利，如“私斗、铸币、修建城堡等，均被威廉一世出于妒意加以限制”（Rights of private war，coinage，and castle-building，were jealously circumscribed），以至于“没有一个英国伯爵可称得上欧洲大陆意义上的伯爵——是其受封地真正的统治者”（No English earl was a ‘Count’ in the continental sense of a real ruler of a ‘county’）②。而他自己不但可以调用民军（fyrd），宣布所有城堡归国王所有，还垄断了铸币权。

1085 年，他下令清查全国土地。清查结果所形成的《末日审判书》（*The Domesday Book of 1086*）令英格兰所有土地都转化为“从国王手中”持有③，土地再也不能像从前那样可由私人转让，这就从根本上提升了国王作为最大领主的封建权利，王权亦因此强化到了历史学家称之为“威权主义”的程度。1086 年，土地清查刚刚结束，威廉一世就召集英格兰所有土地持有者前往索里兹伯里，向他立誓，“全英格兰所有土地持有者，无论他们是谁的附庸，均臣

① Frank Barlow，*The Feudal Kingdom of England，1042～1216*，London：Routledge，2014，p.70.

② William McKechnie，*Magna Carta*，p.8.

③ 罗宾·弗莱明：《诺曼征服时期的国王与领主》，翟继光、赵锐译，北京：北京大学出版社，2008 年，第 236 页。

服于国王,是为其附庸,对其效忠”(All the landowners of substance in England,whose vassals server they were,and they all submitted to him,and became to his men and swore oaths of allegiance that would be faithful to him)①。立誓完毕,威廉一世宣布,“其附庸所获得的土地,终将所有权属于威廉及其继承人”②。

至于国王与僧侣贵族的关系,威廉一世从未允许教会凌驾于世俗王权之上。哪怕面对罗马教皇,他也未肯屈膝。格里高利七世(Pope Gregory VII)登基不久,要求他臣服、效忠于罗马教廷,威廉一世傲然回复,“我不会也不愿向您效忠,因为我从未作出如此允诺,我之前的国王也未曾对您的前任作过如此允诺”(I refuse to do fealty nor will I,because neither have I promised it,nor do I find that my predecessors did it to your predecessors)③。

征服者威廉的气概传给了他的幼子亨利一世(Henry I,1100~1135 年在位)。与父王相比,亨利一世扩充王权的意识更强烈。他不满足于仅仅通过限制封臣权利,提升其作为最高领主的威权,他还要在封建制度之外创造更多王权。

他亲平践贵,将出身低微者引入御前会议(Curia Regis)。虽然老贵族并未受到严格排斥,但从前由其把持的御前会议现在受国王属意的新人操纵。如此一来,国王的意志便可更少约束地得以体现。王权扩张虽不能说在君王颐指气使间,但欲变身贵族的新人们为图自身权力的巩固,主动地将主子权力也扩张。因此,尽管亨利一世在登基加冕时曾允诺绝不滥用封建习俗:保证封地继承金恰当、公平;指定婚姻时无须缴纳金钱;寡妇允许单身;未成年的封臣不由国王而由其亲属监护;动产可通过遗嘱或由死者家属分配;财产没收依照诺曼征服前的惯例来定④。但他并未履行诺言。封地继承金由其专断决定,不许协商;罚金照旧沉重;女继承人出嫁,婚姻指定金不能免除;未成年人的监

---

① William Stubbs,*The Constitutional History of England in its Origin and Development* Vol.1,London:University of Oxford Press,1873,p.289.

② 迈尔克·亚历山大:《英国早期历史中的三次危机》,林达丰译,北京:北京大学出版社,2008 年,第 39 页。

③ William McKechnie,*Magna Carta*,p.13.

④ Frank Barlow,*The Feudal Kingdom of England*,p.138.

护权依然在他手里①。封臣们传统的封建权利在他治下受到严重侵蚀,无力抗辩。

意义更为深远且更具创新性的手段是组建财政署(the Exchequer)。在亨利一世的得力助手索尔兹伯里主教罗杰(Bishop Roger of Salisbury)主持下,财政署一年两度,即每当4月的复活节(Easter)与9月底的米迦勒节(Michaelmas)时,审计地方治安官即各郡郡守以及其他人上报的账目②、裁决他们之间的纠纷,因之而产生的罚金等收入归王室所有。这意味着财政署在财务收支管理之外,兼具司法职能。另外,各郡郡守原来由当地贵族世袭担任,亨利一世将此世袭制打破,改由王室任命;奖励、罢黜等,决于财政署。由是,财政署不仅成为"王室收入的来源,还令国王意志遍为英伦所知"(as a source of royal revenue, and as an instrument for making his will felt in every corner of England)③,显示出一种"普天之下,莫非王土;率土之滨,莫非王臣"的封建集权趋势。

财政署有规制的中央审查之外,亨利一世还派出官员前往各地不定期地巡视。这些原本为财务审查而来的巡视官,在各地遇到了不满于地方封臣之暴政的申诉。处理申诉的结果,是他们逐渐获得地方事务的司法权。到亨利一世统治晚期,这种司法权与其财务审查权已经变得同等重要,甚至更为重要④。王室巡回法庭就此形成。若非有此一举,其外孙亨利二世由以扩张王权的三级司法体系——国王法庭、王室巡回法庭、地方法庭,无有根基。

再就国王与教会的关系而言,1106年3月,亨利一世为履行登基时的诺言——给予教会自由,虽与罗马教皇帕斯卡(Pope Paschal)就圣职授予权(Investiture)达成妥协:"国王放弃圣戒、法衣等授予权,条件是大主教与主教向国王宣誓效忠"⑤;但是,国王提名大主教、主教与修道院长的权力,并未因此

① Frank Barlow, *The Feudal Kingdom of England*, p.147.

② 记录账目的档案称之为"国库档卷"(Pipe Rolls, or Great Roll),每一份档卷由两张羊皮纸首尾相连而成。

③ William McKechnie, *Magna Carta*, p.9.

④ William McKechnie, *Magna Carta*, p.10.

⑤ Frank Barlow, *The Feudal Kingdom of England*, p.144.

而被削弱。圣职选举由国王创议,并在王宫进行。虽然各修道院的代表应诏出席,但国王的意旨与世俗贵族大臣的同意更为重要。“1120年时,所有的主教职位都由国王的教士与亲朋充任”①。教皇特使能否进入英伦、英国教会与罗马教廷的关系等,亦需国王首肯,或在其监视之下。可见,亨利一世对王国的宗教事务保持着强大的控制力。1109年4月,坎特伯雷大主教安塞姆(Archbishop Anselm)去世,亨利一世竟延至1114年才遣使报告教皇,以至于大主教职位空缺长达五年。在此期间,英国教会当奉送罗马教廷的“1便士税金”(Peter's pence)②亦拖延未交。随后产生的坎特伯雷大主教则由国王径行挑选罗切斯特主教担任。这都是国王僭越权力的表现,是对罗马教皇的轻视与诺言的违背。然而罗马教皇并未予以重责③。王权上升之势,在亨利一世治下,确然“达到了诺曼王朝的最高峰”④。

及至斯蒂芬(Stephen,1135~1154年在位)即位,这一趋势暂时停歇,贵族们反而大张其势。其原因正如弗兰克·巴罗(Frank Barlow)所言,“亨利一世将王权推之过猛、行之过急,对其臣属约束过重,超出其承受能力与效忠能力之外(The son of the Conqueror had pushed the royal powers too hard and had strained the capacities and loyalties of their servants far too severely),而继任者又是一个软弱的国王”⑤。

然而一俟安茹王朝建立,亨利二世(Henry II,1154~1189年在位)登基,王权扩张之势便再度活跃,并且由于“前朝的混乱与内战而使王权的强化显得愈加急迫”⑥。亨利二世在其外祖父所创立的基础之上,纵深开掘,不遗余

---

① Frank Barlow, *The Feudal Kingdom of England*, p.148.

② “1便士税金”(Peter's pence)指教众们须每年每户向罗马教皇供奉1便士税金的规定,开始于盎格鲁—撒克逊时期(Anglo-Saxon times),1534年英王亨利八世与罗马教廷交恶时曾中断。Peter(彼得)系耶稣的信徒之一,他被罗马天主教廷认定为罗马教会的第1个主教。公元67年左右,彼得被罗马官方所害,基督教徒尊奉他为圣徒(St.Peter)。彼得原名西门,见到耶稣,甘愿为其使徒,耶稣改其名为彼得。“peter”是希腊语,意为“stone”。耶稣以之为名,寓意彼得坚如磐石的个性;也有解释说,这暗指彼得将修起第一座基督教堂。

③ Frank Barlow, *The Feudal Kingdom of England*, p.148.

④ Frank Barlow, *The Feudal Kingdom of England*, p.137.

⑤ Frank Barlow, *The Feudal Kingdom of England*, p.137.

⑥ John Cannon & Ralph Griffiths, *The Oxford Illustrated History of British Monarchy*, Oxford: Oxford University Press, 1988, p.112.

力地将王权全面扩充，到他统治结束时，也就是"12 世纪末，英格兰已成为欧洲最复杂、有效的君主政体"（By the end of the twelfth century，England had the most sophisticated and effective monarchy in Europe）[①]。其举措涵盖行政、司法、军事、宗教、经济诸领域，且相互交织。

御前会议地位之显赫，超出诸前朝。它不止负责宫廷内务、王室财务，还是王国的行政管理中心与王室司法机构，权力大张。

财政署作用之强大，为亨利一世治下所不及。亨利一世统治晚期，地方郡守权力坐大，郡守世袭制卷土重来。经历斯蒂芬王统治下的内乱，地方贵族再度垄断郡政大权，中央政府控制力削弱。为收回中央政府权力，亨利二世充分发挥财政署同时作为行政管理机关与司法机关的职能，对地方郡守、执行官（bailiffs）、护林官（foresters）等严加监控，时常更替，不仅逐渐废除郡守世袭制，郡守人选亦由国王从宫廷大臣或内府吏员中任命，不由地方贵族置喙。

郡法庭、百户区法庭、封建法庭受到中央政府更有效的羁束。伴随着普通法[②]的奠基，国王向各地遣送司法官员已成定规。司法官跑遍全国，将御前会议与王室法庭制订的法律传至王国全境。《克拉伦敦法令》（*The Assize of Clarendon of 1166*）的颁布，将王室巡回法庭正式确立为国家制度，"古老的地方法院通过巡回法院与王室法庭建立了联系"[③]，国家司法机构三级体制形成。

司法程序改革中的"令状制度"（writ system），进一步规约领主法庭，几近架空领主司法权。它规定；只要自由民缴纳一笔金钱，向大法官法庭（Chancery）申请，获得王家令状（royal writ），便可自主决定将其诉讼从领主法

① John Cannon & Ralph Griffiths，*The Oxford Illustrated History of British Monarchy*，p.158.另：关于亨利二世与其父的成就，亨利二世的母亲、亨利一世的女儿玛蒂尔达（Matilda）在其墓志铭上的一段文字饶有趣味：Here lies Henry's daughter，wife and mother；great by birth—greater by marriage—greatest by motherhood。笔者注：玛蒂尔达先嫁给了德国皇帝亨利五世，后因无子被亨利五世离婚，再嫁给了安茹伯爵 Count Geoffrey，生下了亨利二世。

② "Common Law"中的 common 意指 general。如何理解普通法？首先，它不是经过制订或颁布的法律，因此，它区别于制定法与条例；其次，普通法适用于整个王国，于是它区别于地方习惯法；再次；普通法是世俗法庭的法律，因此它区别于教会法（Canon Law）。参见梅特兰：《英格兰宪政史》，第 16 页。

③ 梅特兰：《英格兰宪政史》，第 47 页。

庭移至王室法庭;若自由民认为领主法庭不能秉持公正,申诉至王室巡回法庭,王家令状有权要求领主法庭陈述其裁决理由;若无王家令状许可,任何法庭均不得审理土地诉讼。总之,亨利二世强有力的手虽未将领主法庭取消,然而封建领主传统的司法权已被严重削弱;相应地,领主们原可从司法管辖权中获得的经济收益也转移至国王的金库。

盾牌金的征收,直接壮大了国王的军事力量。自 1156 年起,亨利二世将亨利一世创制、偶尔才征收的盾牌金改为常用措施,多次征收此税(1156、1159、1161、1162、1165 年)[①],用以招募雇佣军。此税影响之深远,不仅在于国王可在很大程度上摆脱对封臣骑士役义务的依赖,凭借他独立的武装力量,震慑诸侯;还在于它先例一开,便逐渐成为继任国王理所当然的权利与勒索金钱的手段。亨利二世死后,两个儿子——狮心王理查与约翰王——无不利用它一而再、再而三地侵扰封臣贵族、害及小民(这是封臣将税务转嫁给农民的结果),并且变本加厉,提高税金。

《克拉伦敦法规》(*The Constitution of Clarendon of 1164*)的颁布,显示王权对教会权力的强力干预。1162 年起,亨利二世因不满宗教法庭对犯罪教士量刑过轻、屡屡以宗教罪名迫害其臣民,同时也是为了抵制教会权力在斯蒂芬统治期间越出边界、趁乱侵犯世俗权力的结果,开始采取措施,恢复王权对宗教事务的控制,要求教会权力收缩至亨利一世时的范围。1164 年,坎特伯雷大主教托马斯·贝克特(Archbishop Thomas Becket)口头上勉强允诺国王,作出让步。不想亨利二世将贝克特口头上的允诺形诸文字,制订为《克拉伦敦法规》,颁之于众。《克拉伦敦法规》共 16 条,涉及僧俗两界争议如何裁决、圣职推荐与选举、革出教门等宗教惩罚如何实施、国王财产不得被教会侵犯、高级教士离开英国需国王允准等,着重强调教会权力须尊重王权、领有国王领地的僧侣须臣服于国王作为其领主的权威,并且规定:犯重罪的教士必须送达国王的法庭。《克拉伦敦法规》一出,立刻招致罗马教皇谴责、英国僧侣不满。亨利二世与贝克特的争执也就由此发生。1170 年,贝克特被害。亨利二世迫于

① Frank Barlow, *The Feudal Kingdom of England*, p.258.

教皇压力,取消了《克拉伦敦法规》中关于犯罪教士必须送达国王法庭的两条规定①,然而其他条款俱都融入了英国普通法。国王虽未获得全胜,然而他维护乃至扩张王权的目的实已达到。只不过,王权与教权的争执从此更趋激烈,到约翰王统治时发展至危机。

然而无论征服者威廉、亨利一世与亨利二世,其王权扩张都有节制。他们深知:封建王权的行使有它不可逾越的边界;懂得在革故鼎新的同时,尊重封君与封臣间基本的权利义务关系,重视与教会的妥协与合作。即便如亨利二世如此强有力的王者,也不讳于声称:"他的立法经过了大主教、主教、男爵、伯爵和英格兰贵族的建议和同意后才颁行"②。再者,诸王有着高超的统治才能与用人能力;王权的行使也"主要是为了国家利益"(Powers used moderately and on the whole for national ends)③,而非个人私心。因此,在他们治下,没有出现因王权扩张而导致的大规模、成气候的封臣抗议与叛乱。虽然也时有贵族表示愤懑,"但这种愤懑不能解释为整个贵族阶层普遍不满于国王的统治"(Yet it would be wrong to interpret such hostility and resentment as evidence of a general baronial opposition to the whole tenor of Henry II'rule)④。

及至狮心王理查德(Richard I,1189~1199在位)与约翰王掌权,二人治国才能远不及乃父乃祖,但他们承继了先辈的遗风与遗产,将王权扩张视为自然之理;不同于乃父乃祖者,王权在他们手里主要成了营私的工具,而非国家的需要。理查德对金钱之贪婪使他不惜出卖任何官职,甚至宣称"如果能找到一个买家,伦敦也可以卖了"(I would have sold the London if I could find a buyer),显见国民福祉从来不在他心上;约翰王比其兄有过之而无不及,纵情放荡,一味榨取。其结果,是王权无节制的滥用与封臣子民们无可容忍的反抗。这反抗在理查德一世统治时期已显露端倪。1196年,伦敦爆发抗议,其缘由正是国王不公平地征收重税。1197年底,当理查德一世要求英国贵族为其提

① 这事实上等于废除了《克拉伦敦法规》。

② W.L.Warren,*Henry II*,Berkeley:University of California Press,1977,p.381.

③ William McKechnie,*Magna Carta*,p.20.

④ W.L.Warren,*Henry II*,p.381.

供长达一年的骑士役义务时,林肯与索里兹伯里主教们群起而谴责①。大规模叛乱之所以未出现在理查德统治时期,主要源于四点:

其一,在尚武的封建时代,理查德以其英勇善战的声名获得人们尊重。他的“勇气与无畏,即便在那样的浪漫时代,亦无人比肩,因此赢得‘狮心王’名号”(No man, even in that romantic age, carried personal courage and intrepidity to a greater height; and this quality gained him the appellation of the lion-hearted)②。第 3 次十字军东征,理查德遭遇强劲对手、穆斯林英雄萨拉丁(Saladin, 1137 或 1138~1193,当时埃及、叙利亚、也门和巴勒斯坦的苏丹),虽则未能占领耶路撒冷(Jerusalem),仅令基督教徒获得前往圣地的自由通行权,但狮心王出类拔萃的军事天才使他无愧为基督教世界最伟大的战士。其二,受他委托行使权力的王家大法官、大主教休伯特·沃尔特(Chief Justiciar of England, Archbishop Hubert Walter)才干出众,颇善周旋,僧俗两界都愿与之交好。历史学家评论他,“由休伯特·沃尔特来治理英国,实在比理查德亲政要好。他不仅推行了王法,维持住治安,而且开始了一种新政策:信任乡镇里的中产阶级”(Hubert Walter, indeed, governed England better than would have done in person. He not only enforced the King's peace, but began a new policy of trusting the middle classes of town and country)③,从而获得其好感。和平、稳定的局面因此在他治下得以维持。其三,理查德一世统治时期,开启了市政自治的黄金时代。与亨利二世严厉压制城市自治萌芽,并将城市作为其自领地大肆抽取税金、利润不同,理查德一世的时代,一些城市建立了拥有较多自由的市政府。休伯特“颁了很多的特许状给各个城市,且让它们拥有特权:自选官吏、自主管理”(He granted charters to various towns, conveying the privilege of self-government through elected officials)④。因此之故,城市与市民利益较少受侵夺。其四,国王常年征战在外,不在国内。理查德一世统治英国整十年,十字军中度过近三年,被俘受拘 14 个月,亲理朝政不过半年,大部分时间都在对法作战或

① Barlow, *The Feudal Kingdom of England*, p.323.

② David Hume, *The History of England*, p.403.

③ Trevelyan, *The History of England*, London: Longmans Green and Co, 1952, p.165.

④ Trevelyan, *The History of England*, p.165.

准备对法作战。国内便有不满亦不能直接加于他身。

但约翰王在位时,情况就大为不同。他既不如狮心王拥有赫赫战功,反而一再败退,丢师弃甲,国人号之以“软剑”(softsword);也不如他知人善任,有忠实、能干的股肱之臣可以辅佐。1205 年休伯特·沃尔特去世,政府失去了可与教会保持友好关系的中介。他不以为憾,反以为喜,自以为去除了妨碍其专制的障碍。而新任大主教的选举直接导致了他与罗马教皇的冲突。后来他征战于外,任命摄政,此人却是众人痛恨的外国人与暴发户彼得·罗杰(hated alien and upstart,Peter des Roches)。他不施良政,将政府机构、王室法庭只当作他盘剥、泄愤的工具;同时又掠夺成性,专以侵夺封臣权利为好,无论进步与保守的贵族都不满于他。他的个性狂傲自大,沉迷于权力、猜忌于大臣,进而将王权行使发展至专制的地步,以至于举国上下,无论贫富贵贱、商人农民,没有不畏惧又痛恨他的。他缺乏政治远见与外交才能:先与教皇交恶,令国人精神上受尽折磨;后与教皇和好,却将国家主权与教会自由拱手相送,僧俗两界同感威胁。再有一点:他败退国内,将各种苛捐重税的罪名直接延揽于身,无可推脱。人们不能指望通过更换臣工而改变受压迫的现状,只好竖起反旗。各方力量汇聚起来,王权已完全处于弱势,而封臣力量占据了上风。叛乱不起,更待何时?

由此可见,导致《大宪章》的危机发生于约翰王统治下,而非其他时期,既是封君与封臣间权力与权利争执的必然结果,也有他个人乃至时运的因素在内。

恰如沃尔特·厄尔曼(Walter Ullmann)所言,“约翰对神权性王权(笔者注:即以上帝的名义实施统治,将王的意志视为法律,而且是不受限制的法律)的运用太拙劣了,结果引发了贵族们的对抗,乃至公然的敌对”①。而在本质上,正是代代扩张的王权,膨胀了约翰王傲慢的神权性王权观,削弱了他的封建王权观,未曾意识到封君作为封建制度的一部分,其实“没有多少余地来像至高无上的统治者一般实现君王的意愿”②;倘若不顾封君权力的有限性,

① 沃尔特·厄尔曼:《中世纪政治思想史》,第 143 页。

② 沃尔特·厄尔曼:《中世纪政治思想史》,第 141 页。

一再破坏他与封臣间的封建契约,必然招来贵族的反抗。也正如乔治·特里维廉(George Trevelyan)所言,"封建主义与专制是对立的。它虽然时常可为暴君政治,有时也可为无政府政治,但从不能为独裁政治。因为国王与封建地主间的权利义务在封建制度的安排下维持着缜密的平衡,不容某一方有过度的逾越"(For feudalism is the opposite of despotism.It may often be tyranny and it may sometimes be anarchy,but it is never despotism;for it is an elaborate balance of defined rights and duties as shared by the king and various holders of land)①;当诺曼—安茹王朝诸君主将此权利义务平衡关系打破,封君义务渐次减少,封臣负担渐次加重,不满情绪已在长期蓄积中时,约翰王趋向独裁的统治必然导致封臣叛乱与双方间权利、义务的重新认定,封君与封臣间的权利义务关系也必须调整至双方可接受的程度,达成新的平衡。

谈判与和解,权利义务关系的回归——《大宪章》之作成

《大宪章》就其目的来说,是一份和平协议(a treaty of firm peace)。君臣间各自权利义务界定下来后,贵族们向国王重新表示效忠,国王宽宥其叛乱,双方重修旧好的一份协议。这份协议究竟如何产生?由谁草定?何时谈成?国王签署又在何时?历来学者持论不一。

《大宪章》文本的形成以《贵族的条款》(*The Articles of the Barons*)②共 49 条为基础,此为学界共识;但《贵族的条款》是谁拿出来的呢?从叛乱一方为贵族,起事原因为争取贵族权利,以及该条款的名称来看,似乎应推定由贵族拿出。以研究大宪章而知名的威廉·麦克奇尼(William McKechine)、莫里斯·波威克(Maurice Powicke)、托马斯·陶特(Thomas Tout)等,均执此见解。叛乱贵族首领罗伯特·沃尔特还因之被视为"为英国人争取自由的第一位战

① Trevelyan,*The History of England*, p.167;屈勒味林:《英国史》,钱端升译,北京:东方出版社,2012 年,第 177~178 页。

② "The Articles of the Barons"(贵族的条款)并不是当时人对它的称呼,而是后人的命名。首次见于 19 世纪英国历史学家 William Stubbs 的著作 *Selected Charters*.

士"(the first champion of British liberty)①。但是,反对意见也不是没有。如莱恩·普尔(Lane Poole)就认为,依据政治经验与政治智慧判断,只有国王或其支持者才能拿出那样的文本;瑙盖特(Norgate)则指出,从宪章体现出的崇高境界来看,其作者应为大主教兰顿等②。意见执中者,有19世纪英国著名历史学家、宪政学家威廉·斯塔布斯(William Stubbs)与20世纪研究大宪章的另一名权威詹姆斯·霍尔特(James Holt)。二者均认为,贵族至少部分地参与了文件的起草。霍尔特的看法尤有说服力。他指出,从文字上看,《贵族的条款》具有鲜明的王室法庭文书特色,必定是熟悉法律文书者所为,很可能是贵族与国王谈判过后,由一位大法官法庭的书记官(a chancery clerk)将其意见综合整理撰写而成;《贵族的条款》盖有王印,也说明,它必然经历王室官员之手③。另外,《贵族的条款》第一句:"这些是贵族们要求并得到国王许可的条款"(These are the articles which the barons ask for and the lord king grants)④,更加有力地提示出:这份条款在双方讨论过后才产生,绝非某一单方意愿的表示。

设若霍尔特推论成立,一副王权与贵族封建权利争峙的短兵相接图就呈现出来。国王,为了王权的维护与扩张,在他面对最强大的挑战时,依然未肯过分示弱,无条件地退让;贵族,在他们控制首都,有力量提出权利要求时,也不得不考虑王权的尊严与自身的臣属地位,不得不考虑他们的安全与将来的命运。双方都懂得:须在坚持与妥协间寻找平衡,从中建立新的权利义务关系。

这一妥协与坚持的过程,必定显示出双方就权力与权利相争的激烈程度,所以接下来应探讨的问题是:《贵族的条款》何时拟定?《大宪章》又在何时

---

① J.C.Holt,"The Barons and the Great Charter",*The English Historical Review*,Vol.70,No. 274 (Jan.,1955),p.1.

② J.C.Holt,"The Barons and the Great Charter",*The English Historical Review*,Vol.70,No. 274 (Jan.,1955),p.1.

③ J.C.Holt,"The Making of Magna Carta", *The English Historical Review*, Vol. 72, No. 284 (Jul.,1957),p.403.

④ Harry Rothwell ed., *English Historical Document*, *1189 ~ 1327*, London: Eyre Spottiswood, 1975,p.311.

谈成?

19 世纪英国最杰出的历史学家,并在整个欧洲享有盛名的威廉·斯塔布斯,在其 3 卷本《英国宪政史》中,虽未讨论《贵族的条款》何时拟定,但明确说明了约翰王在 6 月 15 日前已经同意了《贵族的条款》,并加盖了王印;《大宪章》的发表就在 6 月 15 日,他与贵族在兰尼米德会面的这一天。在他看来,这是因国王失去伦敦,形势紧迫,亟须与贵族们妥协的缘故。①

比斯塔布斯晚一代的麦克奇尼则认为,《贵族的条款》由贵族们于 6 月 15 日(周一)出示于国王,并在那天盖上王印,标志着它拟定完成;《大宪章》各项条款则于 19 日(周五)得到双方确认,并抄出数份复本,盖上王印。中间的 3 天即周二、周三、周四,是在对各条款做细节的调整。一切都在周五那天全部确定,包括反叛贵族对负责监护《大宪章》执行的 25 人贵族委员会的提名,并获得国王同意;《大宪章》定稿后抄出复本、盖上王印;贵族向国王重新表示效忠等②。

20 世纪的霍尔特推翻了上述看法。笔者对之颇为认同。依据霍尔特的解释,从反叛贵族占据伦敦,到他们与国王谈判并拟定和约,重新宣誓效忠,前后经历四个阶段③。

预备阶段,5 月 27 日~6 月 10 日,双方敌意暂收,为和谈作准备。自 5 月 27 日至 6 月 8 日,兰顿大主教与各方贵族代表陆续与国王见面,讨论和谈事宜。5 月 29 日,约翰王启动首轮谈判。当着教皇使节的面,他向贵族们表示:议定的条款需得到教皇的许可。这一次谈判约持续至 6 月 5 日。5 月 31 日,他从汉普郡的奥迪厄姆(Odiham)移驾温莎城堡,住到 6 月 26 日④。通过中间人兰顿大主教及其他主教的调停、斡旋,约翰王与贵族们议成《贵族的条款》。6 月 10 日,国王与贵族会面于兰尼米德草地,在条款上盖上王印。

---

① William Stubbs, *The Constitutional History of England in its Origin and Development* Vol.1, London: University of Oxford Press, 1873, p.569.

② William McKechnie, *Magna Carta*, pp.38~40.

③ 参见 J.C.Holt, *Magna Carta*, Cambridge: Cam bridge Universtiy Press, 1992, pp.237~266; J. C.Holt, "The Making of Magna Carta," *The English Historical Review*, Vol.72, No. 284(Jul., 1957), pp.401~422.

④ 其间,即 6 月 5 日,国王曾前往温彻斯特,但在 9 日时,他已返回温莎。

第一阶段，6月10~14日。《贵族的条款》盖上王印，表示国王已显示诚意与贵族谈判；贵族的大部分要求已得到国王口头认可，并可将之作为预备协议用于正式谈判。因此，它立刻被送达尚未加入谈判的其他贵族代表手中。正式谈判开始，谈判以《贵族的条款》为基础，但参与谈判的贵族依然只是部分代表。

第二阶段，6月15~18日。15日，全体贵族代表集结于兰尼米德，与国王正式会面。18日，《大宪章》基本拟定，贵族们向国王表示，将于第二天向国王宣誓效忠。

第三阶段，6月19日。贵族们向国王宣誓效忠，《大宪章》盖上王印。但日期仍署为6月15日，表明贵族们接受预备用以谈判的《大宪章》草案。与《贵族的条款》同样，《大宪章》文本出于大法官法庭的一位专业人员之手。而它抄送各地，则在数日之后。

总之，《贵族的条款》不可能晚至6月15日才拟定，否则，难以解释《大宪章》与《贵族的条款》之间较大的篇幅差异与复杂程度；《大宪章》也不可能发表于6月15日，尽管国王与贵族面临危机，均亟图早日寻得解决方案，但谁也不可能不经历一番坚持与争峙，就轻易妥协。在笔者看来，这不符合权力与权利竞争之逻辑。

王权与封臣权利的博弈当然不止表现在过程，它必须体现为结果。《大宪章》与《贵族的条款》究竟有何不同？二者在哪些方面体现了封君与封臣间权力与权利的竞争？

仔细比较，不难发现，这一轮封君与封臣的较量中，国王是彻底的输家。《大宪章》不仅基本保留了《贵族的条款》，少有删除，还增加了一些条款与许多细节性的说明。

最引人注目的是第1条与第63条，指明"英国教会应予自由，其权利仍旧不动，其自由权不得侵犯；英国人民应安然、泰然、全然享受一切增加之自由权"。这两项增加的条款应出于大主教兰顿的影响。作为僧俗贵族的领袖，他为教会争得了自由权；作为英国人民的精神领袖，他也为英国人民的自由权不受国王侵犯建立了屏障。

《大宪章》第2条关于继承金缴纳数额的具体规定：伯爵与男爵的继承人

缴100磅、骑士继承人缴100先令,系《贵族的条款》已然说明留待将来讨论的内容。从约翰王历年来滥用此项领主权利的记录来看:1202年,他曾要求一名骑士为继承其封地缴纳300马克;又有一次,他向一名伯爵勒索5000马克(相当于3300磅)①,国王收取继承金的权利被大大缩小了。

《大宪章》第21条,"伯爵与男爵犯罪者,只应由其贵族并视其犯罪之程度科以罚金",也属《贵族的条款》所无。它进一步将国王作为领主的裁判权限定在最古老的传统内。约翰王再也不能随心所欲滥施权力,敲诈贵族。

无疑,国王与其支持者在谈判过程中必然提出了不少反对意见,因为"《大宪章》最后一稿的起草至少花了4天"②,但在大主教兰顿明显倾向并支持反对国王的贵族一方时,国王一方显得那样的无力,除了退让,似乎无有出路。无奈与压迫之下,约翰王只好同意《大宪章》,但他拒绝亲署其名,只是令人盖上了王印。反对国王的贵族们在这3个星期的谈判中,的确"为他们自己干得很漂亮"③(In three weeks the barons had done very well for themselves)。然而,正是这种博弈过程中的力量过度失衡为《大宪章》的迅即被取消埋下了伏笔。

封君与封臣权利、义务的重新界定——《大宪章》之性质与内容

1215年《大宪章》凡63条,不少学者视之为英国宪政的开篇与英国宪法之精神的体现。前文所提英国历史学家威廉·斯塔布斯曾言,"整个英国的宪政史都不过是对大宪章的注解"(The whole of the constitutional history of England is little more than a commentary on Magna Carta)④。从大宪章对英国宪政体制所产生的影响来说,如此说法不可谓错。然而,在当时,它只不过是封

① William McKechnie, *Magna Carta*, pp.198~201.

② J.C.Holt, *Magna Carta*, Cambridge: Cambridge Universtiy Press, 1992, p.250.

③ J.C.Holt, *Magna Carta*, p.242.

④ William Stubbs, *The Constitutional History of England in its Origin and Development* Vol.1, London: University of Oxford Press, 1873, p.572.

君与封臣间权利、义务的重新界定而已。倘若依照它在后世发生的影响来解释它在13世纪的涵义，必然是对历史的误解与封建政治的误判，似乎封建政治的一开始就有了宪政的思想，而忽略了宪政思想在英国经由数百年发展而来。

大宪章在中国通常又被称为“自由大宪章”，细究起来，这样叫法有违原意。追溯《大宪章》的拉丁文标题“Magna Carta Libertarum”，其中“Libertarum”是复数形式，转译为英文即为“Liberties”。查《牛津大辞典》与《牛津高阶英汉辞典》“liberty”词条，都解释得很清楚：当它以复数形式出现时，意为“权利”(right)或被赋予的“特权”(privilege)。再读西方学者专门研究大宪章的著作，不难发现，无论他们在形式上视大宪章为“权利的宣言”(a declaration of rights)，一部法律(a law)，或有关权利的“条约”、“协议”或“契约”(a treaty, or an agreement, or a contract of rights)等，均将其内容解释为“权利”(rights)或“自由权”(liberties)。研究大宪章达半个世纪的詹姆斯·霍尔特(James C. Holt)还特意指出，“大宪章是一份自由权的陈述而非自由的声明”(The Great Charter is a statement of liberties rather an assertion of liberty)①。中国学者戚国淦先生在《大不列颠百科全书》中译本“大宪章”词条中，也将“liberties”译作“自由权”而非“自由”。这都说明，“自由大宪章”的译法其实不当，改为《权利大宪章》方贴近原意。除非读者能将“自由”二字作广义的理解，懂得它意为“自由权”或“权利”；就像我们在读洛克的《政府论》时一样，知道他有时所说的自由指的是“生命、自由、健康、财产”等权利。

《大宪章》的内容确定为有关权利的保护之后，又一个问题接踵而至：保护谁的权利？贵族的权利还是英国全体民众的权利？对此，学界意见分歧。其中两派观点颇为对立。

一派认为，大宪章所谓权利非只局限于贵族之权利，而是对全体民众公共利益的同等保护；历史学家亨利·哈勒姆(Henry Hallam)声称，“大宪章美就美在它将公民权平等地分配给了所有阶层的自由民”(An equal distribution of

---

① J.C.Holt, *Magna Carta*, p.5.

civil rights to all classes of freemen forms the peculiar beauty of the charter)①;威廉·斯塔布斯也说,大宪章的诸项条款"确实表示,贵族们并未自私地只为自己要求特权"(This proves,if any proves wanted,that the demands of the barons were not selfish exactions of privilege for themselves)②。20世纪之前,持此观点的学者颇占主流,著名法学家爱德华·科克(Edward Coke)、威廉·布莱克斯通(William Blackstone)等均属此派③;但现在来看,已经越来越少。

另一派则坚持:在13世纪的英国,上下不同阶层的利益绝无可能得到同等照顾,平等实为一现代观念,而非当时人的思想。即便说《大宪章》有少量条款涉及佃农权利的保护,其原因也只在于"他们是其领主的珍贵财产"(they formed valuable assets of their lords)④,保护他们的权利也就是保护领主的权利。何况,《大宪章》大部分条款针对的是拥有地产、庄园的领主,而非城市商人与自由民。再者,封建社会构建于分层严格的等级之上,其"本质是阶级特权与阶级私利,个体自由权与之抵触不相容"⑤。《大宪章》只能是一份贵族纲领,而非全民权利书。广大人民既不为贵族关心,也不为他们所考虑。历史学家特里维廉着意强调,"诸贵族之动机实出于私心与阶级意识,其程度,不多不少,与英国其他阶级与派别是一样的"(The barons were acting selfishly and class consciously to just the same degree—no more and no less—as other English classes and parties)⑥。若说这些贵族们认为,最低贱的佃农也可拥有与其相等的权利,那他们必然不会同意。詹姆斯·霍尔特也明确指出,尽管《大宪章》比当时大部分欧洲大陆国家的妥协条款更多地照顾到了自治城市、商人与自由民的利益,但它并没有表现出多少平等意识⑦。

① Henry Hallam,View of the State of Europe during the Middle Ages,Vol.2,Charleston:Nabu Press,2010,Vol.2,p.447.

② William Stubbs,*The Constitutional History of England in its Origin and Development* Vol.1, London:University of Oxford Press,1873,p.571.

③ William McKechnie,*Magna Carta*,p.113.

④ William McKechnie,*Magna Carta*,p.119.

⑤ William Stuart,"The Constitutional Clause of Magna Carta," *Virginia Law Review*,Vol.2, No.8(May,1915),p.567.

⑥ Trevelyan,*The History of England*, p.169.

⑦ J.C.Holt,*Magna Carta*, Cambridge:Cambridge Universtiy Press,1992,p.276,344.

倘若接受后一派观点，就必须再回答一个问题，即，大宪章为什么如特里维廉所言，可称之为“全民族的文书”（a national document）[①]——凡加入大宪章运动的各阶级都得到了若干利益。解释不难得到。此乃因诸贵族为借重各阶层自由民的力量赢得反叛的胜利而采取的策略。他们将各阶层自由民的利益加入其中，并非确实为了平等地主张各阶层的权利与自由，而是为了充分、完全地获得自身利益。当然，其动因中可能也掺杂些正义原则。

封臣权利握有之域便是封君权力退让之处。由于封君与王权的先天独大性，封臣或国民权利的获得与维护，首先取决于国王之权利与义务的界定，因此，《大宪章》从两个方面对封君与王权加以限定，一是国王的权利以何处为界；二是国王的义务如何履行，即他如何实施良政。这也是《大宪章》最为鲜明的特色之一：一份以封君封臣权利义务关系为主要内容的文件。

从封君的权利界限来看，《大宪章》涉及范围甚多。包括教会干预权（第1、22、46条）、继承金权（第2、3、43条）；监护权（第3、4、5、37条）；婚姻指定权（第6、7、8条）；债务处置权（第9、10、26条）；征税权（第12、14、15条）；伦敦管理权（第13条）、征取劳役权（第16、23、43条）；司法权（第17~22、24、34、38、39、44、45、52~54条）；封地复归权（第26、27、32条）等。

学界关于《大宪章》对君权的界定，有一种看法，即《大宪章》是对英国古老习俗的重新认定，或者说对“虔敬者”爱德华（King Edward the Confessor）所制订的法则的恢复，“基本上没有新东西”（the charter contains little that is absolutely new）[②]。这个观点经由法学大家布莱克斯通、弗雷德里克·梅特兰（Frederick Maitland）、历史学家斯塔布斯等传播，追随者甚众。然而结合王权扩张历史细读条款，不得不说，这个结论较为粗疏，稍欠细致。《大宪章》中关于封君权利的认定，既有对英国封建传统的恢复，也有不少是对诺曼征服以来王权扩张的承认，有的甚至是亨利二世也不拥有的权利。

开宗明义第一条，“英国教会应予自由”的承诺，无疑仅将英国教会的自由权推回到威廉一世时。它明确规定，教会对高级教士的选举权不受国王羁

---

① Trevelyan, *The History of England*, p.171.

② Frederick Pollock and Frederick Maitland, *History of English Law before the Time of Edward*, Vol.1, Cambridge: Cambridge University Press, 1898, p.172.

束,因为国王已经主动将此权利交回教会;同时又委婉地、不卑不亢地向罗马教皇表示,“英国教会”的自由也不应受罗马干预,英国教会宁以坎特伯雷大主教马首是瞻,而不唯教皇意志是听。联系到兰顿不依教皇指令惩罚反叛贵族、着意维护英国利益的行为,此意涵不难推测。然而英国教会的自由权回到了虔敬者爱德华时期吗?恐怕不能这样说,因为国王对教会的权利显然比虔敬者爱德华要多。

缴纳继承金诸条款同样是对威廉一世君权扩张的承认。自威廉一世将英国所有土地定为“从国王手中”持有,缴纳继承金就成为封臣普遍认可的义务,并传之于后代。约翰王时代的贵族正是因为对此王权扩张的承认,而在《大宪章》中为封地继承金定出他们认为合理的金额。

第12与14条显然反映出,贵族们同意了亨利一世与亨利二世的举措——征收盾牌金。只不过,他们恨透了狮心王查理与约翰王对此税权漫无边际的滥用,所以规定盾牌金与援助金的征收仅限于3种情况:赎回国王、国王长子受封骑士与长公主出嫁,而且必须召集贵族与官员讨论,经过他们同意后才能征收。

第13条关于伦敦保有一切自由权与自由风俗习惯的规定,则说明,这是对理查王期间才发育起来的城市自治权的认可。伦敦,在亨利一世以及他之前,一直被视为国王的自领地,不存在如《大宪章》中所说的自由权。只是到了理查王时代,休伯特·沃尔特替王理政时,伦敦市民才被允许自己选举市长,自主管理城市事务。

而《大宪章》赋予国王派遣法官参与地方法院司法的权利,简直近于新的王权的创建。尽管大宪章有力地收缩了亨利二世建立起来的司法管辖权,如第17条规定:民事诉讼不得向王座法庭提起;然而在第18条规定:关于收回土地、收回遗产、最后举荐等涉及封主权利的诉讼,国王有权派遣法官2人,每年4次,前往郡法院参与审判。这一项权利,是亨利二世也未曾想到过的。

当然,《大宪章》确有很多条款回到了古老的盎格鲁—撒克逊时代。第9条要求王室不得强取封臣财产以抵偿债务;第16条保护领主要求臣属服劳役的权利;第21条强调伯爵与男爵犯罪,必须由与其身份同等的贵族审判;第24条规定郡守、执行官等不得受理刑事诉讼;第25条说明各地方行政单位按照旧有田地继续存在；第 30 条含蓄声明领主有权征用臣属马匹、车辆；第 31 条明令国王及其官吏不得强取城堡木材；第 34 条废弃王家令状强制土地诉讼中的被告到王室法庭申辩；第 39 条保留领主对其臣属的封建司法权；第 47 条规定国王应归还人民在森林中的权利等等，不一而足，都是对英国古老的封建传统与习俗的重申。

总之，尽管《大宪章》将诺曼征服以来历代君主逐渐扩张了的王权大大地推了回去，约翰王丧失了其父祖苦心经营、累积壮大的诸多权力，但这不意味着 13 世纪的英国王权与封君权利回到了盎格鲁—撒克逊时代。它站在了新的起点上。国王一方面不得不表示遵循古老的传统，另一方面也获得了虔敬者爱德华不曾有的权利与权力，并且负载着新时代的君主所应承担的义务与责任。

依据《大宪章》所列，这些义务包括：召集会议以听取贵族意见（第 14 条）；保护城市自治权（第 13 条）；约束官员不得强取暴夺（第 28～31 条）、不得在无证据的情况下任意执法（第 38 条）；任命负有司法、执法、保安等职责之官员，必须以其具有法律知识为条件（第 45 条）；统一度量衡（第 35 条）；允许通商自由、保护外国商人（第 41 条）；革除森林管理之弊端（第 47、48 条）；不得滥用、拒绝或延搁权利与赏罚（第 36、40 条）；保证英国教会与英国人民的一切自由权、权利与特权（第 63 条）等。

在界定封君权利与义务的同时，《大宪章》也规定了封臣的权利与义务。由于封君与封臣权利、义务的对应性，所以不难看出，《大宪章》很多条款既针对封君，也针对封臣。换言之，封君所拥有的权利便是封臣该尽的义务；封君所不能要求的权利与他所应尽的义务便是封臣的权利。另外，《大宪章》还着意强调，国王的封臣在对其下级臣属拥有权利时，也应同等地履行义务，即保护其下级臣属主要是自由民的权利。譬如第 15、20 条分别规定：贵族只能在为赎回该贵族的身体、长子受封为骑士以及长女出嫁时向自由民征取贡金；自由民犯罪须按轻重公平处置。另外，第 16、39 条，即“凡服务于武士之采地或其他自由保有地之人，不得强制其承担额外役务”；“自由民除经贵族依法判决或遵照法律之规定外，不得加以扣留、监禁、没收其财产、褫夺其法律保护权，或加以放逐、伤害、搜索或逮捕”，虽主要是为限制国王的权利而言，但也规约了贵族的权利范围。地位不及贵族的自由民，其权利同样受到保护。之所以出现这样的条款，乃因诺曼征服以来颇具效力的王权扩张主要通过法律改革的程序进行，当国家法律必须遵循的精神渗透至传统的封建权利义务观时，全体自由民都有权受到法律平等保护的观念也就体现在《大宪章》中。尽管当时的自由民仅指土地持有者，在总人口中所占比例相当低①。《大宪章》在后来一再被确认，其原因也正是因为法律应该受到尊重这一观念主宰了英国人的思想，哪怕君主也不例外。

与封君封臣权利义务为主要内容的《大宪章》，还有一个同样显著的特征：强制性。若非贵族们武装起事，大主教兰顿要求国王保证国内和平，约翰王一时间又在军事上占不了上风，他绝不肯同意这“如同将自己置于奴役之下”的宪章。1215 年 4 月底，当贵族们提出条件，与之交涉，要求各种自由权时，约翰勃然大怒，叫道：“这些贵族们为什么不把我的王国也要走?”(Why the barons did not also demand of him his kingdom?)②。恼怒而不肯及时妥协的国王招来了贵族的报复，《大宪章》因此出现了不少惩罚性的条款。如第 47~52 条、第 55~59 条，要么要求国王归还人质，退还被他夺走的信物、文契、土地、城堡等；要么要求他解除贵族们所痛恨的官吏的职务，永不录用；要么要求他将外国兵士、仆役与雇佣兵赶出英国，以削弱其武装力量。最为甚者是第 61 条：一旦发现国王及其臣仆不遵行宪章，由 25 名贵族组成的委员会必须对他施加压迫——面折君前，奏请改正；倘若国民不愿发誓跟随贵族委员会作压制行动，国王应命令该国民宣誓跟从。

显然，这个委员会如同一个专门监督国王及其臣仆是否遵行宪章的审判团。而国王及其臣仆在什么情况下算是违反了宪章，第 61 条并无明确规定，只说只要 25 人中的 4 人发现国王或其臣仆不遵行宪章，就有权施行压迫，其压迫手段包括夺取君主之城堡、土地与其他财产。这意味着，国王所面对的审判团权力武断、手段严厉。胁迫性如此之强，不要说个性傲慢的约翰，任何一

① 《土地清查报告》即《末日审判书》记载，英格兰总人口为 30 万，只有 1 万 8 千人被列入自由民，自由民比例仅占总人口的 6%左右。William Stuart,“The Constitutional Clause of Magna Carta”, *Virginia Law Review*, Vol.2, No. 8(May, 1915), p.572.

② David Hume, *The History of England*, Vol.1, p.442.

位君主都难以接受。《大宪章》刚刚发布,国王便已准备撕毁和约,英国最终未能免于内战。教皇英诺森三世得悉《大宪章》发布,也立刻声明:“国王是出于畏惧而接受这份协议,它的签署不仅非法而且不正义”①。消息传回英国,《大宪章》问世刚及三月便归于无效。从其永造和平、避免战争的目的来说,《大宪章》确然如霍尔特所言,“它在当时是一个失败”(In 1215 Magna Carta was a failure)②。麦基奇尼也指出,“第61条手段暴烈,处处都可能即刻引发危险;其设计对英国将来的宪政发展有害无益”(It was a violent measure, full of immediate danger, and calculated to exercise a baneful influence on constitutional development in the future)③。大宪章后来历经确认或恢复,但这一条以及那些明显是为了惩罚约翰王的条款从来也没有再写进去。

英国宪政第一步——1215年《大宪章》之后

1215年《大宪章》虽然马上被取消,但它没有死亡。约翰王死后,大宪章立刻恢复生机。1216年,年仅9岁的亨利三世(1216~1272年在位)继承王位,贵族们为声明并确保其权利,要求国王重颁大宪章④。当然,它经过了删改⑤。胁迫性过强的条款,以及因形势需要无法执行的条款如第51条遣散外国兵士等,均不见于1216年《大宪章》。1217、1225年,大宪章经过再度修改后被确认⑥。后一个版本成了法律,因为这是已经成人的国王自由意志的表示,并且将之付诸执行。此后,大宪章一再重颁均以1225年版本为准。

---

① Harry Rothwell ed., *English Historical Document, 1189~1327*, p.326.英诺森此段声明原文如下:He did not dare to refuse what the barons had dared to demand. And so by such violence and fear as might affect the most courageous of mean he was forced to accept an agreement which is not only shameful and demeaning but also illegal and unjust, thereby lessening unduly and impairing his royal rights and dignity.

② J.C.Holt, *Magna Carta*, p.1.

③ William McKechnie, *Magna Carta*, p.473.

④ 这里所说大宪章,非特指某一年份的大宪章,因而不加书名号。

⑤ 1216年《大宪章》共42条,删去22条,补入第42条。余下条款略有更改。

⑥ 1217年《大宪章》共47条。新增第39、43、46、47条。删除1215年《大宪章》第36、38条。其余条款在顺序上稍有调整,内容有合有分,文字亦有删补。1225年《大宪章》共37条。删除1217年《大宪章》第47条,其余条款基本保持不动,但部分有合并。

有趣的是,此后大宪章的重颁,有时是贵族与国王继续争峙权利与权力的结果,类似 1215 年危机的重复,虽则程度不同;有时则是国王为恢复或巩固王权主动采用的手段,表示愿意遵循传统,希望臣民效忠、支持于他。无论哪一种情况,大宪章的重颁都是为了确认"王在法下"的原则。大宪章也正是在这样的一再确认中,渐渐地脱离了它原来狭隘的意图,而迈向了宪政的方向。

宪政的开端伴随着议会(parliament)的发展。1258 年,由莱斯特伯爵(Earl of Leicester)、西蒙·德·蒙特福特(Simon de Montfort)领导的贵族团体(a community of realm)为使议会经常召开,作为代表整个王国表达意见的场所,并使国王受制于它,利用大宪章作为其政治改革的合法资源,组成牛津议会(Oxford Parliament),起草《牛津条例》(*Provision of Oxford*),将议会权力大大扩张。1264 年,西蒙宣布从各县召集骑士参与议会。议会成员构成得以发生前所未有的变化。它不再局限于一小群大贵族,而扩及王国的中下层骑士。尽管西蒙的议会改革运动于次年失败,然而扩大了的议会并未因之而缩小。14 世纪时,贵族、骑士齐聚议会的场景已成常态,甚至有城市中的自由民加入。其中原因皆因大宪章作为根本大法的地位已然确定,国王难以否认其中所赋予国人的自由权。

也就是在 14 世纪,使大宪章成为"英国人幸运的宪法"(our happy constitution)①的"误读"过程开始。爱德华三世(Edward III,1327~1377)在位期间,议会先后通过了六项法规(six statutes,1331~1368 年),将大宪章某些条款的涵义广为延伸。其一,将第 39 条即 1225 年《大宪章》第 29 条,"由身份与之平等的贵族合法裁决"(lawful judgment of peers)解释为"由贵族及陪审团审判"(trail by peers or trail by jury)。大宪章中仅见萌芽的权利保护条款长成了有力量的枝条。其二,"王国的法律"(law of the land)被定义为"正当法律程序"(due process of law),这就把普通法法庭之外的其他机构譬如国王的议事会(council)或特殊委员会(special committees)的司法权排除在外,确立了普通法法庭至为重要的地位。其三,"没有自由人"(no free man)的措辞先改为"没有人"(no man),再改为"无论身为什么等级或处于什么情况下,没有人"

① Trevelyan, *The History of England*, p.169.

(no man of whatever estate or condition he may be)。因大宪章而受益的人群,从范围狭隘的自由人即土地持有者,扩及整个社会。①

有了这样的"误读",再加上大宪章的一再被确认——14 世纪,它被确认 30 次,以及国王在西敏寺大教堂加冕登基时需将大宪章宣读于众,大宪章真正成了全民族的权利文书,其神圣不可违背的法律地位亦深植人们心中。当时,无论是面向"律师还是普遍士绅的法律书籍,均将大宪章列为英国普通法正当程序传统中的第一部法规"(Lawbooks listing the Charter as the first of the statutes taught not only the lawyers but also the country gentry the common law tradition of due process)。有人呼吁,将牛津、剑桥大学的罗马法与教会法(cannon law)课程代之以大宪章。甚至连农民也懂得用大宪章捍卫其权利。他们在向庄园法庭抱怨时,会说"这是不合理的,违反大宪章的"(against reason and Magna Carta)②。

15 世纪,大宪章似乎显得"功效已收,退居幕后,不复为世人所注意"(In the Fourteenth and Fifteenth century it fell into the back ground,its task apparently accomplished)③,仅仅被确认了 8 次。然而它不为世人注意的真正原因并非因其"功效已收",乃因英国战乱频仍。百年战争(Hundred Years of Wars,1337~1453)结束不久,很快又爆发了玫瑰战争(Wars of Roses,1455~1485),人们关心的是王冠落入谁手,而不是王权滥用与否。贵族们趁乱把持权力,行恶地方,人们反而希望加强中央政府权力。大宪章本质上是为限制王权滥用而设,在王权虚弱、亟待加强的时代,它自然无有太大用武之地。然而即便如此,也不能说大宪章在 15 世纪完全被人遗忘。法庭上,依然可见申诉人、辩护人、律师、法官引用大宪章条款解决争议。一位法官,约翰·福特斯克爵士(Sir John Fortescue)撰著阐明两个政府原则:1.法治;2.法律的权威来自于人民的意志,议会立法需经人民同意并得到国王认可④。这种有限君主制与混合政府的思想来自大宪章。

---

① 参见 J.C.Holt,*Magna Carta*,pp.9~10;Ralph Turner,*Magna Carta*,pp.123~124.

② Ralph Turner,*Magna Carta:Through the Ages*, Pearson Education Limited,2003,p.113,127.

③ Trevelyan,*The History of England*,p.172.

④ Ralph Turner,*Magna Carta*,p.134.

及至 16 世纪,都铎王朝建立,大宪章比前一个世纪更受冷落。其原因出自多方面。首先,先后经历百年战争与玫瑰战争的英国人,渴望结束混乱无序与贵族势力霸道横行的局面,对于中央政府权力的强化持欢迎态度,甚至宁愿牺牲一些自由权而换来社会秩序的安定。其次,都铎王朝的君主们也并未将其统治发展至专制的地步。他们承认王国的最高权威属于王在其中的议会(king in the parliament);尊重普通法所建立的正当法律程序传统。不少君主,如亨利八世、伊丽莎白一世,工于统治,颇得民心。动不动就造反、叛乱,颠覆王权的行为在当时民众看来,是为大逆不道。时移势转,可想而知,莎士比亚在其剧作《约翰王》(*The Life and Death of King John*)对 1215 年《大宪章》只字未提,实与其时代背景相关。再次,亨利八世与罗马教皇对抗,在英国人看来,是为英国教会争取自由权,反对者不多。而大宪章背后罗马教皇强悍的身影,反而使它一旦被拿出,就会显得不合时宜。最后,议会下院社会基础扩大,骑士阶层越来越多地进入议会下院。他们既然有发表政治见解的机会,也就无需倚靠或诉之于古老的大宪章,申诉其权利。有趣的是,就在这个时候(1534 年),拉丁文写就的《大宪章》第一次被全文译为英语印刷出版。虽然它译笔拙劣,语句冗赘,时或语序颠倒,然而大致意思已然表达出来。译者乔治·菲勒斯(George Ferrers),既以诗名见著,又是积极的政治活动家,通过他的努力传播,大宪章未至于彻底湮没于历史的陈灰。

17 世纪王权的专制使大宪章焕发华彩。斯图亚特王朝两国王詹姆斯一世(1603~1625)与查理一世(1625~1649)遵奉王权神授论,以为"君主的意志就是法律的来源,法官不过是'王座下的狮子',必当秉承圣意"(the will of the Prince was the source of law,and that the Judges were 'lions under the throne', bound to speak as they directed them)①。王权的绝对专制主义遇到了捍卫普通法至上原则与独立精神的法学家与政治家的抵抗。

身兼大法官与议员两职的爱德华·柯克爵士(Sir Edward Coke,1552~1634)将大宪章奉为"奠定英格兰法律基本原则的宣言……是对普通法缺陷的额外补充",一再用古老的宪章陈述王在法下的传统。面对强横且以削职

① Trevelyan,*The History of England*,p.391.

相威胁的查理一世，他坚持，“国王自应在万人之上，却也应在上帝与法律之下”（King ought to be under no man，but ought to be under God and law）①。他还援引13、14世纪以来的英国普通法解释，指出君王意志不当超越边界，这边界就是古老而传统的自由权；《大宪章》早有条款规定国王须得征求议会同意方可征税等等。

另一位法学家约翰·塞尔登爵士（Sir John Selden，1584～1654）援引1225《大宪章》第29条，即1215《大宪章》第39条，宣称“所有自由人都不应被拘禁，除非遵循了英国的法律传统”②。他第一个将大宪章与人身保护联系起来，且将自由民的概念拓宽至13世纪的贵族绝不肯承认的范围。

尽管科克与塞尔登曲解了大宪章，因此受到学者批评，谓之为反历史或伪历史的解释；但他们把大宪章高立于“英国自由之神”（the goddess of English Freedom）的地位实有助于英国君主制趋向宪政的方向。1628年6月，一份与大宪章性质类似的文件——《权利请愿书》（*The Petition of Rights of 1628*）诞生。与当年的约翰王一样，查理一世企图高于法律与传统之上，结果导致臣民反抗乃至内战。只不过，这次反对君主的不是贵族，而是议会；起草新的权利宪章的不是代表狭隘的贵族利益的罗伯特·沃尔特等，而是捍卫英国人民自由权的科克与塞尔登等。

由此权利请愿书驱动，光荣革命（Glorious Revolution）前后，又有《人身保护法修正案》（*The Habeas Corpus Amendment Act of 1679*）与《权利法案》（*The Bill of Rights of 1689*）通过议会摆在御案前。英国宪制的稳固根基从此奠定。英国人民不但有了更为强大的捍卫自由的武器，议会至上的概念也使其主权渐渐归于代议机关。17世纪，正当整个欧洲的君主制越来越趋向绝对专制时，英国的君主制却离它越来越远。

18世纪，大宪章已经“成为整个英国宪法精神的象征”（It had become a symbol for the spirit of our whole constitution）③，受到所有英国人的遵奉。无论是托利党人布莱克斯通（William Blackstone，1732～1780），还是辉格党人埃德

---

① Ralph Turner，*Magna Carta*，pp.147～154.

② Ralph Turner，*Magna Carta*，p.156.

③ Trevelyan，*The History of England*，p.172.

蒙·伯克(Edmund Burke,1729~1797),“都在通过英国最古老的改革——大宪章,孜孜以求英国人自由权的渊源”(Our oldest reformation is that of Magna Carta.You will see that Sir Edward Coke,……and indeed all great man who follow him,to Blackstone,are industrious to prove the pedigree of our liberties)①。威廉·皮特(William Pitt the elder)还将大宪章比喻为“英国宪法的圣经”(The Bible of English Constitution)。一部封君与封臣间的权利义务契约已然完全演变为英国宪政思想的活水。之所以有此演变,大致有如下缘由:

首先,大宪章是一份封建契约,封建主义的权利义务关系中内含着制约王权的力量。其制约力来源于封君对封臣的效忠依赖。若无封臣的效忠,王权难以维持;而封臣效忠与否,取决于封君是否履行其义务。这种权利义务观投射于王权,令国王不得不遵循王权行使的规则。此规则,在封建主义时代,乃为国王遵守与其封臣间的契约,而在封建主义作为一种社会制度逐渐解体,土地契约不再成为君主要求臣民服从的主要来源时,王权的行使规则就必须转换为赋予并尊重臣民的自由权,凭此换取他们对王权的效忠。英国人自由权的确立,不能不追溯至大宪章。

其次,大宪章的产生,实有赖于普通法的立基。普通法虽为强化王权而创造,但它一旦产生,便超越于王权,具有神圣不可违背的独立性与至上性,并且成为判断王权行使是否正义的标准。大宪章能成为英国宪政发展的第一步,就在于普通法赋予了它诸多可供超越的萌芽。也正是在这个意义上,特里维廉指出,英国“宪法实为封建主义的女儿与普通法联姻者”(Our constitution was the child of feudalism married to the common law)②。

再次,大宪章作为抵制专制最有效的一次行动,为后人提供了示范作用。利用大宪章抵制暴政、申诉权利的人,并不理会它原来的意思,而是按照自己的需要理解和解释它。解释的次数多了,它就褪去了封建色彩,披上宪政的光辉。恰如一位学者所言,“大宪章最大的宪政价值不在于它自身的构成,而在

① Edmund Burke,*Reflections on French Revolution*,London:The Temple Press,1951,p.29.

② Trevelyan,*The History of England*, p.167.

于它被误构；不在于它真实的意图，而在于后世的人想要它有什么样的涵义”①。援引大宪章者，有些人并不知道大宪章到底说了些什么，只是按照他自己的愿望加以引用和延伸。大宪章某些条款的语焉不详，也为解释的延展提供了便利。再加上大宪章很早就拥有了无可辩驳的崇高地位，一再被确认。利用其权威地位，申诉权利，对于英国人来说，没有比大宪章更合适的选择。

最后，大宪章的诞生，依靠的是英国政治两种颇有张力的传统。中世纪的英国，实行的是一种“试探性”的政治体制。这种体制，一方面让国王明白：王权的安全取决于他是否知道“国民们会容忍什么和不能容忍什么；也就是说，他可以干些什么，不能干些什么。关于这一点如果他有闪失的话，就会出现反叛”②。另一方面，也让英国人形成了反抗权威的自然冲动③。英国政治的妥协与对抗传统因之而形成；大宪章就在这样的传统中诞生。大宪章之后，英国政治依然沿着这样的轨道运行。所以人们援引大宪章，并且逐渐使之适应宪政的需要，实乃自然之理。

总之，尽管大宪章在本质上属于一份封建契约，但由于它包含了王权有限、王在法下、依法治理、遏制暴政等宪政发展的核心要素，英国政治本身的传统也给它提供了扩展解释的空间，经过四个多世纪的“误读”与诠释后，它终于演变成为英国宪政史上最重要的第一步。

---

① William Stuart, "The Constitutional Clause of Magna Carta," *Virginia Law Review*, Vol. 2, No. 8 (May, 1915), p.581.

② 沃尔特·白芝浩：《英国宪法》，夏彦才译，北京：商务印书馆，2010 年，第 282 页。

③ 沃尔特·白芝浩：《英国宪法》，第 292 页。

延伸阅读

William Sharp McKechnie, *Magna Carta: A Commentary on the Great Charter of King John*, Glasgow: James Maclehose & Sons, 1914(威廉·夏普·麦克奇尼:《大宪章的历史导读》,李红海编译,北京:中国政法大学出版社,2016 年)。麦克奇尼是 19、20 世纪之交研究大宪章的权威,其研究特点是:考证细致、以"法"眼(法学视野)观之。譬如本书,对 1215 年《大宪章》63 条逐一做了细致解析,实为研究大宪章不可或缺的资料。不过,对于一般读者而言,其导言也许比正文的逐条解析更值得推荐。这正是中译本仅将导言译出的原因。

J.C.Holt, *Magna Carta*, Cambridge: Cambridge University Press, 1992. 作者霍尔特,比麦克奇尼晚一代,被誉为 20 世纪"大宪章研究的带头人"(the dean of Magna Carta Studies)。此书出版,立刻超越了有关大宪章研究的前代作品。

Ralph Turner, *Magna Carta: Through the Ages*, Pearson Education Limited, 2003. 20 世纪以来,大宪章研究可举三人为代表,或可说划分为三代。第一代以 McKechnie 为代表,着重于大宪章各条款的解释及其法律意义。第二代执牛耳者为 Holt,从大宪章产生的政治、政府管理与政治思想为背景阐述其诞生过程及其性质。第三代学人 Ralph Turner 主要研究《大宪章》产生之后对英国各时代政治、法律思想的影响。这本书即为 Turner 三十余年研究成果的归纳。

Frank Barlow, *The Feudal Kingdom of England, 1042~1216*(5th ed.), New York: Routledge, 2014. 适如巴洛所言,"没有故事的历史毫无意义(History without story is meaningless)",人类心理与行为的复杂性正是借助历史学家的故事点缀而得以充分呈现。这本书笔触细腻,行文生动,通过讲故事的方式再现了英国 11 至 13 世纪大主教、贵族与国王之间亦亲亦仇、时和时斗的封君封臣关系,对于了解《大宪章》的历史背景颇有意义。

W.L.Warren,*Henry II*,Berkeley:University of California Press,1977. 此书所写,不止是亨利二世的人生,也涵盖了中世纪英国的政府与政治,可为研究中世纪英国史的案头书。

David Hume,*The History of England*, Vol.1. 大卫·休谟的 6 卷本《英国史》,历史学界无人不知。他也正是因为这部书,首先以历史学家而非哲学家的身份获得公众普遍认可。直到现今,休谟的名字在不列颠图书馆的作者编目中,依然被归入"历史学家"一类。该作甫一出版,便被誉为是"一本将传之于后代的《英国史》"。尽管批评它的声音并非没有,后世也从未断绝;但即便是认为休谟的这部著作"不幸充满偏见",建议将之"放在最后读"的美国《独立宣言》起草人托马斯·杰斐逊也承认,"休谟的风格和笔调是如此迷人"。哪怕不为读史,仅为学习语言,这部著作都值得一读。

梅特兰:《英格兰宪政史》,李红海译,北京:中国政法大学出版社,2010年。文字浅显、叙述清晰,是为研习英国宪政史的入门读物。

马克·布洛赫:《封建社会》,张绪山译,北京:商务印书馆,2002 年 ;佛朗索瓦·冈绍夫:《何为封建主义》,张绪山、卢兆瑜译,北京:商务印书馆,2016年。何谓"封建"? 这是一个在 20 世纪的中国被特定的政治语境搅浑了的概念,好在目前的史学界对于它已经有了正本清源的解释,至少已经承认:学术意义的"封建"有别于"半殖民、半封建"下的政治概念,而要研习西方的封建社会与封建主义,就必须读读布洛赫与冈绍夫的这两本书。尽管从学术成就来看,前者更受称誉,其篇幅也比后者厚重得多,但要了解西欧社会封建主义的起源、何为狭义的封建主义(即封君与封臣的关系)、何为广义的封建主义(即封建社会的经济、政治、文化各方面),这两本书就必须并置案头,而且最好先读《何为封建主义》,再读《封建社会》。

《大宪章》文献研究网址:http://www.bl.uk/treasures/magnacarta/

责任编辑:杨美艳
封面设计:石笑梦
责任校对:胡　佳

图书在版编目(CIP)数据

世界历史名篇译读·卷一,自由与权利/梅祖蓉 编著. —北京:人民出版社,
2018.1
ISBN 978-7-01-018339-8

Ⅰ. ①世…　Ⅱ. ①梅…　Ⅲ. ①世界史课-双语教学-高等学校-教材
Ⅳ. ①K1

中国版本图书馆 CIP 数据核字(2017)第 271609 号

《世界历史名篇译读》卷一:自由与权利
SHIJIE LISHI MINGPIAN YIDU JUAN YI ZIYOU YU QUANLI

梅祖蓉　编著

人民出版社 出版发行
(100706　北京市东城区隆福寺街 99 号)

北京市文林印务有限公司印刷　新华书店经销

2018 年 1 月第 1 版　2018 年 1 月北京第 1 次印刷
开本:710 毫米×1000 毫米 1/16　印张:14.25
字数:220 千字

ISBN 978-7-01-018339-8　定价:39.00 元

邮购地址 100706　北京市东城区隆福寺街 99 号
人民东方图书销售中心　电话 (010)65250042　65289539